THE SPANIARDS
IN THEIR HISTORY

Ramón Menéndez Pidal, Hon.Litt.D., Oxford
Director of the Royal Spanish Academy

THE SPANIARDS
IN THEIR HISTORY

Translated with a Prefatory Essay
on the Author's work by
WALTER STARKIE, Litt.D.,
Corresponding Member of the Royal Spanish Academy

LONDON
HOLLIS & CARTER

MADE AND PRINTED IN GREAT BRITAIN
AT THE BROADWATER PRESS, WELWYN GARDEN CITY
FOR HOLLIS AND CARTER LTD, 25 ASHLEY PLACE, LONDON, S.W.I

First published 1950

Preface

The celebrated Essay of Ramón Menéndez Pidal on the Spaniards in their History, which we publish for the first time in English, has awakened a great deal of interest, not only in Europe but also in America. It was the first official utterance after the tragic Civil War by one who is acknowledged to be the patriarch of humanism in the Spanish world, and at the same time it sums up a great deal of the achievement of the last fifty years in research into the Spanish Middle Ages. To understand the full significance of this Essay it is necessary to be well acquainted with the life-work of this doyen of Spanish scholars. For this reason I have preceded the Essay by an Introduction on his life work, and my intention was that it should appear in 1949 in time for the eightieth birthday of Don Ramón, a small contribution among the many that will swell the volume of homage which is being published in Spain in the Master's honour.

To understand Menéndez Pidal's personality it is not enough to follow him through the libraries, the lecture halls, or the research laboratories. My earliest meetings with him were during the years 1921-4 and even then I remember how significant were his remarks about his wanderings through the pueblos of Castile. His book on the minstrels was my favourite 'knapsack volume' when I roamed through La Mancha and Andalusia in the years 1928-35. Hence the immense importance of his life study of the Romancero and its derivatives throughout the world. At times his ballad-chasing recalls the magic personality of our own Cecil Sharp in the Appalachians, and Menéndez Pidal would certainly nod assent to that king who said that he did not mind who made the laws of the country but it was vitally important who composed the ballads.

The Essay on the Spaniards in their History was written by the man who, more than any other Spaniard, has tried to collect together the complete ballad lore of Spain, in the belief that the Romancero is a kind of everlasting plebiscite in favour of

Hispanic writing. For Spain always remains staunchly loyal to her ancient traditions and constantly strives to revive them and adapt them to the spirit of modern times.

W. S.

Contents

INTRODUCTION

THE SPANIARDS IN THEIR HISTORY

INTRODUCTION
by Walter Starkie

Chapter I

Ramón Menéndez Pidal

G. K. Chesterton, in his life of Chaucer, said: 'Why do I sometimes seem to be writing about modern politics instead of about mediaeval history? I am left with an overwhelming conviction that it is because we miss the point of mediaeval history that we make a mess of modern politics.'[1] Chesterton's statement is singularly applicable to Ramón Menéndez Pidal, the doyen of Spanish scholars and foremost humanist of the Hispanic world, who has devoted his life to the gigantic task of unravelling and explaining the history of mediaeval Spain. And it is his unrivalled knowledge of the learning and literature of the Middle Ages that gives such significance to the present essay which he composed as preface to the monumental history of Spain which was published in Madrid in 1947. It is a happy omen for the future that this acknowledged *maestro di color che sanno* should have returned in 1947 to his accustomed throne of scholarship in the Royal Spanish Academy, for he had presided over its deliberations until the outbreak of the Civil War in 1936. The Academy, which was founded in 1713 by Philip V on the model of the French Academy, bears as its motto the phrase: *Limpia, fija y da esplendor*, and concerns itself primarily with the Spanish language. The main task of the forty-two 'immortals' is to compile the monumental Academy Dictionary of the Spanish language after collecting, discussing and analysing the words that are sent in by scholars from all over the world. Every Thursday the academicians meet around the long, oval-shaped table covered with green baize in a room that was two years ago the rendezvous of Hispanists from Europe and the South American continent, who were invited by Spain to commemorate the fourth centenary of the birth

---

[1] G. K. Chesterton, *Chaucer*, London, 1932.

3

of Cervantes (1547–1947). It is significant that during the
War, when Spain was cut off from many countries beyond the
seas, even Spanish-American republics whose governments
were politically unsympathetic to Spain yet sent through their
Academies cordial messages to the Mother of all Spanish Academies, thus providing an admirable proof of the strength of
cultural ties between countries of the same language. Cultural
relations are all the more valuable because they are not swayed
by politics; they go deeper and link up scholars and humanists
whose minds have not been perverted by the passions and mass-
produced slogans of warring political parties. Indeed it is true to
say that the Hernán Cortés celebrations in Seville, and the two
sessions devoted to Cervantes in 1947 and 1948 have drawn the
nations of Hispano-America closer to the mother country.
Prominent philologists, scientists and men of letters from overseas have lectured in the universities throughout Spain, and
they have been followed by groups of students who have been
given by their respective governments facilities to attend courses
and become acquainted with their Spanish companions. Cultural questions are given great importance in American countries no less than in Spain, and it is noteworthy that the inaugural
lecture of the Cervantes celebrations in Seville in April 1948
was given by the Colombian minister to Spain, Don Eduardo
Caballero Calderón, academician and author of widely-read
books on Cervantes. We in Great Britain do not always understand how closely connected business and cultural relations are in
Hispanic countries, where it is customary to send out celebrated
scholars and writers on delicate diplomatic missions. In the case
of disputes between Hispanic countries, frequently arbitrators
have been invited from Spain and we may mention as an early
tribute to Menéndez Pidal the fact that he was invited to act as
Comisario regio in the settlement of the frontier question between
Ecuador and Peru in 1904–1908. It is significant to note that this
honour came to him when he was thirty-five years of age, and at a
moment when he was deeply immersed in his work on mediaeval
texts. But Don Ramón has never withdrawn himself into an ivory
tower; his learning has never been devoted to selfish ends, and
throughout his long life of investigation we can trace a distinct
process of evolution from the early days when he was a philologist, through the years spent in investigating the history of the

Spanish Epic and the Romancero, ever widening and expanding his horizon until it enclosed the whole Hispanic world. Don Ramón, indeed, has become a modern patriarch of learning, and can gaze back in retrospect over the whole history of Spain, as he does in the present essay, for he possesses, too, what Goethe called 'a sense of the past and present as being one; a conception which infuses a spectral element into the present'.

To-day this small, bearded man, with his gentle voice and serene manner, holds a privileged position in the Hispanic world owing to his qualities as a humanist. In every one of his works we observe this spirit of detached scientific investigation, forever in quest of the deeper issues. His works resemble a series of classical marble figures which seem to be illuminated from within by magic power. All his science he has used to determine the boundaries separating history from legend, thus revealing the complex Spanish Middle Ages in a way that enables us to understand better the modern history of the country. He is the prototype of the modern philologist who is the antithesis to the ancient grammarian; he possesses that universal curiosity which leads him to probe indefatigably the racial struggles of the past and establish parallels between the specimens of speech he has collected far and wide. Being, however, also an artist and a philosopher, he has divined the deeper harmonies of history and has discovered traces of the prehistoric past in the babblings of primitive languages. As the eminent humanist, Americo Castro, said of him: 'A hundred lines of a piece of parchment sufficed for him to reconstruct a lost epic poem of Roncesvalles; the analysis of a number of Pyrenean names enabled him to plot the area of the Basque language in Roman times; a comparative study of the celebrated ballad of "Gerineldo", in 160 versions, enabled him to construct an unsuspected folk-lore geography.'

There is a sense of unity throughout his work. His whole life has been devoted to the Spanish Middle Ages, but so profound is his knowledge of the obscure workings of the human race in those centuries that he has become universal, and his researches are no less significant to the Hispanists of England, France, Holland or Italy than they are to those of North and South America. For this reason his prestige has united the scholars of both hemispheres, and it may well be said that the celebrations in Spain to commemorate the fourth centenary of the birth of Cervantes

(1547–1947), to which scholars were invited from the South American republics as well as from the Western European nations, was a definite reminder of Spain's spiritual significance in the world to-day.

Ramón Menéndez Pidal was born in 1869 in La Coruña in Galicia, the north-western province of Spain, a region echoing with Celtic traditions. Any one who knows Don Ramón well is conscious of the underlying characteristics that we find in Celtic peoples. These show themselves in his unfailing interest in minstrelsy, and they inspired him to write his celebrated book *Los Juglares*, which is a treasure-house of minstrel lore. There lurks, indeed, in the soul of this scholar, whose life has mostly been spent in libraries, a tiny imp who has led him from time to time to forsake books and parchments and set off on vagabond tours on the trail of the Cid or the Seven Infantes of Lara. In Ireland we call such an imp a leprechaun, a tiny fairy that haunts certain families gifted with magic sensibility. This elusive quality appears here and there through the works of Don Ramón; it gives a touch of romance which Keats immortalized in:

> . . . magic casements opening on the foam
> Of perilous seas in faery lands forlorn.

It was in 1893 that he obtained his doctor's degree in the university, and from that moment he began his career as a scholar. From February 1896 to 1899 he occupied the post of Reader in the school for Higher Studies of the Ateneo in Madrid, and in that year he was appointed Professor of Romance Philology in the University of Madrid.

In order to understand the full significance of Menéndez Pidal's early works it is necessary to study the forces moulding Spain in the last twenty years of the nineteenth century. Among the humanists of Spain no one at that time was so significant as Menéndez y Pelayo, the great master of Menéndez Pidal. Indeed it was Menendez y Pelayo who, referring to the early works of his disciple, quoted a phrase from the old ballad: '*Si no venci reyes moras—engendre quien los venciera.*' (If I did not vanquish Moorish kings, I begat one who would do so.) The phrase is an illuminating one; it explains the relationship of our great mediaevalist to the preceding generation.

Chapter II

The Forerunner

Menéndez Pelayo was the great forerunner. He, too, came from the north of Spain, from the highland region of Santander, the prolongation of Castile to the sea. His youth had been spent in the world of tradition hallowed and perpetuated in the novels of Pereda; a world of proud hidalgos and God-fearing country folk. Menéndez Pelayo, too, had been an infant prodigy and had won his Professorship at a very early age with record marks. In his early works he had been a polemist, especially in 'Ciencia Española', 1876, which attacked the scientific methods of Spain in the eighteenth and nineteenth centuries. In 'Heterodoxos Españoles', 1882, he had continued this attack on a higher level, and by that impressive book established his name as a great critic and as one who refused to allow his mind to be swayed by political prejudices. Dr Marañón, in a brilliant essay,[1] has described Menéndez Pelayo as the forerunner of the modern neo-liberals, who make such a profound appeal to the thinkers of to-day possessing balanced minds. Menéndez Pelayo handed the torch on to Menéndez Pidal and his generation of scholars and professors, who were eager to make Spain take her rightful part in the humanism of Europe.

Together with Menéndez Pelayo we should mention the name of Ramón y Cajal, who in 1880 published his first scientific work, 'Investigaciones experimentales sobre la génesis inflamatoria' (two years before the first edition of 'Los Heterodoxos'). In his fascinating autobiography, 'Recuerdos de mi Vida', written in latter years,[2] he has described the attitude of mind of the young scholars and scientists of 1880–1890. They were in revolt against the rhetorical

[1] G. Marañón, Tiempo Viejo y Tiempo Nuevo, Madrid, 1943, p. 97.
[2] S. Ramón y Cajal, Recuerdos de mi Vida, Madrid, 1923, 3rd edition.

7

bombast of their elders; they wished to strike out on a different path, rather than follow the example of their predecessors who wasted their energies in fruitless political discussions in the various Ateneos and filled the newspapers with facile articles on every conceivable subject. Menéndez Pelayo, Cajal and their companions shut themselves up in their studies and in their laboratories. Being conscientious scholars and scientists, they shunned giving opinions on subjects with which they were not deeply acquainted; they noted with surprise and misgiving the blatant self-confidence of their elders who trumpeted their political views to the four winds; and they faced imperturbably those who accused them of being fools and upstarts. The generation of Menéndez Pelayo, Cajal, Ribera and Hinojosa was one of scientists and scholars in contrast to the former which had been one of preachers and orators. It was a generation of peace, for the revolutionary spirit of 1868 had died down, owing to the restoration of the monarchy, and Menéndez Pelayo, though he was a polemist, yet fought with equal zeal against the fanatics on both sides. He saw that the nineteenth century had been one long dreary record of intolerance and prejudice, and he was determined to discover some method for uniting Spaniards in brotherly concord, and thus diminish the violent antagonisms which made intellectual relationships impossible. Marañón, in his essay, has referred to the great antagonism that existed in those years between Perez Galdós and Menéndez Pelayo, for the former had recently published 'Doña Perfecta' and 'Gloria', embodying his anti-clerical theories in positive nineteenth-century fashion, and Menéndez Pelayo in the first edition of 'Historia de los Heterodoxos' attacked the position of the novelist with great bitterness. Nevertheless, the two men were to the last close friends and no nobler tribute was ever paid to Galdós than the speech pronounced in the Spanish Academy by Menéndez Pelayo in commemorating the former's election to that august body. The lesson of tolerance taught by Menéndez Pelayo sank into the minds of those who, like Menéndez Pidal, were to open up new fields for Spanish investigation. Tolerance and sense of reality were Menéndez Pelayo's watch-words: 'Let us,' he said, 'cast away those old-fashioned declamatory history books with their everlasting commonplaces about Pavia, San Quintín and Lepanto:

they serve only to lull us to sleep and fill us with foolish vanity. We must turn the thoughts of our countrymen to the real internal problems of Spain.'[1] It was such sentiments that prompted him to utter paeans in the style of Costa and Macías Picavea to the rigid geometry of large metallic bridges and factories with waving trains of smoke, and when celebrating the virtues and excellencies of the great Catalan scholar, Milá Fontanals, he was even able to find words of praise for the grotesque architectural excrescences of Gaudí as symbolizing the unconquerable urge to progress of industrial Barcelona, 'which God may destine to be the heart and head of a regenerated Spain'.[2] Laín Entralgo, in his significant biography of the master, has summed up the various generations of the late nineteenth century as follows: 'The generation of Menéndez Pelayo was not one of poets but of scholars. The generation of preachers (Costa, Galdós and Macías Picavea) was followed by one of scholars (Menéndez Pelayo, Cajal, Ribera and Hinojosa), and this was followed by a generation of men of letters and literary artists—the so-called "Generation of 1898".'[3] Each of these generations, concludes Laín Entralgo, faced the problem of Spain in the crucial hour of disaster in 1898. Galdós and his contemporaries had lived through the years when the monarchy of Isabel II was crumbling, and events were leading Spain on to the 'Revolution of September'. Menéndez Pelayo and his contemporaries were fortunate enough to spend the impressionable years of their youth in the peaceful days of the monarchical restoration. The 1898 generation, to which Menéndez Pidal and his literary contemporaries belong, spent their youthful years in an atmosphere of pessimism and heart-searching.

---

[1] P. Laín Entralgo, *Menéndez Pelayo*, Madrid, 1944, p. 110.
[2] Menéndez Pelayo, *Estudios*, V, 168.
[3] P. Laín Entralgo, *op. cit.*, pp. 112–113.

B

Chapter III

The Disaster of 1898

A great deal of the success afterwards won by the Modernists of the 1898 Movement was due to the patient toiling of their predecessors in those dark years when Spanish misfortunes were approaching their climax. On the one hand we see the signs of an approaching dawn of interest in literature during the nineties evidenced by the frequent performances of the works of Aeschylus, Shakespeare, Goethe; on the other we behold the murky darkness of the political atmosphere. The old repressive spirit of Spain's colonial policy continued until 1898 when the Cuban War broke out. In spite of the heroism of the fighting men, in spite of glorious deeds worthy of an epic, the war ended disastrously and Spain lost her remaining colonies. But the sailors who sank at Manila singing hymns to their country had not died in vain.[1] The disaster marked the end of a chapter. Every year since has seen the introduction of new ideas into Spain. The harsh terms of the Treaty of Paris after the war, when all Europe looked on with indifference, showed the Spaniards that they must bring their country into line with modern Europe. A new liberal spirit began to inspire the youth of the country. Up to 1898 the administration of railways, mines and other sources of national wealth had been, to a large extent, in the hands of foreigners. After this Spaniards began to invest their money in their own country, and to the lotus-eater's spirit of *hasta mañana* there succeeded an eager activity. We find that the word 'Europeanize' came into Spanish. Many brilliant writers and statesmen took up with great fervour the question of introducing foreign methods. The *Unión Nacional* was formed, led by philosophers like Joaquin Costa. Do not let us think, however, that the Cosmopolitans had it all their own

---

[1] W. Starkie, *Jacinto Benavente*, Oxford, 1924, p. 15.

way; Spain never loses her heart altogether to any foreign ideals. At the beginning of the new century Miguel de Unamuno, one of the 1898 generation of new writers, represented the traditional Spaniard, and from his watch-tower at Salamanca he hurled pamphlets at Costa and the Europeans. 'So far from being Europeanized,' he cried, 'I should not be ashamed of being African—yes, as African as Tertullian.' The remark is a striking one and goes a long way towards giving us a key to the Spanish soul. Spain can never be entirely European—she has always resisted with tenacity any invader, and the spectacle of the chief men of Saguntum throwing themselves and their treasures into the flames of their burning city has been repeated many a time in her history. However far her intellectuals may assimilate the ideals of her neighbours there is always the leavening of '*Españo-lismo*' in her literature and art. All Spanish writers who start their careers by trying to be European, inevitably, sooner or later, return to the national tradition.

The movement of 1898 started brilliantly in literature under the guidance of young writers whose minds were concentrated on the idea of rebirth after the disaster. They were severely analytical and eager to make war on false values. They faced facts, and stripped away ruthlessly the flowers of rhetoric and hollow-sounding phrases. They made a cult of the intellect and worshipped the visionary art of El Greco and the primitive poets. Their watch-word was precision. 'Each thing in written language,' said Azorín, one of the masters of the generation of 1898 and the one who had given it that name, 'must be called by its exact name.' And the important fact is that Castile absorbed all those poets and artists, no matter from what region of the country they came, and we discover that in contemporary Spanish literature the best pages on the Castilian scene come from the pens of the Basques Unamuno and Baroja, the Andalusian Antonio Machado, and Azorín of the Mediterranean region. The generation of 1898, too, loved old towns where life still preserved the eternal qualities of the Middle Ages, and in literature they turned to the Castilian troubadours and minstrels of these early centuries such as Gonzalo de Berceo, Juan Ruiz and the Marquis of Santillana. I remember on one occasion hearing Ignacio de Zuloaga, the great painter, exclaim: 'Though I am a Basque, and a patriotic one at that, I am most active in my work when I live in Segovia, for there I never fail to find queer, grotesque types as models. Here in this Basque garden of Zumaya life is too soft and easy. In my studio at Pedraza, not far from Sepulveda in the province of Segovia, I can gaze at a great stretch of Castilian sky and landscape. Up there I can live the timeless existence of the traditional Castilian. For you should remember that though I am born a Basque from Eibar yet I refuse to sacrifice my universal heritage for any regionalism. It was Castile made Spain, and every one of us, whether we are Basques, Galicians or Andalusians, must go forth from our narrow regions and become Castilian, for it was Castile that made the Spanish World.'[1]

These words might have been uttered by Ramón Menéndez Pidal, for all through his works runs the central theme of Castilian unity, and it is this sense of the eternal unifying mission of Castile in the Spanish world that gives such significance to the great works on the Cid and the Romancero. It is thus necessary to extend the scope of the 'generation of 1898' to include the humanists such as Menéndez Pidal, whose works of scholarship were published in those troubled years. Indeed, as modern writers like Laín Entralgo[2] have shown in recent studies, the term 'generation of 1898' is a misleading one when applied to many of the writers. The term was first used by Azorín when describing his own position in the modern Spanish movement of the time, but it has been rejected by his colleague Pío Baroja in no uncertain terms. When we consider these writers we should remember that it was Azorín himself who explained the origin of the movement when he said: 'To Galdós the new generation of writers owed the very essence of its being, for it was he who introduced the spiritual atmosphere of things, the dark, grey, uniform everyday life.' His work was that of an analytical critic as much as of an artist. In the field of scholarship it was to Menéndez Pelayo that the humanists of Menéndez Pidal's generation owed their being. His mind with its immense range of vision illuminated the past scene of Spanish history; here and there his disciples saw vast panoramas, whose existence they had never formerly suspected. They felt impelled to devote their lives to investigating the count-

---

[1] W. Starkie, *Spanish Raggle-Taggle*, London, 1934. p. 97.
[2] P. Laín Entralgo, *La Generación del 1898*, Madrid, 1945.

less relics of the early centuries lying in the shrines throughout Spain. They hearkened to his voice as to that of the prophet Ezekiel.

When we consider the works of Menéndez Pidal we should remember that they were produced in the same years as the literary works of the modern masters who had so deep an influence upon contemporary Spanish literature. There is thus a reciprocal influence between the writers and the research scholars, and we can understand the significance of Menéndez Pidal's mediaeval researches in the Spanish world when we recall the personality of Unamuno, the seer Tiresias, as he was called by Ramón Pérez de Ayala. All his life he acted as a modern Don Quixote, riding full tilt against hypocrisy, smug consciences, dogmatism, and shibboleths. He was the *enfant terrible* of modern Spain, in spite of his air of puritanical austerity at times, which caused Salvador de Madariaga to compare him very aptly to an elder at an Eisteddfod. But Unamuno all his life was obsessed by the Spain of the Middle Ages. 'I feel that my soul is mediaeval,' he cries, 'and that the soul of my country is mediaeval: I feel that it has passed perforce through the Renaissance, the Reformation, the Revolution, learning from them but never letting its soul be touched; and Spanish Quixotism is nothing but the despairing struggle of the Middle Ages against the Renaissance.'[1]

[1] M. Unamuno, *El Sentimiento Trágico de la Vida*, Madrid, 1913.

Chapter IV

The Story of the Seven Sons

The first book of Menéndez Pidal, '*La Leyenda de los Infantes de Lara*', which was published in 1896, immediately set the author in the very front rank of mediaevalists. Menéndez Pelayo in reviewing the book called it the second great contribution to the history of Spanish epic poetry, worthy to stand beside the famous treatise on the Castilian epic by Milá y Fontanals which had appeared in 1874. The French Hispanist, Morel Fatio, prophesied that Pidal's book would lead to a renaissance in Spain of historical and philological studies on mediaeval themes. The story of the Seven Infantes was a local incident that took place in the storm-tossed tenth century, when Almanzor, the celebrated Moorish king of Córdoba, was ravaging Castile. The incident would have faded from men's memories had it not been for the anonymous minstrel—the blind rhapsodist who strung the events together and sang them as a long narrative. Once the story was launched on the wings of poetry it began to fly far and wide. It became a symbol of Spain in the sense that the drama of the Oresteia was a symbol of Greece. In studying the story from its origins through the centuries down to modern days as Professor Menéndez Pidal has done, we can study the evolution of literature. It is instructive to note the scientific way in which the author plans out his work. First of all he establishes the correct text, solving one by one the multitude of philological problems as they present themselves; then he studies the theme and the poem or fragment of a poem in their relation to the history of the time. From this analysis he was able to prove that the story of the Seven Infantes was originally a local one concentrated in the small region of Castile between Barbadillo, Salas and the River Hebros within a radius of six or eight leagues. But the 'juglar' or minstrel who recited the poem was a man who knew many lands,

14

and as he recited the narrative he included many references to his own travels in order to dazzle the simple minds of his audience. Thus the scope of the poem gradually widened as the minstrel described many towns between Salas and Córdoba. When the minstrel departed the people preserved in their memories the salient points of the rhapsodic poem he had recited to them, and recalling a turn of phrase here and a dramatic touch there, they recited them to one another around the fire in the long winter evenings. Such was the origin of the old Spanish ballads which were the multiple offspring of the epic poems. The ballads consisted of striking passages from the old epic songs remembered by the people and handed down orally from one generation to another, but with many changes due to the method of transmission. At the same time there is one very significant point about the original epic poem which should not be forgotten, for it gives a special historical significance to the Spanish epic. In the Spanish chronicles of the Middle Ages we find many of the poems prosified, and we come to realize that from the outset Spanish mediaeval history is mingled with epic poetry. And these old epic poems, after being prosified in the chronicles and split up into the small ballads, progress a step further and become the themes for drama. The dramatic ballads of Spain such as those that deal with the blood-curdling story of the murder of the Seven Sons were the seeds from which sprang the great dramas of the Spanish Golden Age of Lope de Vega, Tirso de Molina, Calderón, and others. And after the Golden Age had passed, Menéndez Pidal studies the treatment of the story by the romantic poets of the nineteenth century. We are thus enabled to follow the development of a significant theme from the dim ages of antiquity up to modern days, thereby tracing the peculiarities of Spanish psychology and sensibility. It is interesting, in this connection, to note that the vengeance motive, which became the mainspring of so many bloodthirsty 'Honour' dramas of Calderón such as '*A Secreto Agravio Secreta Venganza*', and '*El Médico de Su Honra*', is to be found in all its tragic force as far back as the tenth century. Doña Lambra, the haughty wife of Ruy Velázquez of Burgos, feels that she has been insulted at her wedding feast by one of the Seven Sons of Lara and she plots their destruction. As a result of treachery, they are led into a Moorish ambush and slain. The

seven heads are then sent to the Moorish king who displays them
at a banquet to the grief-stricken father. But retribution comes in
the second part of the poem, for Mudarra the Avenger was born
to the old father in captivity at the Moorish king's court, and it is
he who returns to Castile and exacts vengeance from the guilty
Ruy Velázquez and his evil spouse. At the end of the book the
author, pursuing his exhaustive scientific method, actually
visited the countryside of Lara, Salas and Barbadillo in order to
discover what traces of the legend remained in the folk-lore of the
region. Even to-day the inhabitants of Barbadillo still call themselves 'Alambraos' in allusion to Doña Lambra who possessed
estates there. Although there are very few traces left of the Seven
Infantes in folk-lore, their heads are preserved in a coffin in the
church at Salas. As for Doña Lambra, the Lady Macbeth of the
ballads, her ghost still haunts the popular mind. She rises at
times from the black lake up in the mountains where tradition
says that she threw herself. Menéndez Pidal in studying the folk-
lore development of the ancient story points out how to-day there
is confusion in the minds of the folk concerning Doña Lambra
due to the fact that they have amalgamated her sinister personality with that of her victim, Doña Sancha, the mother of the
Seven Sons. In modern days when a woman gives birth to trip-
lets, quadruplets or quintuplets, she is fêted and given the King's
Bounty, but in olden days it was not so. Even a woman who bore
twins was frowned upon, because it was considered a sign that she
had committed adultery, for how was it possible to give birth to
two children at the same time unless there had been two fathers?
Popular tradition supposes that the mother of the Seven Infantes
bore them at one birth and the people tell the story thus: 'A poor
woman was begging for alms one day at the gates of the palace for
her five children, and Doña Sancha rebuked her for having so
many children. The latter then cursed Doña Sancha, saying:
"May God grant that you bear seven babes at one birth." When
her time came, Doña Sancha was delivered of her monstrous
brood, and in shame she ordered her servant to put six of the
seven children in pails and drown them in the river. But Gonzalo
Gustios, the father, arrived just in time to save his six sons and he
reared them in secret. When they were seven years old he dressed
them all up in the same coloured costume and invited them to the

palace to a banquet with Doña Sancha and the other son. When she saw them she exclaimed: "May God grant that a black lake open in the ground and engulf me".' According to Menéndez Pidal, the tradition of the woman who was delivered of seven children at one birth is associated in the Castilian mind with the famous Count Diego de Porcelos of Burgos. His name, which was derived from the Latin *porcelli*, or little pigs, according to ancient tradition, commemorated his own birth, for his mother bore him and his six brothers in her womb just as pigs bear a litter of seven. Hence in the modern ballads that are recited by the villagers around Salas and Barbadillo even to-day we find the words:

'Doña Urraca, Doña Urraca, well may'st thou praise thyself; Thou hast given birth to seven sons like any dunghill sow'

which are actually the same as those used by Doña Lambra in the epic poem. It should be added that the country-people do not call her Doña Lambra, but Doña Urraca, perhaps confusing her with another Lady Macbeth of the Middle Ages—the Infanta Doña Urraca, sister of Alfonso VI, who was supposed to have plotted the murder of her brother Sancho.

This early work explains in detail the method which Menéndez Pidal has followed faithfully throughout his life. He considers the ancient traditional story not merely from a literary or historical point of view, but as a living organism, and he studies its progressive evolution through the centuries, watching the modifications imposed upon it by the varying moods of the different ages. Each book thus gives us a vision of the workings of the Spanish mind.

Chapter V

The Origins of Epic Poetry

Gaston Paris, the doyen of French mediaevalists, in reviewing 'The Seven Infantes of Lara' expressed the hope that the author would next devote the same passionate interest to the Poema del Cid, 'the national poem of the Spanish race'. '*Nous attendons avec confiance qu'il consacre la même ardeur, le même savoir et la même pénétration à la reconstruction de l'époque du Cid, plus belle encore et plus importante à tous les points de vue, et qui, tout en étant aussi profondément nationale que la première, offre un intérêt autrement considérable pour l'ensemble de la littérature européenne. Il aura bien merité, quand il aura accompli cette grande œuvre, et de la science et de sa patrie.*'[1]

It was in 1911 that Menéndez Pidal published the final and definitive edition of the '*Cantar de Mío Cid*', reproducing palaeographically the Bivar Codex and adding such a wealth of notes and vocabulary that it became in itself the greatest monument of learning concerning the Middle Ages. Furthermore, in the preceding year he had published in Paris '*L'Épopée Castillane à travers la Littérature Espagnole*'[2]—a volume of lectures which he had delivered at the University of Johns Hopkins in Baltimore in 1909. In the first two chapters of this book the author places before us the results of his long years of patient investigation concerning the beginnings of the Castilian epic. It was the discovery of a whole series of mediaeval poems of chivalry that caused the scholars in the second half of the nineteenth century to modify their theories concerning epic poetry. Previously the study of epic poetry was limited to Homer, Virgil, Tasso, Ariosto, and their imitators. Now, however, it was seen that there were two categories: on the one hand the primitive epic poem, of spon-

[1] G. Paris, two articles in *Journal des Savants*, May and June, 1898.
[2] Spanish translation published Buenos Aires, 1945.

18

taneous and traditional character, such as the 'Iliad', the 'Chanson de Roland', the 'Nibelungenlied'; on the other there existed a later form of epic poetry, of a more learned and artificial nature, written in a more personal and erudite style, such as the 'Aeneid', the 'Orlando Furioso', the 'Araucana', the 'Henriade'. Whereas the poems of traditional character were by anonymous authors, and were written to be chanted in public, the erudite poems, on the contrary, were by individual authors conscious of their literary reputation, who wrote for a restricted public of connoisseurs.

Many peoples possess a traditional lyric poetry of their own, but few countries have created the higher and more complex form of heroic narrative poetry. Indeed, it is held that epic poetry is the special creation of a small number of countries of Aryan race, namely India, Persia, Greece, Brittany, Germany, and France. To those the name of Spain was added only after 1874. Before that date, even those who were most deeply acquainted with the Spanish Middle Ages, such as Ferdinand Wolf and R. Dozy, not only insisted that Spain had no epic poetry but gave every plausible historical reason why she could never have had any. Spain, they added, might rest satisfied with her Romancero which had aroused universal admiration, and they compared the case of Spain with that of Serbia and Scotland, countries that had never completed the process of evolution beyond mere sketches of epic poems. Two long Spanish poems were known in those days, the 'Cantar de Mío Cid,' and the 'Mocedades de Rodrigo,' but Wolf saw in them no more than crude attempts to imitate a French type of composition. Even the great master of Romance philology, Gaston Paris, maintained in 1865[1] that Spain had no epic poetry, but after Milá Fontanals had proved the existence of the Castilian epic he retracted his former opinion and admitted that many of the ballads of the fifteenth century were essentially fragments of the ancient *Cantares de Gesta*, and, moreover, he recognized that the Castilian epic was richer and more varied than had hitherto been believed. Gaston Paris, however, still maintained his thesis that the Castilian was derived from the French epic, basing himself on the argument of metrical similarity and on the fact that epic poetry only began in Spain after epic poetry in France had already reached its peak point.

[1] G. Paris, *Histoire Poétique de Charlemagne*, Paris, 1865, p. 203.

Menéndez Pidal at the outset demolished these arguments of the French scholar, showing that the metre of the Spanish poems was not imitated and had evolved slowly in a different way from the French, and, moreover, that the phenomenon of the paragogical (e) which existed in the Spanish was unknown to the French *chansons de geste*. He also proved that the first active contact between the brilliant French civilization and the Spanish took place at the end of the eleventh century under Alfonso VI, whereas the first accounts of the introduction of *chansons de geste* into Spain date from the beginning of the twelfth century in the '*Historia Silense*' and in 'Turpin'. Meanwhile, the events described in the epics of Fernán González and the Infantes of Lara belong to the tenth century, and, in view of the surprising accuracy of historical, geographical, and genealogical details in these poems, we are led to believe that they must have assumed their original form very soon after the events they describe.[1] Pidal then goes on to show the Germanic influences in the Spanish epic. From early times the Germans had been in the habit of singing the annals of their race. Tacitus refers to this in his 'Germania', and in the 'Getica' of Jordanes we are told that the 'Visigoths sang the high deeds of their great heroes, accompanying themselves on the *cítara*'. And a proof of the existence of epic poetry among the Visigoths, even after their settlement in Gaul and in Spain, is the story of the Visigothic hero, Walter of Spain, which was celebrated throughout the Germanic world. This legendary hero, who lived in the days of Attila and was called Walter of Spain and Walter of Aquitania, was the ruler of the vast territory of Spain and Aquitania, which in the period of the Hunnish monarch was actually under the power of the Visigoths. The stories of his deeds became the subject of narrative poems among the Visigoths, and, as Menéndez Pidal shows, their memory persists through the early literature of Spain, even as far as the ballads, for to our amazement, we find an echo of the epic of Walter in the popular minstrel ballad of the sixteenth century which relates how Gaiferos fled from Sansueña with his bride Melisenda who was captive there.[2] So close are the analogies between the struggles of

---

[1] R. Menéndez Pidal, *Leyenda de Los Infantes de Lara*, 2nd edition, Madrid, 1934, pp. 453-458.

[2] R. Menéndez Pidal, *La Epopeya Castellana a través de la Lit. Esp.*, Buenos Aires, 1945, p. 26.

Gaiferos against his Moorish pursuers, and the flight of Walter with his bride Hiltgund, that Pidal sees in the sixteenth-century ballad, so effectively staged for Don Quixote by Maestro Peter's puppets, a relic, preserved by chance, of the mysterious bond uniting the heroic poetry of the Visigoths and the Castilian epic. In support of this link between the Castilian epic poems and the legends of the Visigothic epoch, we find that the society described in the *Cantares de Gesta* has a marked Germanic character. In the Castilian epic the king or lord consults his vassals before taking action. Also the duel between two warriors reveals God's purpose and it is held in war to decide an issue between two armies; and in peace to decide the guilt of the accused. Another characteristic custom of the Germans which existed among the Castilians was the vow which the knight uttered on solemn occasions. Other Germanic customs appear in the epic poems, such as that of giving a special name to the sword of the knight. The German warrior used to bring his wife and children into battle so that their presence might inspire him to perform prodigies of valour. In the same manner the Cid insists that his wife and daughters should be witnesses of his battle against the King of Morocco. Their presence, he says, will add strength and courage to his arm. This patriarchal feeling is characteristic of the primitive chivalry of the epic poems and is a contrast to the later more artificial gallantry of the knight-errant who invoked the name of his lady when he raised his sword. Another significant trait that comes into the Castilian epic from Visigothic source is the punishment of adultery. In the 'Germania' of Tacitus adultery was punished severely by the offended husband and society. The guilty woman's hair was cut off, and the husband, in the presence of his kinsmen, stripped her naked and cast her out of his house, and flogged her through the streets. In the epic poems it was customary to degrade the adulteress by cutting her garments above the knees. It is interesting to notice that though this insulting procedure disappeared, the implacable chastisement survived, and the outraged husband could only preserve his honour on condition that he put his guilty wife to death by his own hand. For this reason the Count Garci Fernandez of Castile, the hero of the epic poem '*La Condesa Traidora*', even abandons the government of his realm and sets off alone to France in pursuit of his unfaithful wife and her lover. Only after killing them both by his own hand does he consider himself fit and worthy to govern his Castilian subjects. Such is the first 'Honour' drama in Spanish literature, and the theme is one that will appear again and again in many forms, especially in the tragic works of Calderón.

In spite of the cruelty we observe in the warriors' society of the Middle Ages, the influence of Christianity predominates in the lives of men. Whenever the Cid and his followers were preparing for any serious undertaking they spent the night before in prayers and watching in a church illuminated by candles, and they attended Mass at dawn, when it was customary to make rich offerings to the shrine. Before battle the armed bands devoutly heard the Mass of the Holy Trinity and the bishop gave absolution to those who would die fighting in the sacred war against the Moors with their faces to the foe. Through the epic poem we meet with long prayers imitated from the French *chanson de geste*, as well as short invocations and religious war cries—all of which show us how deep was the trust in God's protection. It is noteworthy, too, how frequently we meet with references to pilgrimages to famous sanctuaries. The Cid, for instance, goes devoutly to Santiago de Galicia, which in the Middle Ages rivalled Jerusalem and Rome as a centre of pilgrimage. There is, however, an antithesis between the French and the Castilian Epic in the matter of the supernatural. The ideals of the French are best reflected in the '*Chanson de Roland*', which was written in the early days of chivalry, when coat of mail had only just replaced the primitive leather jerkin and when 'chivalrous' meant the admiration for the physical qualities of the knight. But Roland, as well as being of great physical strength, was God's agent on earth, and under His special protection. When he lies dying the angel picks up the gauntlet which he stretches towards heaven. The angel Gabriel spends the night keeping watch by the bedside of Charlemagne, and the sanctity of the Emperor's mission is symbolized by his sword '*Joyeuse*', for in its hilt are fragments of the Sacred Lance. The supernatural appears again and again through the poem; the sun halts its course for him, the waters of the rivers part so that he may pass, the walls of cities fall of their own accord before him. The background of chivalry is made up of dream-like visions, the geography is fantastic, and

supernatural forces intervene in the lives of men. Armies of
360,000 and 450,000 knights battle: five French knights kill
4,000 infidels: the horn of Roland is heard thirty miles away. It
must be remembered that the '*Chanson de Roland*' was written
nearly 300 years after the death of the hero, and in the meantime
a host of legends had grown up around his exploits, whereas the
'*Cantar de Mío Cid*' was composed within forty years after the
death of the Campeador in 1099. The '*Cantar de Mío Cid*' strikes
us by its Homeric simplicity and its patriarchal character. There
is very little of the supernatural in the poem. The angel Gabriel
does appear in a dream to the Cid to comfort him in his exile,
but when the moment for battle arrives the hero needs no help
but that of his sword and we never find him doubting the power
of his own arm. He always invokes the name of Saint James, but
he does not expect the Apostle to descend from the clouds
mounted on a white charger. There is only the one supernatural
element which we find in the Castilian epic, namely the observation of the flight of birds. This form of augury played an important part in Castile, though it was unknown in French epic poetry.
Every *ayo* or preceptor entrusted with the education of youth had
the duty of interpreting the flight of birds, especially eagles, and
there is one very significant passage in the poem of the Seven
Infantes of Lara. When the seven youths pass through the pine
woods of Canicosa on their way into Moorish territory, they see
two ravens and an eagle flying on the sinister side, and the old
ayo Nuño Salido points out the evil omen, begging them not to
proceed, but to return to their house and wait until the omens
should change. 'My sons', said he, 'in truth I like not this journey,
for the omens say that we shall never more return to our house.
Wherefore I say that if ye break these omens you must send a
herald to your mother, telling her to cover with black cloth seven
biers and set them in the courtyard of the palace and weep over
you all as dead.' This course of action suggested by the *ayo* was the
customary method of warding off the evil influence, by exorciz-
ing the omen and pretending that the prophesied misfortune had
already taken place. The seven warriors pay no heed to the prudent counsel of their aged tutor, and ride on to their doom. The
anonymous minstrel author from Medinaceli used the incident of
the adverse omens to convey to his public the atmosphere of

mystery and tragic foreboding. Augury was considered in Europe in those days to be an essential Spanish art, and William of Malmesbury tells us that Pope Silvester II had learnt it from the Saracens in Spain.

It is necessary to stress the influence of the French epic poems on the Spanish as regards subject matter. This was shown especially in the transplantation into Spain of the stories connected with Charlemagne and his Twelve Peers. The French poems celebrating their deeds not only spread to Spain but to England, Ireland, Germany, Norway, indeed to the whole of Europe. But Spain and Italy so deeply assimilated these tales that each became a second fatherland for the heroes of the Carolingian romance. Looking back to my own personal experiences years ago in Sicily, I remember with what feeling of amazement I suddenly found myself transported back into the world of Roncesvalles. It was in one of the tiny puppet *teatrini* in Palermo patronized by the *facchini* and street-arabs of the quarter. The curtain rose, disclosing a scene from one of the romantic stories of Charlemagne and his paladins. The cloth-painted scene changed from baronial hall to battlemented wall, and then to the forest of the dragon. The puppets were of varying types—those who played the secondary parts in the drama were simply made, but those who acted the heroic parts were carved with all the loving care of Sicilian artisans, who had inherited the traditional craft. Orlando was one of the gorgeous puppets: he was decked out in brilliant costume and could move his body with as much agility as if he had been an acrobat. This was necessary because he was the favourite hero of the audience, and the great scene of the whole piece was his duel with his rival in the fatal battle.[1]

In Spain so deep an influence did the *chansons de geste* on the rout of Roncesvalles have upon the Castilians, that they created a famous character, Bernardo del Carpio, who, though purely a legendary figure, became the third hero in the Spanish Walhalla, rivalling even the historical Fernán González and the Cid. Spain became naturally associated with Charlemagne because of his wars against the Saracens. Nevertheless, when we compare the French and Spanish, we are struck by the profound differences that exist between the two, in spite of the fact that both sprouted

[1] W. Starkie, *The Waveless Plain*, London, 1938, p. 281.

from a Germanic seed. As Menéndez Pidal shows conclusively in his masterly chapters on the origins of the Castilian epic, the Castilian is incomparably more historical than the French epic.[1] Whereas the *chansons de geste* limit the historical element to one central incident, the Castilian heroic poems are historical even in their unimportant details. And this strongly historical character can be easily explained because various texts are preserved referring to incidents that occurred at the same time as, or a little later than the events described in the epic poems.

[1] R. Menéndez Pidal, *La Epopeya Castellana*, pp. 38–39.

C

Chapter VI

Spain's National Hero

It is deeply significant that right in the centre of Spanish epic poetry rises the gigantic figure of the Cid, the national hero of Spain, who died in 1099, and the poem celebrating his deeds was written only forty years afterwards. The central figure of the French Epic, Roland, on the other hand died as far back as 778, and the *chanson* consecrating his heroic exploits was not written until three centuries later. Consequently, whereas the incidents in the French poem take place in an atmosphere of legend and fantasy, the Cid and his knights behave as normal heroes and perform deeds of valour which are in no way more unusual than the exploits of such crusaders as Godfrey de Bouillon, which were described by eyewitnesses. The anonymous creator of the '*Poema del Cid*' is at great pains to show throughout the kindly, tolerant and patriarchal simplicity of his hero. At the beginning he has been exiled by his king, and, after saying farewell to Burgos, he rides through the night accompanied by his retainers to the monastery of San Pedro de Cardeña, for there he had left his wife, Doña Jimena, and his children. Instead of an arrogant hero with feudal wealth and privileges, we find a tender husband and father driven into exile by an ungrateful monarch. The streets of Burgos are silent and deserted, and no one will open his door or receive him, for fear of the King's wrath, but he meets a child of nine years who consoles him and bids him Godspeed. When the Campeador reaches the gates of the monastery, the cocks were crowing amain, and the day was beginning to break. The abbot was saying Matins and the church was a blaze of light. Then Doña Jimena and her ladies, with tapers in their hands, meet the hero at the gate, and the Cid said farewell to his wife and children, while the bells of the monastery tolled through the cold morning

air the message that the Campeador was departing for exile and
needed the loyal help of his friends. The Cid never forgot San
Pedro de Cardeña through those years when he fought for the
Moorish King of Zaragoza, and later, after the capture of
Valencia, he sent his doughty friend Minaya there to bring his
wife and daughters to share in his triumph over the Infidel. Here
and there the minstrel poet by subtle touches brings out the
human, chivalrous nature of the Cid. He is often represented as
'beautifully smiling' ('fermoso sonrrisando'). He is quick to feel
emotion and cannot restrain his tears in joy nor in sadness:
tears fill his eyes when he says farewell to his palace at Bivar and
sees the doors wide open, the postern gates without hinges, the
perches without falcons: he rejoices when his wife and daughter
watch him fighting, and he says to them: 'Be not afraid to see me
in the combat, my heart grows mightier within me when you
watch me fight.' And when he wins the battle, his first thought is
to send booty to his King and master, for he is ever a loyal vassal,
despite the monarch's cruel ingratitude. To the beaten Moors at
Valencia he is humane and chivalrous, and his trait of restraint
and measure is stressed again and again throughout the poem in a
way that contrasts with the ferocity and cruelty which are im-
puted to him in the later version called 'Las Mocedades de Rodrigo',
describing the deeds of his youth. In the 'Cantar' there are also
little humorous touches which serve to bring out the drama of the
story, as in the scene of the lion where the minstrel contrasts the
calm courage of the hero with the cowardice of the arrogant
Infantes of Carrión, one of whom takes refuge behind a wine-
press and emerges all covered with grime after the Cid has led
the escaped lion back to his cage. Another instance of this naïve,
humorous comment occurs in the pathetic scene after the cow-
ardly Infantes of Carrión have outraged their wives, the daughters of the Cid, and left them for dead in the oak-woods of Corpes.
Bleeding and insensible they were found by the nephew of the
Campeador, the youth Fernandez Muñoz. 'The tissues of his
heart were torn' (partiéronsele las telas de dentro del coraçón) and he
cried out to the fainting girls: 'Cousins, my cousins, Doña Elvira
and Doña Sol! Wake up, cousins, for the love of almighty God!'
When one of the girls calls out for water he runs to fetch it in his
hat, and the poet adds: 'it was a new one, for he had only recently

bought it in Valencia.' This naïve remark uttered aside by the *juglar* is a relief to the pathetic tension of the preceding verses. Even after this terrible insult by the arrogant Infantes of Carrión against the honour of his name, the Cid acted with admirable restraint and Menéndez Pidal adds that 'it is astonishing to find moderation poetized as a characteristic of the most redoubtable of warriors; yet not only did he always subordinate his own strength to the law but he knew how to temper justice with mercy.'[1] When he first heard of his dishonour he swore by his beard, which was the most solemn oath a knight could take. Then he complained to the King who was responsible for the unfortunate alliances, and Alfonso convoked his magnates for the trial of the case against the Infantes at Toledo, and appointed the *alcaldes* or judges to try the case. Then the Cid appeared accompanied by a hundred knights wearing armour beneath their rich robes and he wears his long beard tied up to avoid the grave insult of having it 'pulled'. When the session began he asked that the Infantes should return his swords 'Colada' and 'Tizon' which he had given them, and also the wealth he had bestowed upon them at Valencia. Finally he accused them of having dishonoured his daughters—a wrong that could only be settled by duel. To this García Ordoñez and the powerful nobles of the Carrión party answered that men of such proud descent as those of Carrión could never desire, even as paramours, the daughters of a mere miller like the Cid. (This was an allusion to the mills owned by the Cid's father on the banks of the river Ubierna.) The King, however, decided that three of the Cid's vassals should fight the two Infantes and their brother. Just at this juncture two messengers appear on behalf of the Princes of Navarra and Aragon to beg the Cid for the hands of his two daughters. As before, the Cid leaves the decision to the King, who authorizes these new and much more important marriages. Thus the Cid obtains complete satisfaction, and after giving encouragement to his challengers, returns to Valencia. The Infantes fight their challengers in the Vale of Carrión and are defeated. According to the Germanic procedure of ordeal by battle the Infantes on falling to the ground vanquished were bound to utter the formula, 'I am defeated', and the arbiters replied, 'That we hear'. The final trial

[1] R. Menéndez Pidal, *The Cid and His Spain*, London, 1934, p. 441.

scene in Toledo is the grand climax of the whole poem and as a picture of mediaeval society it is unsurpassed. The memory of the Cid lived on in the minds of men and became a perennial theme of poetry. While still alive he inspired the *Carmen Roderici* and possibly other contemporary poems which have since been lost. The '*Poema del Cid*' appeared soon after, at a time when Romance was still too humble a vehicle for great literary conceptions; and it was the Cid's ideals, already deeply rooted in the spirit of the nation, that lifted the language to heights hitherto unknown and made this poem the expression of the ideas and aims of primitive Castile.[1] One after another there followed Spanish epics, which, breathing the loftiest national spirit, sang of the Cid down to the fifteenth century. And then came the ballads in which the hero was sung in the most vigorous traditional poetry ever known and which for hundreds of years were recited by all classes and are still echoed in the popular songs of to-day current from Galicia and Catalonia to Tangier and Chile. Not only did the Cid cause in his own country an efflorescence of poetry such as no hero of any other nation has ever done, but later he fired the imagination of foreign parts. Crossing the Pyrenees, he reigned supreme in French tragedy, and Corneille was followed by Victor Hugo, Leconte de Lisle and Hérédia. Beyond the Rhine, Herder's verses rendered the love-story of the Cid and Jimena as famous as the tragic tale of Siegfried and Kriemhild. In England we might mention the short poems of Lockhart and Gibson, and the longer poetical narratives of Dennis and Southey; in Italy the romances of Monti; in Denmark the fragments composed by Carl Baggers . . . and a last voice in the concert of nations reaches us from the antipodes, where the Tagals also have their poem '*Buhay ni don Rodrigo at ni doña Jimena*'.

---

[1] R. Menéndez Pidal, *The Cid and His Spain*, pp. 435 *et seq.*

Chapter VII

Spanish Chivalry

The '*Poema del Cid*' teaches us that the chivalry of mediaeval Spain rested on a broad democratic basis, and this was a necessity in the secular struggle culminating in the reconquest of the Peninsula. Spanish chivalry partakes of the popular and anti-feudal character of all early Castilian institutions.[1] In practice every one was a caballero, who served in war with a horse, even if he was not an Hidalgo. Thus the horse Babieca was the emblem of chivalry, for he prolonged the legs of the Cid Campeador as his sword Tizona prolonged his arm. So precious was such a horse to the mediaeval knight that when he retired for the night he would keep it tethered in the same room in which he slept with his wife.[2] And when the Cid lay at the point of death in Valencia he commanded that his body be carried, so one of the old ballads tells us, 'in full armour upon his horse Babieca to the Church of San Pedro de Cardeña outside Burgos'. We can imagine that sad procession of knights and retainers, tearing their hair, beating their breasts, throwing ashes on their brow, as they followed the corpse of the Cid, clad in full armour, mounted on the loyal steed. Another ballad tells us that 'Babieca himself understood his sad mission and looked as crestfallen as the mourners.' No horse that ever lived has such a proud history as the Cid's loyal companion of whom he wrote in his last will, 'When ye bury Babieca, dig deep, for shameful thing were it, that he should be ate by curs, who hath trampled down so much currish flesh of Moors.' And this deep traditional affection for the horse that we find in primitive Spanish chivalry passed on to the Conquistadores beyond the seas. 'For, after God, we owed the victory to the horses' is a frequent

[1] A. Pastor, *Essay on the Chivalry of Spain*, in *Chivalry*, ed. by E. Prestage, London, 1928, p. 117.
[2] R. Menéndez Pidal, *La Epopeya Castellana*, p. 112.

phrase in many of the contemporary records of the Conquest. In
the words of Cunninghame Graham, a modern conquistador, if
ever there was one, 'the Conquistadores (after God) owed their
conquest to their horses, and there was an intimate companionship between them that is well-nigh impossible to understand
to-day. A companionship and pride at the same time, such as a
man may feel for a younger brother who has accompanied him in
some adventure. This love of horses pervaded every class and all
conditions of the Spaniards of the time.'[1]

The Cid did not belong to the highest nobility, but to the
Hidalgo class whose members were called *Infanzones*, and the
anonymous author of the poem is entirely in sympathy with the
class of his hero, who was a squire deriving his income from his
mills on the river Ubierna, and spares no pains in satirizing the
vices and failings of the higher class of nobility to whom be-
longed the powerful family of the Infantes of Carrión.

From the outset the chivalry of the Cid was felt to be national
and not merely Castilian, but as Menéndez Pidal says, the poem
is not national because of patriotism in it, but rather as a picture
of the people amongst whom it was written.[2] Prescott in his
history of Ferdinand and Isabella says that in the same way as the
Homeric poems were the most important bond between the
Greek states, the *Cid*, which expressed some of the greatest
national memories, affected deeply the national feeling of
solidarity.[3] There is no allusion to 'Spain' in the manner in which
Roland speaks of 'La France' (170 times), giving that name to the
whole empire of Charlemagne, and looking upon the French as
the chosen people of God. The Cid feels '*quant grant es España*', and
he puts all his loyalty and faith in the King-Emperor whose
dominions include Portugal, Galicia, Leon as well as Castile.
And the pathos of the drama arises from the ingratitude of the
monarch towards his great captain. A really invincible leader has
arisen in Spain, only to find his efforts frustrated by the antagonistic peers and kinsmen who were envious of the Cid's achievements. The charge of *invidia* so often preferred by the Latin
historian connotes a lack of vision: '*Castellani invidentes*'. Such an
invidente was Alfonso himself who found it convenient to promote

---

[1] R. B. Cunninghame Graham, *The Horses of the Conquest*, London, 1930, p. 2.
[2] R. Menéndez Pidal, *The Cid and His Spain*, p. 431.
[3] Prescott, *History of the Reign of Ferdinand and Isabella*, London, 1854.

García Ordoñez in preference to the Cid. But in spite of all this blind, malignant envy, the Cid showed no ill-feeling. When exiled he sought no vengeance; nor did he like Achilles sulk in his tent. On the contrary he went to the help of the King again and again, and, in spite of all the rebuffs from his countrymen, he withdrew to a place where envy could not reach him. The Cid in addition to his qualities as leader had the gift of conciliating his antagonists. He was courteous towards the humble and ready to humble himself before his lord and master. When he became reconciled to the King he humiliated himself before him. As the poem says: 'he bites the grass, tears stream from his eyes, so great was his delight'. And Menéndez Pidal at the end of his monumental historical work '*La España del Cid*', which was published in Madrid in 1929, added the following comment: 'The contemporaries of the Cid pointed to his readiness for conciliation and his public spirit as essential features of the heroic character. Nowadays, and especially since the black year of 1898, how many are there who, feeling themselves cut adrift from the body politic, instead of being irresistibly drawn back to it, do their utmost to bring it into disrepute, as if they took a delight in rending their own flesh. This unedifying attitude has become the fashion amongst our intellectuals, and having spread to the people at large, has led to the proud despotism of the governors and the placid resignation of the governed, as if neither had at heart the interests and the welfare of their country.'[1] Those words were written by the author in 1929, two years before the fall of the monarchy. They were to be even more tragically prophetic than the author believed when he penned them. But it is significant to quote from an article by Edward Herriot entitled '*El final de una Dictadura*' published in the Madrid daily newspaper '*El Sol*' under the date of 25 February 1930. Herriot in the article stated that what precipitated the fall of the Dictatorship was the decided action taken by the Spanish universities; 'to the Universities belongs the honour of having struggled manfully in the past few years for dignity and spiritual independence. The letter, addressed on 27 March 1929, to General Primo de Rivera by Sr. Menéndez Pidal, President of the Spanish Academy and Professor of the University of Madrid, will remain as a document of interest in the history of freedom of thought.'

[1] R. Menéndez Pidal, *The Cid and His Spain*, London, 1934, p. 445.

By the publication of his monumental work on the Cid and his history, Menéndez Pidal had brought to completion the result of many years' intense research. It was a public example of the immense range of his mind. His method resembled that of the great architects of the Middle Ages erecting stone upon stone a gigantic cathedral. Pidal the architect traced out the scheme and drew the plans for his edifice, but then he would call to his assistance his other personalities—Pidal the philologist, Pidal the historian, Pidal the folk-lorist, not forgetting Pidal the biographer. First of all Pidal the philologist and palaeologist published the text, grammar and critical edition of the 'Poema del Cid' in the years 1908–1911. Then came the turn of Pidal the lecturer and literary historian with the book on the Castilian Epic in 1910; and finally, to complete the edifice, we have Pidal the architect and biographer gathering all the themes together in the great unified work portraying the universal figure of Spain's national hero against the vast background of the mediaeval world. When the book appeared Luis de Zulueta wrote the following imaginary dialogue in 'El Liberal': 'We must,' exclaimed Joaquin Costa, 'double-lock the tomb of the Cid to prevent him from riding out again on Babieca.'

'Why?'

'Because the Cid personified collective vanity, external pomp boasting of past glories, and bellicose adventures, whereas the Spanish people needs to remake itself internally, silently, by hard work and culture.'

The Cid rides out again. But this time even Costa himself would congratulate the distinguished director of the Royal Spanish Academy, for this Cid of Menéndez Pidal is not the disfigured and falsified Cid, whom it was necessary to repudiate. After centuries, the Campeador again became the victim of false accusations and endured a spiritual exile. But now we see him return victorious, after triumphing over his enemies, to his loved Castile . . . and again he may cry out the words:

Albricia, Alvar Fañez, ca echados somos de tierra
mas a gran honra tornaremos a Castiella!

(Be of good heart, Alvar Fañez; they've driven us from our land, But we'll return in greater honour to Castilla.)

Chapter VIII

The Ballads

The primitive epic poem of the Cid, and, indeed, all ancient epic poetry, paid but scant attention to the themes of love and courtship. Love occupied in social life a less important place than it does to-day, and marriage was a subject of family concern in which the individual had but little to say. The *cantares de gesta* were baronial poems of war and public life, and love was restricted to the courtly poetry of the town dweller. Nevertheless, there came a time when heroic poetry began to lose its power and domination, and it was then that the tiny blind-folded god, armed with bow and arrows, began to seek his victories among the bearded heroes of the epic sagas.[1] Where we notice this intrusion of Cupid is in '*Las Mocedades de Rodrigo*', describing the youth of Roderick the Cid and his courtship of his wife Jimena Diaz. Older authorities such as Amador de los Rios upheld the theory that this poem was anterior to the '*Cantar de Mío Cid*', but Menéndez Pidal proved conclusively that this latter was the older. As Pidal says, the poetical Cid lived his mature life in the '*Cantar de Mío Cid*', and only later, practically at the end of his life in epic poetry, did he reappear in '*Las Mocedades de Rodrigo*' as a young hero 'treading the primrose path of dalliance'. The first account that is known of the '*Rodrigo*', as this poem is called, is to be found in the 'General Chronicle' of 1344—a chronicle which was not known to Amador de los Rios, for it was only in 1895 that Menéndez Pidal himself identified it and began to make it known to scholars. He was then able to prove that the '*Rodrigo*' was not known to the authors of the 'First General Chronicle', which was composed under the orders of Alfonso el Sabio, and continued after his death in 1289. Thus Menéndez Pidal was able to show

[1] R. Menéndez Pidal, *La Epopeya Castellana*, pp. 107–108.

34

that the poem appeared in the fourteenth not the thirteenth century. In accordance with the usual custom the entire story of Rodrigo's courtship is prosified in the Chronicle of 1344. The chronicle describes how the house of Vivar quarrelled with Gomez, Count of Gormaz, and in the mêlée Rodrigo killed the count. A daughter of the victim then appeared before the King and, kneeling before him, said: 'I am the younger daughter of Count Gormaz whom Rodrigo de Vivar has slain: give me him as husband, for well do I know that he will be the most powerful vassal of your kingdom, and if you grant him to me as husband, I will pardon him the murder he has committed.' The King hearkened to her petition and bade the young Rodrigo to come to Palencia, and thus the marriage was celebrated, but Rodrigo on his return to his house with his wife swore a mighty oath that he would never consort with her in town or countryside (*yermo ni en poblado*) until he had won five pitched battles by the strength of his arm; and so he departed to the Moorish frontier. These incidents have no foundation in historical fact. The Jimena mentioned in the '*Cantar de Mío Cid*' was not Jimena Gomez, but Jimena Diaz, daughter of Count Diego de Asturias, a woman of royal descent, for she was the niece of King Alfonso VI. All the details of the '*Rodrigo*' are conventional incidents that appear again and again in narrative poems. It was common for a girl of noble birth, were she orphan, to appeal to the King, asking him to act as father and find a husband for her, but the characteristic point of the story is that the bridegroom is the murderer of the bride's father, and this was the origin of the great dramatic scene of the Cid in Spanish and French literature. After the poem of *Rodrigo* had been prosified in the Chronicle of 1344, we find a further poem (attributed by Pidal to the beginning of the fifteenth century) which makes still greater alterations in the story, for the desire of the adapter was to exaggerate the deeds of so popular a hero and pander to a sensation-loving public that read with avidity fantastic Romances of Chivalry such as Amadis of Gaul. Instead of the 'beautifully smiling' hero 'who girded on his sword in a happy hour' we find an arrogant and insolent young man, devoid of measure or good sense, who, when he opens his lips, utters threats and blood-curdling oaths. The more affably the King behaves to him the more his insolence increases, and at last the King cries out in wonder: 'This is no man but the devil himself!' This fierce young Cid captured the imagination of the people and roused their affectionate interest. They applauded the betrothal scene, and after rewarding the minstrel with money or gifts of garments, they would take leave of him, humming to themselves the verses and they would spread them far and wide. The fragmentary verses of the old epic form thus became the substance of what is called a popular or old ballad, which was orally transmitted from generation to generation. Even at the beginning of the sixteenth century the ballad describing the scene with the King was remembered by the folk, but so shortened that no explanation was given why the young Cid Roderick and his father went to court; nor did the ballad refer to the betrothal with which the interview with the King terminated. All that caught the imagination of the people and remained in their memory was the fierce, indomitable spirit of the young warrior, who feels it a humiliation to do homage to his liege lord. When Menéndez Pidal says that the people or folk was the author of the old ballads he means the sum total of all the individuals who invent, remember or recite a ballad, a story or a traditional legend, which is repeated from generation to generation.[1] In the poems repeating this ballad, each performer introduces changes and variants, according to his own tastes, with the result that in the course of time it becomes rounded and polished like a stone that has been rolled along by a river flood. Menéndez Pidal gives to such anonymous ballads the name 'Traditional Poetry'. They are the work of many authors, who successively have elaborated the theme. The publicity of a poetical work was not made by the number of copies written out, but by the performance of the reciter, who was its best editor and publicity agent. He it was who performed it in every house and *plaza*, so that eventually it became known as a *cantar muy dicho*. All knew it by heart a hundred leagues around, as Villasandino, one of the minstrels in the *Cancionero de Baena*, said of his own ballads:

> '*Mas lueñe de cien jornadas*
> *son mis dezires sabidos.*'

The perpetuation of a well-known ballad did not take place

[1] R. Menéndez Pidal, *Poesía Popular y Poesía Tradicional en la Literatura Española*, p. 126.

without many modifications, for the minstrels and performers were not faithful to the text in their singing. They lost their memory and adapted. As an instance, we may quote the anecdote of the shoe-maker *juglar*, who sang before the famous poet Juan Manuel, but misquoted some of the latter's lines. 'You are wrong', cried the poet angrily, and he tore the cobbler's shoes to bits.[1] Juan Manuel dreaded any adaptation or re-editing of his works, and was even afraid of the errors of copyists. He therefore corrected with his own pen his own manuscript and deposited it in the Monastery of Peñafiel, forbidding any one to reproduce the poems unless he previously consulted the original manuscript in the monastery. This attitude was the opposite to that of his contemporary, the king of minstrels, the arch priest of Híta, who recommended that his ballads should be tossed from one person to another like a ball in a game played by ladies, and gave special instructions to posterity in his '*Libro de Buen Amor*', saying:

> '*Qualquier omne que lo oya, si bien trobar supiere,*
> *puede mas añadir e emendar lo que quisiere.*'

(Let any one who is an accomplished poet add and correct as best he will.)

Those who sang the old ballads based on the '*Mocedades de Rodrigo*' followed the method of the archpriest and modified the traditional story, adding new touches until they had created a new personality for the Cid, which was a complete contrast to the patriarchal figure of the '*Poema del Cid*'. Professor Entwistle in speaking of the aggressive young Cid of the ballads makes the following very apt comparison: 'As the embodiment of reckless force of will the young Cid is the Don Juan of the Middle Ages; the Don Juan of the classical period is inferior to the young Cid inasmuch as his field of conquest is much more trivial. He resembles those great nobles of the later Philips, full of great ambitions without adequate outlet owing to the jealous royal policy. If the young Cid is Don Juan, the old Cid is Don Quixote; but a Don Quixote not frustrated, not tilting against windmills. He seeks justice, but he obtains it; he releases not galley-slaves, but loyal vassals unjustly suspected. The two immutable por-

---

[1] Juan Manuel tells this anecdote of a Troubadour from Perpignan, *Bibl. Aut. Esp.*, vol. 51.

traits of the Spanish mind thus emerge from the Romancero of the Cid, less complete than when later sketched with all the increased literary power of the Renaissance, but more masters of their fate.'[1] The theme of the young Cid and his marriage became the theme of drama, and in the seventeenth century Guillen de Castro in his play 'Las Mocedades del Cid' increased the dramatic tension by supposing that the Cid and Jimena were in love before the quarrel between their parents, which led to the murder of her father by the Cid. In this way there arises the dramatic struggle between love and vengeance which takes place alternately in the minds of the Cid and Jimena. Corneille then took the subject of Castro, and as Boileau said: 'Tout Paris pour Chimène eut les yeux de Rodrigue.'

---

[1] W. J. Entwistle, European Balladry, Oxford, 1939, pp. 171–172.

Chapter IX

The Vogue of the Ballads in Spain

Even in the earliest days we note the existence in Castile of a profoundly democratic spirit; in her original constitution she was as free as any nation needs to be for all the purposes of social security and individual happiness. Her kings were her captains and her judges, the chiefs and the models of a gallant nobility, and the protectors of a manly and independent peasantry; but the authority with which they were invested was guarded by the most accurate limitations, nay—in case they should exceed the boundary of their legal power—the statute book of the realm itself contained exact rules for the conduct of a constitutional insurrection to recall them to their duty, or to punish them for its desertion. Every order of society had, more or less directly, its representatives in the national council; every Spaniard, of whatever degree, was penetrated with a sense of his own dignity as a freeman—his own nobility as a descendant of the Visigoths.[1] And this fundamental democratic sense instead of suppressing the nobility actually extended it to those below, so that each peasant might become an hidalgo. In the fourteenth and fifteenth centuries, in proportion as the ancient noble families became broken and more disorganized, the municipal orders living on the Andalusian frontier became strengthened in patriotism, owing to their struggles against the enemy, and both nobles and lower orders combined together on equality in the national effort. Every day witnessed situations where a simple farmer, as in Lope de Vega's play '*Peribáñez*', might become a knight and prove as staunch a champion of his own *pundonor* as one of the nobility. And we discover the same spirit in other dramas of Lope,

[1] J. G. Lockhart, *Spanish Ballads*, London, Introd., p. xxv.

39

such as *'Fuenteovejuna'*, *'El Mejor Alcalde, el Rey'*, and *'El Alcalde de Zalamea'*, where the peasant is conscious of his own dignity and proudly claims that his honour has the same right to be respected as that of the noble. As Menéndez Pidal shows, this democratic spirit caused the spirit of heroic poetry to change its course. The poems of vast proportions, which had been composed to be recited by professional minstrels in the leisurely atmosphere of the banqueting hall, became transformed into shorter poems appealing to men of less leisure and of lower station, who would sing them for their own recreation.[1]

Heroic poetry itself began to lose its markedly military character and seek themes of adventure and romance that would appeal to a wider public, for, in contrast to the later French epic, which was written for a restricted public of connoisseurs, the Castilian epic was always a public performance and never lost its ancient free versification which was more suited to recitation than to reading.

Very few heroic ballads have been preserved in manuscripts of the fifteenth century, and nearly all the oldest that we know descended by oral tradition until the days when printing saved them from oblivion. Professor Entwistle has in his survey summed up the benefits which the Spanish ballads gained by this contact with epical poems. They gained, he says, in gravity, imagination of a literal kind, dramatism and nationality. The old Castilian *gravitas* freed them from the triviality which is so prominent a feature of other balladries; as a repository of all that concerned the Castilian spirit and as a veracious account of Spanish history the Romancero attained a unique authority. Certain cycles of ballads, especially those of the Infantes of Lara, stand out for their exceptional fidelity. It is from them, after all, that we must glean our best idea of the old *Cantares de Gesta*; they give us, as prose cannot, the rush and fury of poetry. Their language is starker, fitted to the stark ferocity of the action. It is in them that we hear the actors speak out their jealousies and hates.[2]

Most of the authorities agree that the Castilian ballads rose to prominence in the middle years of the fourteenth century, when Spain was torn asunder by the Civil War which raged between

---

[1] R. Menéndez Pidal, *La Epopeya Castellana*, p. 138.
[2] W. J. Entwistle, *op. cit.*, p. 169.

King Pedro, the son and successor of Alfonso XI, and his bastard
brothers. Pedro's mind had been poisoned in early youth by the
ill treatment he and his mother had received from his father, who
neglected them for his mistress, Eleanora de Guzmán and the
bastard sons she bore him. Thus when Pedro came to the throne
in 1350 the country was divided into two factions—the king's
party and the opposition headed by the eldest bastard, Henry of
Trastamara. Pedro's task was a grim one, for he had to curb the
power of the nobles and establish his kingly power over territories
that had been alienated from the Crown in a period of feudal
anarchy. Pedro was by nature brooding and revengeful, and
would not forgive the injuries he had received. His position, too,
was complicated by his liaison with Doña María de Padilla, for
whom he neglected Blanca de Borbon, his wife, from the day of
her wedding. He afterwards married Doña María, thus legitimiz-
ing her children and adding to his difficulties, owing to the in-
trigues of her relatives. Meanwhile, Henry of Trastamara and
his brothers were seeking the help of foreign powers against Don
Pedro's government, with the result that the revengeful king embarked upon a course of murder which earned him the name
of Pedro the Cruel. The Civil War between Pedro the Cruel
and Henry of Trastamara became a struggle between foreign
powers on Spanish soil. The French king and Pedro IV of Aragon
were sympathetic to Henry, but Edward III of England, sup-
porting Pedro as the legitimate king of Spain, sent his son the
Black Prince, the flower of chivalry, to his assistance. Nevertheless, in spite of English help, which led to the victory of Nájera,
Pedro's affairs went from bad to worse, and the Civil War came
to a sudden end at Montiel in 1369, when Henry murdered his
brother. The ballads deal with the events of these turbulent
years but nearly all of them were composed in support of the
Trastamara faction and were violently hostile to Pedro. In fact
these ballads resemble anonymous editorial articles of bitter
political comment inspired by the usurper, Henry of Trastamara,
and were used as propaganda of his cause throughout the country, and so effective was this method of propaganda by anonymous ballad that the loyalty of Pedro's own partisans was sapped
by the accusations, and the grave Chancellor Pero López de
Ayala embedded them in his chronicle, with the result that Pedro

D

became a byword of cruelty even after his death. Nevertheless, when we turn to Seville, we find other influences championing Pedro's cause and transforming him into a fantastic hero of the Arabian Nights, a kind of Harun Al Rashid, wandering about the city at night, observing the lives of his humblest subjects and seeking to right the wrongs of those who were the victims of injustice. This was the monarch who became the hero of many plays of Lope de Vega and was known as Pedro el Justiciero—Peter the Dispenser of Justice.

All through the later years of the fourteenth century and the whole of the fifteenth century the ballads, like the modern newspapers, spread far and wide the news of public events. It was in this way that the frontier ballads came into being, for they informed the people of the engagements and skirmishes against the Moorish kingdom of Granada, and the kings continued to make full use of them for propaganda. Henry IV, for instance, in 1462, ordered a ballad to be composed on a campaign against the Moors and made the singers of the royal chapel perform it. Similarly, in the chapel of Ferdinand and Isabel ballads were sung in honour of the latest victories in the war against Granada. Indeed, so many minstrels among the Moors and Spaniards sang of the Granada war that we are reminded of the words of the blind minstrel Homer, when he told the tale of the Argive Danaans and sang the lay of Ilios: 'All this the gods have fashioned, and have woven the skein of death for men, that there might be a song in the ears even of the folk of aftertime.' No war save the Trojan ever inspired such a wealth of ballads as this ten years' conflict which led to the final fall of the Crescent in Spain. The ballads celebrating the exploits of the Christian knights were ever answered by those devoted to the Moorish champions in continuous antistrophe. In reply to the songs of Ponce de León, Gonzalo de Córdoba or Alonso Aguilar, we hear the refrains of the capture of Alhama, the bullfights in the Bibarrambla, the deeds of Muza and the feuds of Zegries and Abencerrages.[1] Reading the ballads in the *Romancero General* to-day we see, as in a vision projected before our inner eye, the succeeding events of those years, and such refrains as '*Ay de mi Alhama!*'—'Woe is me, Alhama!'—echo and re-echo through our minds like a melan-

[1] W. Starkie, *Grand Inquisitor*, London, 1940, pp. 177-178.

choly prophecy of Nemesis to come. And while we read the glowing accounts of the chroniclers describing the triumphal entry of the Christian army into the Alhambra, we hear in the distance the ballad describing the forlorn departure of Boabdil: *'En la ciudad de Granada grandes alaridos dan.'*

There was crying in Granada when the sun was going down,
Some calling on the Trinity, some calling on Mahoun.
Here passed away the Koran, there in the Cross was borne,
And here was heard the Christian bell, and there the Moorish horn.
Te Deum Laudamus was up the Alcala sung.
Down from the Alhambra's minarets were all the crescents flung;
The arms thereon of Aragon they with Castile's display.
One king comes in in triumph, one weeping goes away.
Thus cried the weeper, while his hands his old white beard did tear,
'Farewell, farewell, Granada! Thou city without peer.
Woe, woe, thou pride of Heathendom, seven hundred years and
     more
Have gone since first the faithful thy royal sceptre bore.'[1]

As a result of the War of Granada there followed a period whose spirit we can still recapture to-day, when we gaze at the fifty-four scenes carved by the German artist in 1489 on the choir stalls of the Cathedral of Toledo, under the patronage of the great Maecenas, Cardinal Mendoza. These reliefs tell the story of the events described in prose in the chronicles of Bernaldez, Valera, Pulgar and Palencia, and in verse in the countless songs of the Romancero. Chivalry was becoming a ceremonial display and a ritual, which was being destroyed by the new inventions of the military engineer. Most of the reliefs, indeed, show forces of artillery in action, bombards mounted on ox-drawn carts, engineers firing globular masses mixed with gunpowder; but in spite of those machines of destruction, which were to destroy chivalry, the artist revelled in the final display of that chivalry. We see Isabel, to whose inspiration the triumph of the campaign was due. She appeared among her soldiers like some celestial visitant to cheer their faltering spirits and inspire them with her own energy. The attachment to Isabel was the pervading

[1] Version by J. G. Lockhart, *op. cit.*

principle which animated the whole nation with one common impulse and impressed a unity of design on all its movements. Years afterwards, in 1526, the Venetian ambassador Andrés Navagero, when travelling in Spain, noted how personal heroism had increased among the knights owing to the presence of the Catholic queen and her suite of ladies. 'There was not a knight,' he says, 'but was in love with some lady of the court, and as these damsels witnessed every deed that was performed, and armed with their own fair hands every knight who rode into battle, begging them to prove the strength of their love by their deeds of valour, what man, were he ever so puny or weak, would not have preferred to lose his life a thousand times rather than return in shame to face his lady? Hence one may say that love was the true victor of that war.' This quotation of Navagero explains the spirit of the Moorish ballads—*romances moriscos*—of the sixteenth century, which were but a later form of the frontier ballads we have described. The Spanish poets disguised in Moorish fancy-dress their lyrical sentiments, and these ballads became the fashion among such writers as Ginés Pérez de Hita, who incrusts them like gems in the vivid setting of his prose. With exquisite taste, he weaves fantastic tales around those ballads, evoking for us as in a dream the scenes of the Arabian Nights in flowering corners and patios lulled by murmuring fountains. The enchantment of Pérez de Hita's book made the Moorish ballads famous throughout the world and inspired romantics like Chateaubriand and Washington Irving to embroider this oriental romance.

The capture of Granada, which was the final display of chivalry in all its trappings, also marked the end of national heroic poetry and the inspiration of the Romancero disappeared never to return again.[1] Even the great enterprises culminating in the exploration and conquest of the New World did not inspire a new traditional poetry. In America the same Castilian race was not lacking, and heroism assumed there gigantic proportions; empires were destroyed, and immense territories were gained for God and Caesar. In spite of all, no fresh Romancero appeared. The heroic muse, who had transferred her abode from old Castile, where she had established herself, in the tenth and

[1] R. Menéndez Pidal, *La Epopeya Castellana*, p. 156.

twelfth centuries, to the kingdom of Jaén and Murcia in the fourteenth century, was unable to emigrate to the New Continent. Although America was colonized at the time when the ballads were in the memory of every one, yet it was no longer a creative period. Cortés and the Conquistadores remembered by heart innumerable old *romances*, but they created no poetry like the frontier ballads. The Renaissance made a cult of the Romancero, for it regarded such poems as the products of nature pure and undefiled and far superior in their unaffected simplicity to the conceits and circumlocutions of art.

One of the most universal spirits of the Renaissance, Montaigne, held that it was not reasonable that art should gain the point of honour over our great and powerful mother Nature. 'We have,' he adds, 'so overburdened the beauty and richness of her works with our inventions, that we have quite smothered her. And yet when she shines in her purity, she marvellously puts to shame our vain and trivial efforts.' And in another essay, quoting Plato, he defines Nature as 'enigmatic poetry; as we might say, perhaps, a veiled and shadowy picture with glimpses here and there of an infinite variety of false lights, to exercise our conjectures'.[1] In England many of the courtiers and poets were thrilled by the ballads, and Sir Philip Sidney declared that when he heard a blind minstrel recite the ballad of Percy and Douglas his heart was stirred 'as with a trumpet', and Ben Jonson on one occasion asserted that he would have preferred to have been the author of the ballad 'Chevy Chase' than of all his works. And yet the voice of criticism also made itself felt, as in the case of the Marquis of Santillana, who, when writing in 1445, speaks of 'the lowest order of versifiers, those who without any order, rule or count compose these ballads and songs in which persons of low, menial state delight'. As Professor Entwistle shows in his interesting comparative survey, the ballad people are the whole people organized under its natural leaders: they prefer aristocracy to the proletariat, and often seem to be interested in the lesser nobility. It is the local chief, not the nation's king, who counts for so much in frontier ballads; the Percy and Douglas, Sayavedra, Bishop Gonzalo of Jaén, Fajardo, Kolokotronis. The ballads, in contradistinction to the epic, which was inspired by larger

[1] Montaigne, *Essays*, trans. by E. J. Trechmann, London, 1927, Vol. 1, p. 537.

movements of the folk, are concerned with local heroes, raids, and excitements of no more than episodic value in the nation's history. Even a national movement, such as the conquest of Granada, is broken up by ballad poets into disconnected episodes of personal and local interest.[1]

The important point was that the ballads were directed to an unlettered audience not necessarily illiterate who had ears to hear; not to readers. When the ballads were printed they ceased to be transmitted orally and began to lose their vigour. As the learned poets of the Renaissance began to cultivate the *genre*, the ballad increased in refinement and reflected the poetical ideals not only of Spain but of Italy. The poets revived the old traditional *romances*, refining and elaborating the texts with variants. Menéndez Pidal warns us not to look upon the Romancero as an obscure *mélange* of aristocratic and plebeian elements. Both elements exist in it, but they are perfectly differentiated, and the various versions of the same ballad, which may to-day be collected from tradition, show clearly whether they spring from the educated or the unlettered classes. The versions which were traditionally elaborated among the cultivated classes of the *siglo de oro* are the genuine Romancero that we all know, and thus the Romancero is popular in the highest sense of the word, not low and fit for those of menial condition, as the Marquis of Santillana said, but noble owing to its heroic origins, and it continues to maintain its noble spirit owing to the process of elaboration it received in the period of the Renaissance. Even so strict a humanist as Juan de Valdés praised the ballads for their freshness and simplicity, and contrasted them with the low plebeian style of many of the poems by court poets.[2] The court poets, whether humble versifiers like Sepúlveda, or great poets like Lope de Vega and Gongora, composed many poetical variations on the ancient themes. As a parallel to the pastoral verse which became the 'escapist' form of literature *par excellence* in the sixteenth century, there arose the pastoral ballad with idyllic scenes from Arcadia, peopled with Amaryllis, Phyllis and their lisping swains, and at the same time the process of poetic idealization appears in another traditional *genre*, the artificial Moorish

[1] W. J. Entwistle, *op. cit.*, p. 30.
[2] R. Menéndez Pidal, *Flor Nueva de Romances Viejos*, Madrid, 1943, Intro., pp. 37–38.

ballad of the latter years of the sixteenth century. The *Romancero General* of 1604 is the Golden Treasury containing the new ballads of these modern poets. At the courts of Charles V and Philip II the ballads became so popular that it was customary to carry them about in little volumes of pocket size. They became still more popular in the *salons* at Court and in the palaces of the noble families owing to the vogue given to the old melodies by the players of the *vihuela*, who were very fond of playing variations on them through the necessity of relieving the monotony of the accompaniment during the recitation of a long *romance*.[1] To take one characteristic example, the famous lines of the ballad:

> *Mis arreos son las armas,*
> *Mi descanso el pelear,*
> *Mi cama las duras peñas,*
> *Mi dormir, siempre velar*
> (My ornaments are arms,
> My pastime is in War,
> My bed is cold upon the wold,
> My lamp yon star),

quoted by Don Quixote as he greeted the landlord of the inn whom he took to be governor of a fortress, were set as a song with accompaniment for the *vihuela* by Luys Milán, a Valencian lutenist and composer, who won renown by his '*Cortesano*', a work inspired by '*Il Cortigiano*' of Baldassare Castiglione.[2] In 1535 Luys Milán published the first book of music for the *vihuela* called '*El Maestro*' containing *romances*, as well as *fantasías, pavanes* and *villancicos*. The *vihuela* and the guitar became the typical domestic instruments of sixteenth-century Spain, and accompanied ballads[3]: we meet them in the palaces as well as in the taverns and the barbers' shops, for they were instruments for amateurs as well as for professionals, and the Spanish lute-books generally begin with easy lessons for a beginner. The lute was also the chief instrument for serenading fair ladies beneath their balconies, and as we know from the pastoral novel, the *Diana* of Montemayor, it was customary to include *romances* in their serenades.

[1] J. B. Trend, *The Music of Spanish History to 1600*, Oxford, 1926, pp. 105–106.
[2] J. B. Trend, *op. cit.*, pp. 115–116.
[3] Grove's *Dictionary of Music*, London, 1940. Article on the difference between vihuela, lute, and guitar.

Chapter X

The Ballads and Don Quixote

It is to the works of Cervantes that we should turn if we would understand how closely identified the ballads became with the lives and traditions of Spaniards in the sixteenth century. Cervantes all his life was a ballad-lover, and though lacking the lyrical genius of his great contemporaries, composed some *romances* that are perpetuated in the Romancero. His head echoed and re-echoed with the sound of countless ballads, and no sooner did he sit down to write a story than he began to recall scraps of ballads, tunes, proverbs, refrains, and countless quips and cranks that he had picked up on his vagabond journey through life; for he was of insatiably inquisitive disposition, for ever asking the why and the wherefore. He was, too, he admits, a voracious reader, but of such imperious curiosity that he would pick up scraps of paper in the street to see what was written on them. All was grist that came to his mill. Like his contemporary, Shakespeare, he drew his sustenance 'as we draw air, fast as 'tis ministered, from courtier, scholar, soldier', from tradesmen, from all the mixed public that frequented the taverns, theatres, inns, and above all, the high roads that cross the monotonous *meseta* of Castile and La Mancha. Cervantes absorbed the whole mass and movement of life; the life that surged around him, and the life already recorded in stories, dramas, chronicles and ballads: both became for him raw material which he re-shaped, re-composed and revitalized in accordance with his own genius.

It was Menéndez Pidal's deep study of the Romancero that led him to investigate the ballads connected with *Don Quixote* and enabled him to propound an ingenious theory concerning the origins of the immortal work. He embodied the theory in the Presidential Address given at the Ateneo in Madrid on 1 December 1920.[1] At the beginning he explains how the romance of chivalry evolved from the Breton forms current in France in the twelfth century, and the prose works of the first half of the thirteenth century, down to the Spanish romance of Amadis of Gaul, which indicates what a change had come over society. In contrast to the ancient forms, which were based upon an austere philosophy of life and were patriarchal in spirit, we meet in 'Amadis' a new restless kind of hero who yearns continually for dangerous adventure, and yet trembles and is abashed in the presence of his lady, and hardly dares to look upon her. This new hero represented a new social consciousness. The French mediaeval novel reappeared in Spain at the end of the Middle Ages and lasted on into the Renaissance, when García Ordoñez de Montalvo re-edited and amplified the story of Amadis. As a result there arose in the Peninsula a host of knights—*Esplandians, Lisuartes, Florisels, Palmerins* and countless more who owed their origin to the '*Amadis*'. The romance of chivalry became the favourite reading, not only of the general public, but even of the élite, for we find tributes paid to them by such austere spirits as Saint Ignatius, Saint Teresa and the Emperor Charles V. The success of this form of literature lasted all the first half of the sixteenth century, but then came a sharp decline, and the last really successful book of chivalry, was '*El Caballero de Febo*' by Diego Ortuñez de Calahorra (1562), which became known beyond Spain and inspired the English theatre in the days of Marlowe and Shakespeare.[2] It is interesting to note that there were sharp differences of opinion in those days over the books of chivalry. Whereas moralists like Vives and Fray Luis de León considered them a national plague, other thinkers of no less austere minds, such as the Chancellor Pero López de Ayala in the fourteenth, and Juan de Valdés and Saint Teresa in the sixteenth century, defended them. Cervantes grew up surrounded by passionate enthusiasts of the books of chivalry and no less passionate denouncers of that *genre*, and so he had mixed feelings about them. Undoubtedly in *Don Quixote* he clearly expresses his intention to discredit the

---

[1] *Un Aspecto de la Elaboración del Quijote*, Madrid, 1920. The text of the Interlude is printed in *El Hospital de los Podridos*, ed. by D. Alonso, Madrid, 1936. See also J. Millé y Gimenez, *Sobre el Génesis del Quijote*, Barcelona, 1930, and W. J. Entwistle, *Cervantes*, Oxford, 1940, pp. 103–106, for criticism.

[2] R. Menéndez Pidal, *op. cit.*, p. 10.

books of chivalry, and on this account he has been reproached, first by Lord Byron, who accused him of 'smiling Spain's chivalry away', then by Léon Gautier, the great champion of chivalry in nineteenth-century France, and finally by Falangist intellectuals in an article entitled, '*Porque no nos gusta el Quijote?*' ('*El Español*', 31 October 1942). Menéndez Pelayo, on the other hand, held the view that Cervantes did not set out to kill an ideal but to transfigure and exalt it, and that all the poetic, noble and human qualities of chivalry were embodied, to the highest degree, in his masterpiece. *Don Quixote* was thus the last of the books of chivalry and the greatest.[1]

Between these two extreme opinions Menéndez Pidal takes up an intermediary position. *Don Quixote*, he thinks, is the last of a series of works, which combined both heroic and comic elements. One of the oldest examples of this type of literature was '*Le Pélerinage de Charlemagne*', and in more recent times there were the Italian romances of chivalry, which presented their heroes in satirical guise. Boiardo, for instance, delights in describing Orlando as *babbione* and always tricked by Angelica: Ariosto for ever makes fun of his hero, and nearly a century later Cervantes in determined passages of *Don Quixote* echoes the satiric spirit of the Italian poem. Menéndez Pidal, however, maintains that the original inspiration of Don Quixote did not come to Cervantes from the Italian romances, but from a humble and even unpretentious Spanish literary *genre*, which allowed a franker and cruder criticism of chivalry. In these works the method adopted was to personify the ideals of chivalry in a lunatic, whose crazy notions bring him into collision with the hard world of everyday. One of these works has come down to us—the '*Entremés de los romances*' or Ballad Interlude, which was intended to be a satire on the mania for ballads in Spain during the years 1591 to 1597.[2] Menéndez Pidal was of the opinion that this interlude inspired Cervantes to write the first episodes of *Don Quixote*.

The Interlude describes how a poor farmer, Bartolo by name, goes mad as a result of a surfeit of ballads of chivalry, and he wishes to imitate the deeds that are described in them; so he arms himself *cap-à-pie* in grotesque accoutrements, says farewell to his

[1] R. Menéndez Pidal, *op. cit.*, p. 17.
[2] *Ibid.*

wife, saddles an ass, and accompanied by his squire, Bandurrio, rides out into open country in search of adventure. He believes himself El Almoradi, the Moor Tarfe of the Moorish ballads, and a knight-errant to his finger-tips. He rushes to defend a fair shepherdess from the attentions of her swain, but the latter seizes his lance and lays low the 'righter of wrongs and undoer of injuries'. This episode in the Interlude bears a close similarity to the drubbing of the Knight by the lackey of the Toledan merchants in the fifth chapter of Don Quixote, for even the excuses which Bartolo makes, attributing his defeat to his mount, closely resemble the words uttered by the Manchegan Knight as he lies upon the ground. A further coincidence is that both knights-errant in their despair quote the same ballad, namely that of the Marquis of Mantua, and when the family of Bartolo arrive to give assistance, the latter, like Don Quixote, when the labourer succours him, addresses his family in lines from the same ballad:

> O noble Marquis of Mantua,
> My carnal lord and uncle!

Bartolo, too, is transported home to his village in the same manner as Don Quixote, and on the way both victims in their ravings quote from the *romance* of the Marquis of Mantua and from the Moorish ballads. The follies of the two madmen and the comments uttered by the neighbours and the families in both cases resemble one another closely.

According to the critics, the Interlude was written about 1588, the year of the Armada (though the first printed edition of the work is dated 1611), for Bartolo plans to attack Drake and Queen Elizabeth, and the ballads quoted in the work belong, all but three, to the period 1580–1585, and these others were printed in 1589, 1593, and 1597.[1] Menéndez Pidal, however, holds that the Interlude can be proved to be anterior to *Don Quixote* by the fact that its central theme is a satire on the Romancero, and all the allusions refer to the personalities in the ballads. The main purpose of Cervantes, on the contrary, was to satirize the books of chivalry, but he strays from his theme when he makes Don Quixote rave and rant in the style of the heroes of the ballads,

---

[1] W. J. Entwistle, *Cervantes*, p. 104.

thus following the example of Bartolo.[1] What occurred was that
Cervantes became so impressed by the comic incidents of the
Interlude that, for a moment, he hesitated whether to pursue the
scheme he had embarked upon for his novel. Conscious, however, of the literary value of the Romancero and remembering
that the books of chivalry were execrated far and wide, he no
longer vacillated, and continued to make them the main butt of
his satire. At the same time he used certain details of the Interlude in constructing his general scheme. Menéndez Pidal, in discussing the various inconsistencies in the sequence and arrange-
ment of episodes in the First Part, adds that these inconsistencies
caused some critics to expatiate on the author's impulsive genius
which drove him to write in hot precipitation without re-reading
or correcting; others, on the contrary, held that such statements
were banal *clichés*, for it was well known that Cervantes corrected
and re-wrote portions of his works.[2]

Menéndez Pidal was of the opinion that Cervantes purposely
did not round off the story of Don Quixote with the same precise
care as he did the short exemplary novels, with the result that the
personality of his hero became more and more complex as the
book progressed. 'We start from the supposition,' he continues,
'that Cervantes did not spontaneously create the figure of the
Manchegan Knight out of his imagination, but was, to a certain
extent, influenced by the Interlude of Ballads; nor did he mould
the character of his protagonist according to a definite preconceived plan; and it was only as the work progressed slowly, and,
at times, tentatively, that he extracted and brought to life the
noble complexity of the character which had been lying dormant
in his mind from the start.'[3]

Some critics will disagree with Menéndez Pidal's thesis that
Cervantes did not spontaneously create the figure of the Knight
but was influenced by the Interlude. It seems to us that the first
ten lines of the first chapter are an unmistakable proof that Don
Quixote sprang from the imagination of Cervantes as spontaneously as Pallas Athene from the brain of Zeus. No hero of
fiction has ever stamped himself so indelibly from the outset upon
the minds of his readers. 'At a village of La Mancha, whose name

---

[1] R. Menéndez Pidal, *op. cit.*, p. 20.
[2] *Ibid.*, p. 25.
[3] *Ibid.*, p. 26.

I do not wish to remember, there lived a little while ago one of those gentlemen who are wont to keep a lance upon the rack, an old buckler, a lean horse, and a swift greyhound. His stew had more mutton than beef in it, and most nights he ate the remains salted and cold. Lentil soup on Fridays; "tripe and trouble" on Saturdays, and an occasional pigeon as an extra delicacy on Sundays consumed three-quarters of his income. The remainder was spent on a jerkin of fine puce, velvet breeches, and slippers of the same stuff for holidays, and a suit of good honest homespun for work-days. His family consisted of a housekeeper about forty, a niece not yet twenty, and a lad who served him both in the field and at home, and could saddle the horse or use the pruning knife. Our gentleman was about fifty years of age; of a sturdy constitution, but wizened and gaunt-featured, an early riser and a devotee of the chase.'

This short pen portrait tells us more about our visionary gentleman than a volume of biography. He is no *figurón* (or 'humour', as Ben Jonson would say) like Bartolo, but a man of flesh and bones. Indeed we might even assert in Pirandellian fashion that the Don is more vital than a man of flesh and bones, for whereas human beings are ever-changeable and their reality changes from to-day to to-morrow, and on they pass and die, a character created by the imagination of the artist has his life fixed within immutable bounds. For Nature uses the instrument of human fantasy in order to follow her high creative purpose. A character in a novel comes to life just as a tree, as a stone, as a butterfly, as a woman. And he who has the fortune to be born a character can afford to jeer even at death, for he will never die. And to live for ever, he has no need of amazing gifts or miracle working. Who was Don Quixote? And yet he lives on eternally as a live germ—just because he had the luck to find a fertilizing womb, an imagination which knew how to bring him up and nourish him so that he might live for ever.[1] And let us note that Cervantes will never let us lose sight of his lantern-jawed hero, and from time to time he makes other characters in the novel describe him as: 'a man of tall stature, hair 'twixt black and grey, nose aquiline and somewhat hooked, and the mustachios heavy, black and drooping'. And again: 'his pale, gaunt face, half

[1] W. Starkie, *Pirandello*, London, 1937, pp. 206–207.

a league long, his job lot of arms and his grave courtly manner'.[1]

Where did Cervantes see him? In 1863 Hartzenbusch drew attention to a portrait of a man in a side-chapel in the parish church of Argamasilla de Alba (it is still there) with a young girl kneeling at his side. The face of the man is long and narrow, the eyes a little wild, the mustachios heavy. Underneath is the inscription: 'Our Lady appeared to this gentleman when, seriously ill and despaired of by the doctors, in the Vespers of St Matthew 1601, he lay commending himself to this Lady and promising her a silver cresset and calling on her day and night from the great pain he suffered in his head from a violent chilliness that curdled his wits.' As Azorín tells us in his delightful and fanciful book 'La Ruta de Don Quijote' the gentleman was a local magnate, Don Rodrigo Pacheco. He is still to-day a tradition in Argamasilla, Campo de Criptana and Toboso. For our part, however, we are convinced that Cervantes created the Knight in his own image, as he was in 1597—with his gaunt 'El Greco' face, his aquiline nose and long mustachios. He, too, had dried up his wits through over-reading and life had been hard on him. What could his sterile genius do in Seville gaol 'where all discomfort dwells and all kinds of noise abide', but create in his own image this dried up whimsical child?

The first five chapters of Don Quixote are in the nature of rollicking variations embroidering the central theme of Don Quixote, some of which the author did not develop any further; but he soon discovered that the overwhelming personality of the Knight needed company for, as the proverb says, 'he who talks to himself talks to the devil'. He needed a companion to act as a foil, for how could he go through life as a lonely knight-errant, for ever raving in the style of Amadis of Gaul or the Marquis of Mantua? And so, after the scrutiny of books had blown away all traces of Bartolo and his ballads and opened the lists, as it were, there enters Sancho Panza, mounted on Dapple. Sancho, as the Spanish scholars love to tell us, had his models, for we meet the character of the proverb-spouting squire in the earliest known

---

[1] Robinson Smith, trans. of Don Quixote, New York, 1932, Vol. 1, Intro. p. xxxviii.

book of chivalry—'*El Caballero Cifar*',[1] but again, we maintain firmly that Sancho, no less than his master, sprang spontaneously to life in the imagination of the author, who not only knew La Mancha from the topographical reports published in the sixteenth century, but had plenty of opportunities of becoming acquainted with him during his travels from Andalusia through the villages of the steppes of La Mancha, towards Toledo, Madrid and Valladolid. Sancho sprang to life in the mind of his creator as a result of the divine spirit of Cervantine humour, for humour arises by antithesis. In the mind of a man a thought cannot rise without at the same time causing a directly opposite and contrary one to appear, and so, free, unfettered emotion, instead of soaring aloft like the lark in the clear air, finds itself held back just at the moment that it stretches out its wings to fly. Don Quixote, the hero, begins to soar on the wings of his ideal, but then reflection, which springs from his disposition towards humour, whispers in the poet's ear that idealists are rare in this world of human frailties; and so he creates, by contrast, a character whose feet are firmly planted on the earth, and whose mind is stored with the homely wisdom that flowers spontaneously at Nature's bidding. And as knights-errant must have squires, so this honest son of the glebe entered the service of his master, and so inseparable a companion of the Knight did Sancho become that the author was forced to say at the beginning of the Second Part: 'Let Don Quixote attack and Sancho talk'.

A curious parallel to Sancho's entry into *Don Quixote* occurs in the *Pickwick Papers*, a work that shows by its plan and construction how deeply Dickens studied Cervantes when a youth. Mr Pickwick sallies out accompanied by his colleagues of the Pickwick Club and has a series of jolly adventures, but he, too, felt the need of an attendant no less keenly than the knight-errant of La Mancha, and the novel does not begin really to get under way until the tenth chapter when the benevolent old gentleman discovers Sam Weller in the yard of the White Hart inn polishing boots. And if Sancho followed his master, riding his ass like a patriarch, with wine-skins and saddle-bags and a huge desire to see himself Governor of the promised isle, Sam Weller's

---

[1] Menéndez Pelayo, *Origines de la Novela*, Vol. 1, p. 198.

reflections on entering his master's service were: 'I wonder whether I'm meant to be a footman, or a groom, or a gamekeeper or a seedsman. I look a sort of a compo of every one of 'em. Never mind; there's a change of air, plenty to see, and little to do; and all this suits my complaint uncommon; so long life to the Pickwicks, says I!'

But let us return to our muttons, or rather the ballads. Cervantes, as his work progressed, became more aware than ever that only by weaving a series of parodies on the books of chivalry could he hope to create comic situations for the Knight and his squire, for the episodes of the Romancero were too patriotically consecrated by the Spanish people to become the themes for parody. Moreover, Cervantes, who was a lover of chivalry, intended his work to be a literary burlesque rather than a modern democratic assault upon the gentle castles of romance.[1] The ballads were dear to the heart of the Spanish people and to no one more than Cervantes himself. Likewise, many of the books of chivalry such as Amadis of Gaul were, as Professor Ker says, the Tales of My Landlord, and were equally loved by the host and his wife and his daughter, and by Maritornes as well. Every one in the Spanish society of that time had their minds steeped in such tales, and Dorothea, whom Salvador de Madariaga celebrates as the clever heroine *par excellence*, not only has read them but can talk their language, and straightway becomes Princess Micomicona, in order to lead the crazy Knight home to his village. Cervantes wished to gibe at the ridiculous poverty-stricken style and trivial invention of degenerate prose romances, and his astonishing familiarity with even the worst specimens of the *genre* enabled him to create situations that are profoundly ironical, owing to the perpetual contrast between Don Quixote's noble nature and the absurdities he pours out from his surfeit of romances. Moreover, Hegel in the '*Aesthetik*' has one passage on Cervantes as well as Shakespeare which is profoundly illuminating, where he states that what he admires most in Shakespeare and Don Quixote is the strength of the individual character, and the resistance of the character to all outward pressure. Don Quixote never for one moment doubts in his cause, and his noble nature, added to his surprisingly wide range of intellect, makes

[1] W. P. Ker, *Essays*, London, 1925, Vol. 2, p. 33.

him an unending source of delight to readers of every age and experience. One of the striking characteristics of Don Quixote is
that he is so impregnable a character that at times he resists even
the onslaughts of his own creator. Cervantes tried to make the
best of both worlds—the Arcadian world of literary convention
and the real world, where, in the words of Sancho, 'every man is
as God made him, and even worse very often'. Cervantes in the
First Part from time to time tries to call the Knight to order. He,
as it were, sends him to Coventry, and turns aside to compose a
romantic tale such as 'Impertinent Curiosity' which, he believes,
will prove to his readers that his literary hand had not lost its
cunning. But Don Quixote, like a naughty child, will not sleep
peacefully in the nursery; he fights with the giant in his sleep,
and according to Sancho, cuts his head clean off like a turnip,
and the room is flooded with gore. There is commotion and
uproar, the Knight is awakened by a large bucket of cold water,
and the adventure ends with the landlord bemoaning the rich red
Manchegan wine that flows from his gutted wine-skins. Sancho,
too, has his tantrums, and rebellious moments against his author
when he is left out in the cold, as towards the end of Part I, after
Dorothea has at last become reconciled to her husband, Fernando. Forgetting for a moment that she is Princess Micomicona
she allows Fernando to embrace her, but Sancho, who happens
to be close by, notices the gesture and is shocked to see her
Highness behaving more like a courtesan than the queen of a
great country. The rebellious attitude of Knight and Squire
increases in Part II, for they are puffed up with pride now that
their deeds are already celebrated in history, and they give their
author no peace. He tries to separate their partnership by sending
Sancho off to govern the island of Barataria, but in vain: the
Knight begins to mope, and his mood of melancholy brooding
communicates itself to his readers, even to the author himself, so
that there is no remedy but to overthrow governor Sancho, conclude the ducal *charade* and send the Knight and his squire back
to the high road to continue their wandering. Even where
Cervantes calls the Church to his assistance to chasten his hero he
is not more successful, as in the passage where the worthy Canon
of Toledo tells our Knight in paternal fashion to give up be-
fuddling his brains with Amadises, Emperors of Trebizond and

E

Felixmartes of Hircania, and to study the true chivalry of such historical personages as Fernán González and the Cid Campeador, whose admirable exploits will make him enamoured of virtue and enlightened in all better feelings. At the Duke's banqueting table another ecclesiastic attacks the Knight in fierce terms, calling him Don Coxcomb and bidding him to go home to his family and look after his children, if he has any, and to cease tramping the world o'er, sucking wind, the butt and derision of all. Don Quixote then sprang to his feet, shaking like quicksilver from head to foot, and rebuked the ecclesiastic, who presumed to measure the liberality of the great by the narrowness of his own soul. 'Is a poor pedagogue,' he cries, 'who never saw more of the world than twenty or thirty leagues around him, to give laws to chivalry and pass judgements on knights-errant? Is it, perchance, a vain business or time ill-spent to roam the world, not seeking its pleasures but its hard toils by which good men ascend to the abode of immortality?' On this occasion the Knight has turned the tables with a vengeance and unmasked the true Cervantes. It was no longer the time for the well-worn debate on arms and letters with its opposition between clerk and knight. These words of Don Quixote must have stirred the heart of Lepanto's maimed hero, the ex-service man Cervantes, whose deeds had long since been forgotten by his countrymen. These words, too, fittingly recall the Cid, who, according to one of the ballads, rebuked the monk Bernardo when the latter intervened in a conversation the Cid was having with King Alfonso VI in the cloisters at San Pedro de Cardeña. 'Go up to your pulpit,' he cried, 'and pray to God for victory: your habit's stained with oil but not with blood.' The reprimand of the ecclesiastic to Don Quixote according to Unamuno bears close resemblance to the reprimand which the vicar of the Dominican monastery at Salamanca made to Loyola when he called him and his companions idiots because they had not graduated.[1]

So far we have witnessed the triumph of the character against his author, but there were occasions, such as the adventure in the depths of the cave of Montesinos, when we feel that Don Quixote was beginning his recantation and turning his thoughts towards

[1] M. de Unamuno, *La Vida de Don Quijote y Sancho*, 2nd edition, Madrid, 1913, p. 214.

home. In descending into the cave of Montesinos, Don Quixote, according to Unamuno, was sinking into the cave of tradition of his race and people, and again he draws the parallel between the Visions of the Manchegan Knight and those of Saint Ignatius— the knight-errant of Christ, as he calls him—in the cave at Manresa. But Saint Ignatius, the warrior, who loved the books of chivalry, became disillusioned with the purposeless warring episodes and turned to the lives of the Saints. In the silence of the cave of Manresa he began his great spiritual adventure. Don Quixote, too, in the cave of Montesinos, anticipates the last scene, when on his death-bed he, too, will renounce the books of chivalry with the words: 'Now I see their folly and fraud, and my sole regret is that the discovery comes too late to permit my amending my ways by reading others that would enlighten my soul.' It is significant that Cervantes calls Montesinos, the most fantastical of all the ballad heroes, to aid in quelling the spirit of the wayward child of his imagination.

Chapter XI

The Ballads and the Drama
of the Golden Age

We have seen how the national epics of Spain, which were preserved in the prose of the chronicles, survived in fragments that were sung by high and low throughout the peninsula and beyond the seas, and became, as Menéndez Pidal says, the sum total of the nation's memories. Then came a great period of transformation, when the ballads were taken by the famous poets and woven into the texture of the new art form of the day—the drama. Menéndez Pidal devotes a great part of his book '*La Epopeya Castellana a través de la literatura Castellana*' to this fascinating subject. During the fifteenth century, as a result of the Renaissance, a profound change took place in ancient poetical traditions. In Italy the Renaissance had gradually penetrated into mediaeval forms of culture and had transformed them, but in France and Spain the Renaissance came as a revolution that was hostile to the poetical theories of the Middle Ages. The works of Dante, Petrarch and Boccaccio made such a profound impression upon the Marqués de Santillana, Enrique de Villena and other forerunners that they came to despise their own national poetry, calling it rude and uncouth. The Spanish conquests in Italy from the time of Alfonso V of Aragon increased this tendency, and, as a result, once more we have an illustration of the saying: *Graecia capta ferum victorem cepit*. It was a decisive moment, for the art of the theatre was springing to life and every one turned to Italy as the source of inspiration. Torres Naharro, Lope de Rueda, Timoneda and their followers devoted their energies to imitating Italian comedies and novels, while in lyric poetry, as Lope de Vega said, the native genius of Spain had disappeared owing to the craze for imitating the Italian muse. In the last third of the sixteenth century the only plays that rivalled the Italian-inspired drama were those of romantic character such as the *'Amadis'* and *'Don Duardos'* of Gil Vicente and the *'Duquesa de la Rosa'* of Alfonso de la Vega, and it is significant to note that the books of chivalry were considered the most obvious source of material for dramatists. But then came 1579 when the Sevillian dramatist, Juan de la Cueva, broke new ground by basing his play *'La Muerte del Rey Don Sancho'* on the most famous of national epic stories—the Siege of Zamora. It must have caused a sensation in the theatre to hear the lines of the ballad, which every member of the audience had known by heart from childhood. It was thus possible for the public, through its memories of the Romancero, to collaborate intimately with the actors on the stage, and this imparted to the characters in the play a vitality which had not existed previously in the theatre. Thus the year 1579, when ballads were woven into the texture of a play for the first time, marks an epoch in the history of the Spanish theatre. And Juan de la Cueva, in addition to that play, produced in Seville in the same year two further plays taken from the poetic tradition: *'La Libertad de España por Bernardo del Carpio'*, and the Tragedy of the Seven Infantes of Lara. He must, therefore, be regarded as the first poet to understand the value dramatically of the Spanish heroic themes and he was the first to write in Spanish an Art of Poetry (1606) in which he definitely rejected the rigid rule of the Three Unities.

Although Juan de la Cueva and his followers had caused a revolution in Spanish drama, their plays were more in the nature of experiments. What was needed was a truly national poet, whose genius would revitalize the whole art of the theatre. It was then that Lope de Vega, that 'Monster of Nature' and 'Phoenix of Geniuses' as he was called, appeared in the theatre. Of Lope it may be said that he created the Spanish national theatre and built up an entire dramatic history of the country from chronicles and ballads, interweaving ballad phrases with his verses in such a way that the original cannot be separated from the new. This he could do all the more easily because the best Castilian ballads cut short the narrative, leaving only the dialogue.[1]

Lope de Vega was a case of miraculous precocity; when he was only seventeen he composed a play on the exploits of Garcilaso de

[1] W. J. Entwistle, *European Balladry*, p. 121.

la Vega and the Moor Tarfe, divided into four acts, but with several fragments of ballads interwoven into the action of the play. This work, which has fortunately been preserved, reveals how from his earliest years Lope's poetic imagination was attuned to the traditional ballads. The ballads, as we have seen, were venerated by the people as records of the nation's history rather than enjoyed as poetry, but Lope de Vega was able to breathe into these legends of past heroes the magic of his genius and transform them into drama. And what is still more remarkable is that Lope's vast erudition acquired later, and his enormous reputation among men of letters, did not in the slightest degree diminish this vivid and intensive feeling for traditional poetry. His heart was always open to the artless simplicity of folk-songs, for they awoke in him deeper harmonies. Menéndez Pidal, with his rare acumen, points out how deeply suggestive was the technique employed by Lope de Vega in these plays based on traditional themes. He made use not only of the traditional narrative elements, but also of the short refrains that were sung by the people, and in this way he was able to convey dramatic emotion by subtle touches here and there throughout the play. In a play entitled 'Las Almenas de Toro' ('The Battlements of Toro'), we hear the voice of the sentry on the castle walls driving off sleep by the melancholy traditional song:

> Velador que el castillo velas
> Vélale bien y mira por tí,
> Que velando en él me perdí.

In another called 'La Adúltera Perdonada' we hear the traditional invocation to dreamy green eyes which were in those days, as now, so fashionable:

> despertad, ojuelos verdes,
> que a la mañanita lo dormiredes.

One of the most beautiful of all Lope de Vega's plays, 'Peribáñez', is entirely founded on a folk song, and in 'San Isidro Labrador', a play devoted to the patron saint of Madrid, the same folk song is woven into the play's texture. In this way such plays are priceless records for the study of folk-poetry. It should be remembered that the fragments of ballads and folk songs which abound in Lope's plays are like stray folk melodies used by a great master of musical form, who from them weaves a magic sound-pattern, which, in the end, becomes a complete and original work, but through it runs the slender gold thread of that melody, faint as a ghost of the past, but full of evocation, like a sudden glimpse through magic casements. Sometimes the lines of the ballad conjure up the vision of the heroic age of León and Castile; at another the allusions are allegorical and echo the chants of pilgrims on their way to far off Santiago de Compostela; or again, the author uses the refrains of the ballads and the proverbs to add salt and charm to the dialogue of his *graciosos*, as they called their clowns on the Spanish stage. Lope had the genius to sense the rich dramatic material that could be extracted from the ballads and the chronicles of Spain's past history, and from the chronicles the poet reached the ancient Epic, because his dramatic genius led him straightway to the most poetic passages, which were those derived from the old rhapsodic poems. In this way the spirit of the ancient epic exercised a decisive influence on the nascent theatre of the *siglo de oro*.[1] Menéndez Pidal gives an example of this tendency in '*El Bastardo Mudarra*', which deals with the old epic theme of the Seven Infantes of Lara. In the two earlier plays on the same theme—'*Los Infantes de Lara*' of Juan de la Cueva and '*Los Hechos de Mudarra*' by an anonymous author —only the last part of the grim tragedy of the seven sons was dramatized, namely, the vengeance of Mudarra. Lope, on the contrary, saw the immense possibilities of the theme for the stage, and by quickening the action of the play he made it more effective, and instead of concentrating mainly upon the vengeance, he dramatized the betrayal of the seven sons and even the remote causes of that betrayal, which made the legend such a favourite among the mass of the people. '*El Bastardo Mudarra*' by Lope, is thus, according to Menéndez Pidal, one of his characteristic works—a dynamic type of play, moving onwards in a series of short, impressionistic episodes resembling the effect produced by the modern cinematograph.[2] For this reason Pidal uses the term *cinedrama* to describe Lope's historical plays wherever the dramatist's use of rapid movement enables him to include many themes which formerly were regarded as impossible and unsuit-

[1] R. Menéndez Pidal, *La Epopeya Castellana*, p. 186.
[2] *Ibid.*, p. 187.

able for the stage; but it must be admitted that frequently in the attempt to convey the ever-changing and cinematic impressions the author neglects the drama. Lope's plan was not only to include far more traditional narrative in his plays than his predecessors, but also to recapture far more of the traditional spirit than they had done, by following the two principal versions of the story of the Seven Infantes current in those days, namely those in the Chronicles and in the Ballads of the Romancero. Lope thus, unlike his predecessors, used the poetical touches preserved in the chronicles and the rapid, forceful narrative of the ancient prose for the dialogue of his play; and from the ballads he adopted the metre and turns of phrase, and even in some scenes he inserted whole ballads or portions that fitted into the action of the play.

In this way the Spanish heroic drama became a kind of dramatic epic and the principle upon which it was based was that all that could be narrated could also be represented upon the stage. A good illustration of this principle is the play '*Las Mocedades de Bernardo*', in which the penalty of gouging out the eyes of the Count of Saldaña is enacted in full view of the audience; just in the same way as Shakespeare, who resembles Lope in many respects, shows upon the stage in *King Lear* the tearing out of Gloucester's eyes.[1]

Menéndez Pidal lays great stress on the significance of these heroic plays in which Lope dramatized the chronicles and the mediaeval ballads (over seventy of them are preserved), for it was to them that Spanish literature owed the continuity of the poetic tradition which began to be interrupted by the Renaissance. Thanks to this continuity the Spain of absolute monarchy was able to keep in touch with the past and understand the Spain of the Reconquest. It was in this way that the Greece of Pericles gathered on to the stage the ancient inspiration of the heroic ages. The Spanish epic like the Greek did not die in a decadence of dull poems and prosaic chronicles. The remains of both were preserved and stored away until the poetic genius of the people, when it arrived at maturity of expression, took possession of the theatre, and brought it out of its liturgical infancy; then the epic flooded the new poetic form with national vitality. When we consider that in other countries, France for instance, which also

[1] R. Menéndez Pidal, *op. cit.*, p. 188.

had a vigorous heroic poetry, the theatre developed apart from epic tradition, it is surprising that Greek and Spanish literature should, at an interval of twenty centuries, produce the same phenomenon of transformation from epic into drama.[1] In the case of Lope de Vega, as in the case of Cervantes, it is necessary to take his official declarations at times with a grain of salt. Lope was a man of the theatre and makes a great show of pretending that he had to break the rules of France and Italy in order to please the groundlings and win their applause. Thus he said:

> '*El vulgo es necio y pues lo paga es justo*
> *Hablarle en necio para darle gusto.*'

This may be paraphrased in the words of Dr Johnson:

> 'The drama's laws, the drama's patrons give,
> For we that live to please, must please to live.'

Lope is not sincere when in '*El Peregrino en su Patria*' ('The Pilgrim in his Country') he apologizes to foreign critics for the faults of Spanish drama, saying that he continued the tradition of his predecessors as he did not dare to keep the rules. Such words were more in the nature of an attempt to forestall the criticism of learned critics than an appreciation of the rules for play-making. Instead, in his theoretical treatise in verse: '*El Arte Nuevo de hacer Comedias*' ('The New Art of Playmaking') for once he drops all timid pretence and rebels against the lawgivers with their rigid rules.[2]

Around Lope there clustered a whole school of playwrights and Madrid became the centre of the new theatre, which attracted to itself the important group of Valencian dramatists, owing to the strong ties of friendship uniting the Madrilenian Lope de Vega and the Valencian Guillén de Castro.

Guillén de Castro deserves a permanent place among the dramatists of the Golden Age on account of his two chronicle plays, '*Las Mocedades del Cid*' and '*Las Hazañas del Cid*', which are a series of varied scenes in melodrama style, but Menéndez Pidal prefers to compare them to those admirable Gothic altar-pieces that are separated into different compartments and represent

---

[1] R. Menéndez Pidal, *op. cit.*, p. 189.
[2] R. Menéndez Pidal, *Cervantes a Lope de Vega*, Madrid: article on *El Arte Nuevo y la Nueva Biografía*.

the Crucifixion and the Resurrection. Guillen de Castro's bio-
graphical plays on the Cid form a historical altar-piece, and the
spectator watches the performance just as a reader skims over
the various chapters of a novel or a history book, following the
succession of chief events and episodes, whose only unity comes
from the hero himself. The great merit of Castro's play '*Las
Mocedades del Cid*' lies in the fact that he made the whole drama
centre in the tragic conflict between love and vengeance, first of
all in the heart of Rodrigo, and afterwards in that of Jimena. The
author, more than any of his predecessors, knew how to make use
of the original sources of the Cid story and discover in the verses
of the old ballads the struggle between passion and duty. In this
way he created a new poetical theme which had hitherto remained hidden, and, moreover, such was his knowledge of the
ancient ballads and his technical equipment as a dramatist that
he was able to maintain unity of action, while tacking on to the
main action a series of legendary episodes which had nothing to
do with the hero's marriage, but which served to bring into
higher relief his personality. One of these episodes, that of the
Infanta Urraca, whom the ancient ballads represent as an early
playmate of the Cid, makes her appear as a rival to Jimena, and
her presence serves to raise the prestige of the Cid, as Napoleon
and Schlegel noticed. Corneille in his adaptation of Castro's play
kept this episode of the love of the Infanta for the Cid, and thereby laid himself open to the criticism of the French academic pundits, for whereas Guillén de Castro could permit himself the
luxury of dramatizing all the Cid ballads, had he been so dis-
posed, for he could count on the freedom from restrictions of the
Spanish drama, Corneille, on the other hand, by copying from
his model the love of the Infanta and various other episodes,
violated the sacred and inflexible rules of French tragedy, and
thus drew upon his head the maledictions of the critics.[1] Where
the chorus of pedantic critics raged loudest was over the famous
scene of Corneille's play, where Jimena receives the visit of her
lover, who has just made her an orphan. According to the rules
of tragic decorum, Jimena should have retired, without consenting to listen to the pleas of Roderick, but Corneille did not suppress the scene which he had taken from his Spanish model,

[1] R. Menéndez Pidal, *La Epopeya Castellana*, pp. 196–197.

because of the startling dramatic effect it had upon the public, for at the early performances of the work, when the unhappy lover appeared before Jimena soon after the homicide, there was an excited murmur in the audience denoting the impatient curiosity of the spectator to know what the unhappy pair of lovers would say to one another in such tragic circumstances. The fact that Corneille in his defence referred to this pleasant memory of the early performances, and called upon Aristotle's protection when confessing that he had merely paraphrased the scene of the Spanish dramatist Guillén de Castro, shows that the French public and the progressive spirits were eager for their poets to shed timidity and put up a fight against pedantic, worn-out rules. Even the French Academy had to confess that the rules of poetry and its beauties were sometimes strangely at variance, for they had to recognize that there was an inexplicable charm in '*Le Cid*' in spite of all its faults (*cet agrément inexplicable qui se mêle dans tous ses défauts*—a phrase which explains the disconcerting effect produced by the free, unhampered Iberian muse when she appeared amidst the band of severe Gallic muses). And French literary historians such as Lanson who analysed the psychology of Corneille's hero discovered that with his intellectual conception of *le devoir* he was in complete accord with Descartes. Menéndez Pidal, however, shows that every one of those traits, even the most subtle and psychological, may be found in the Spanish original from which Corneille himself frequently quotes, as in the line:

> '*Qui m'aime généreux, me haïrait infâme*',

which is from Guillén de Castro:

> '*Afrentado,*
> *por infame aborrecieras*
> *quien quisiste por honrado.*'[1]

Menéndez Pidal draws the conclusion that the disputes in Paris among the French intellectuals over '*Le Cid*' only go to show the differences existing between the French and Spanish theatres. The classical rules of dramatic art of Aristotle and Horace were as sacrosanct for Lope as for Corneille, but the difference was that Lope did not think them infallible, and he

---

[1] R. Menéndez Pidal, *op. cit.*, p. 198.

discovered a new art, for he proposed to please rather the public
than the law-givers of Parnassus, whilst Corneille bowed his head
and sacrificed his own inclinations to *Messieurs les Académiciens*.
Corneille envied '*l'irrégularité de l'auteur espagnol*' and lamented
again and again the rigid rule of the three unities, but he sub-
mitted and sacrificed much of the grandeur of his works to them.
In order to save the three unities he had to lump together the
incidents of the Cid and accelerate them so as to bring the action
within the time limit of twenty-four hours, preferring thus, as
Pidal says, to do violence to the laws of human nature than to the
precepts of poetic convention. In obedience to the unity of
time, he purposely fixed the Court of Ferdinand I at Seville, thus
sacrificing historical accuracy to the academic rules, and Voltaire
even haggles with him for letting the Infante utter the word *hier*
which shows that a night's interval had elapsed in the action.[1]
Scudéry and other critics of the time attacked the play for its
excessive piling up of incidents, and they pointed out that the
haste which Jimena shows in consenting to become the bride of
the murderer of her father transforms her into a kind of *parricide*.
It is strange that it never occurred to these critics that the reason
for all these defects was the rule of the three unities; instead they
pedantically concluded that the theme of the *Cid* violated the
principal rules of drama, and was absolutely worthless for tragedy
or poetry. This solemn declaration by the pundits of criticism,
says Menéndez Pidal, makes us understand better the dramatic
talent of Guillén de Castro, for from this subject which was considered useless for drama, that is to say, a subject drawn from
ballads that were full of life but crudely mediaeval, Castro was
able to create what Voltaire called the first true tragedy of the
modern European stage; a work that drew tears from the people
at a time when 'yet no nation had learnt the art of speaking to the
heart.' France had turned away scornfully from the Middle
Ages, saying that such literature was crude and uncouth; but
Spain cherished that age and was able to discover in that
Cinderella hidden beauties which could raise and exalt her to the
lofty regions of classical art. And so great were the strength and
vitality of the Spanish dramatists that they made the French
admire the Spanish Middle Ages more than a century before

[1] R. Menéndez Pidal, *op. cit.*, p. 199.

Voltaire began to reveal the wealth of France's own mediaeval past, and this was all due to '*Le Cid*' of Corneille which was persistently applauded in spite of the bitter criticisms of the pedants.

It should be noted that in Spain itself the cult Lope de Vega and Guillén de Castro made of the heroic ballads did not extend itself to their followers, probably because the followers such as Pérez de Montalbán, who was the apple of Lope's eye, wrote no plays based directly on the *romances*: nevertheless Vélez de Guevara, the author who bears the closest resemblance to Lope de Vega, according to Menéndez Pidal, does not bring on the stage the Cid or the Castilian counts, but uses lyrical and novelesque ballads to embellish and add lustre to important scenes in his plays, such as '*Reinar después de morir*' ('Monarch after Death'), and he has three interesting plays based on non-heroic ballads, namely, '*El Conde don Pero Velez*', '*La Serrana de la Vera*', and '*El Principe Viñador*'. The world knows Vélez de Guevara by his famous picaresque novel '*El Diablo Cojuelo*' ('The Lame Devil') which inspired a brilliant adaptation by the author of '*Gil Blas*', but has neglected his important play '*La Serrana de la Vera*', which remained in manuscript until Menéndez Pidal and his wife published it in 1916. The play centres in a heroine of a ballad which is to-day sung by the folk—a highland lass or *serrana*, who is as athletic and as keen-eyed a huntress as Diana herself. A captain has played her false, so she revenges herself by inviting any luckless male she meets in the mountains to her cabin, where she murders him. Her type recalls the Amazons whom the fourteenth-century vagabond minstrel arch-priest of Hita describes with such glee and with whom he used to wrestle in the Sierra de Guadarrama. Velez wrote the play in 1613 in order that the most famous actress of the time, Jusepa Vaca, might display her arrogant beauty on the stage, and swagger about, shouldering her arquebus. It was for her that Lope de Vega had written his play '*La Mocedad de Roldan*' ('The Youth of Roland'), 'in homage to her gallant figure when dressed as a man', and she had previously acted in another work of the same title and plot as Velez de Guevara's play.[1] In this case it is instructive to compare the works of master and pupil as Menéndez Pidal has done. Strange to relate, it is Velez de Guevara who surpasses his master even in

[1] R. Menéndez Pidal, *op. cit.*, pp. 201–202.

his handling of the traditional theme, for he carries the story as told in the ballad to its inexorable conclusion, and the highland Amazon falls victim to the arrows of the Holy Brotherhood, whereas Lope de Vega turns his heroine into a commonplace Arcadian *serrana*, and he avoids the tragic ending, forcing her, as Millamant would say, to 'dwindle into marriage'.

Another play of Vélez de Guevara we have mentioned, '*El Príncipe Viñador*', is an illustration of the romantic adventures that may befall ballad collectors and *aficionados* to-day. It was not based upon a celebrated ballad nor upon those that became known through the collections published in the sixteenth century, but upon a ballad handed down by oral tradition, whose original form appears only in that play and in another of 1610 by Agustín de Castellanos entitled '*Mientras podo las Viñas*' ('Whilst I prune the Vines'), which is one of the lines of the ballad. The ballad is unknown in Spain but Menéndez Pidal, whose ballad-chasing covers every corner of the world, was able to get twenty-three modern versions from the Spanish Jews in Morocco and in the East. This is an illustration of how obscure ballads from Africa or the Balkans preserved mysteriously by tradition may be the solutions to many problems that scholars find in the plays of the early years of the seventeenth century, and the expert ballad-chaser in his travels may hear, when he least expects it, a street singer perform the very same ballad that one day three hundred years ago inspired the famous author of '*El Diablo Cojuelo*', but had faded completely from the memory of the Spanish people.

It was the enormous popularity of the Romancero that led to its decline. Its great period of brilliance was from 1580 to 1620, that is to say, about half a century. Already the decline in the use of traditional ballads is apparent in a dramatic poet of the first order like Tirso de Molina, who was only about ten years younger than Lope de Vega. Not a single play of his is inspired by ballads and when a character does sing a ballad, as in the play '*Quien habló, pagó* ('The Speaker Paid') it is one by Gongora. Gongora's ballads had the good fortune to become famous on the stage, and we find the great Calderón inserting one in '*El Príncipe Constante*' ('The Constant Prince'). In the latter's dramas, as in Tirso's, there is no trace of the folk-poem atmosphere of Lope de Vega, and this is all the more strange in Calderón, because he was the most musical of poets, both in his *comedias* and in his 'starry autos', as Shelley calls them. The ballad had accomplished its mission, which was to inspire the creation of a genuine national theatre, and it now retired and lived forgotten among the humble classes of society. But the impulse it had given survived through the centuries, for mediaeval themes, bereft of all ballad elements, continued to be dramatized by the authors of the day. These adaptations carried the tales on through the arid eighteenth century to the Romantic Movement of the nineteenth century, when the Duke of Rivas produced the first masterpiece of the romantic revolution—'*El Moro Exposito*'—a poem which, according to Menéndez Pidal, was for the Spanish Movement what '*Le Préface de Cromwell*' of Victor Hugo was for the French.

Chapter XII

The Heroic Themes in Modern Poetry

But before the Duke of Rivas arrived upon the scene as a providential deliverer, there were years when the authorities in Spain did all in their power to stifle any attempt at creating a national literature. The *Afrancesados* or pro-French partisans like Leandro de Moratín believed that French taste could be imposed on Spain by royal decree. In 1799 actually a *junta* or commission was appointed and given absolute power over the theatrical companies and their repertories. The actors tried to resist the tyranny by declaring a strike, but then another royal order was proclaimed declaring the strike a conspiracy against the safety of the state. By another Royal Order of 1800 the *junta* drew up a list of 600 plays to be forbidden in all the theatres of the Kingdom. Among these were such famous works as '*La Vida es Sueño*', '*El Mágico Prodigioso*', and many other plays of Calderón; '*El Convidado de Piedra*', and '*La Prudencia en la Mujer*' of Tirso de Molina, and a multitude of other masterpieces which were regarded with abhorrence by the worthy *junta*. Furthermore, the *junta* declared that all the plays called heroic were unacceptable, for 'though the great Corneille adapted heroic plays with their extraordinary scenic changes, this was the unfortunate result of his close study of Spanish dramatists.' And in this *junta* the most prominent figure was Moratín, who, though he had been resident in London, was incapable of understanding Shakespeare. Moratín and the *junta* in vain tried to impose their reforms, for the public refused to be converted and stayed away, with the result that the government had to dissolve the commission. The first gleam of hope for the national drama came with the arrival in Madrid of the great actor Isidoro Maiquez who had just perfected his art in Paris under Talma. Owing to his great ascend-

72

ancy over the public he was able to perform adaptations of the ancient themes such as '*La Condesa de Castilla*' by Cienfuegos and the popular old play '*Vida y Muerte del Cid y noble Martín Perlaez*'. But those were years of disaster when the invasion of Spain by the French was followed by the absolutism of Ferdinand VII. All material and intellectual progress ceased for more than twenty years, and Menéndez Pidal records the following anecdote as an example of puerile vigilance by the authorities. When Maiquez had to declaim in Quintana's play '*Pelayo*' the lines:

> *A fundar otra España y otra patria,*
> *Más grande y más feliz que la primera,*
> (To found another Spain, another country,
> Greater and happier than the first)

the police guards in the theatre were reinforced for fear of the enthusiasm which the great actor roused in the audience. Ferdinand VII, helped, whenever necessary, by the 100,000 sons of Saint Louis, who came to his assistance from France, imposed his absolutism by all the means granted to him by bayonets, censorships and the Inquisition. And as for the intellectuals, they hid their lack of talent beneath the cloak of another absolutism, namely the tyrannical pseudo-classical rules of the French, and they openly expressed their abomination of the ancient Spanish literature. They ruled in Spain, but political persecution drove abroad a multitude of distinguished patriots, who verified the truth of Victor Hugo's dictum that Romanticism is liberalism in art. Of no country is that saying truer than of Spain, says Menéndez Pidal in his passionate review of this period of his country's fortunes. 'In the peninsula', he added, 'romanticism was not only liberalism in literature; it became also intricately confused with liberalism in politics, for the great romantics were also the great liberals, who suffered persecution under Ferdinand VII, in contradistinction to France where it so happened that the romantics were absolutists and the classicists were liberals.'[1]

The writers who were expatriated found to their surprise a large movement in progress in favour of the ancient Spanish literature which was so despised within Spain's frontiers, and the surprising fact was that the movement started at the same time from England and Germany. In England from the very first

[1] R. Menéndez Pidal, *La Epopeya Castellana*, pp. 215–216.

F

year of the nineteenth century the poet Robert Southey made Spanish legends and epics the source of inspiration of his *García Fernández, King Ramiro, Roderick the last of the Goths*. He also translated the *Poem* and *The Chronicle of the Cid*, the *Amadis* and the *Palmerin*, and he rebuked the Spaniards for not revering the first monument of their own literature, prophesying that they would never create any work in the higher spheres of art until they abandoned their false notions which prevented them from appreciating the high poetic value of the history in verse of the Cid. Then came Walter Scott with his poem, '*The Vision of Don Roderick*' (1811), which fused together the epic material of the chronicles of King Rodrigo with the memory of the glorious geographical discoveries of Spain and the recent Peninsular War.

Simultaneously in Germany Herder, whose mind was so open to the enchantments of what he called 'the voice of peoples', became profoundly interested in Spanish heroic poetry and produced an adaptation of the Cid ballads (1802) which became a classic in Germany. And Herder's example was followed by many other German translators and imitators such as Depping, Friedrich Diez (the founder of romance philology) and others who roused the interest of the public in traditional Spanish poetry. And at the same time the traditional poetry of Spain became a banner of romantic revolution for the brothers Schlegel. They lectured on the ancient theatre of Spain, and one of the two, Frederick, produced in 1802 at Weimar a tragedy based on the old ballad of Count Alarcos, which, he claimed, would lead to the creation of the true German national theatre. The play was received by the public with hostility, which turned to scornful laughter, but then Goethe, the omnipotent ruler of literature in the state, rose indignantly from his seat, imposed silence, saved the work, and handed it over to the passionate controversy of the critics.

As a result of this pioneer movement in Germany and England, the French, too, began, though later, to consider the Spanish epic themes as an essential part of their romantic movement. Abel Hugo in 1822 translated a good part of the Romancero and roused his brother Victor's natural inclination towards things Spanish, for Victor when a child had lived in Madrid with his parents during the French invasion and never forgot his impressions of childhood. It is interesting to note that the invocation of the *almogávares* to their sword: '*Hierro, despiértate!*' ('Iron, awake!') is the motto of one of the '*Orientales*', and the Spanish word *hierro* was the war cry adopted by the five hundred writers of *La Jeune France*, when, dressed in Spanish cloaks, they paraded for battle on the first night of '*Hernani*'.[1]

But it was England that became the favourite refuge of the Spanish *émigrés*, and there they formed an important nucleus. England had been the ally of Spain in the War of Independence, and afterwards the haven of the persecuted liberals, and she now became, as Menéndez Pidal says, the great initiator of Spanish Romanticism, but he is careful to explain that Romanticism in Spain was more in the nature of a restoration than a revolution, for its fundamental idea was the rehabilitation of literature and national traditions. And so the Spanish *émigrés* in London united together and produced a review entitled '*Ocios de Españoles Emigrados en Londres*' setting forth their impressions of *la ciudad de la niebla* (the Fog-bound City).

The Portuguese *émigrés*, too, had their literary *cénacle*, for it was in 1828 that Almeida Garrett published in London adaptations of the traditional ballads of his country: '*Adoçinda*' and '*Bernal-francez*'.

The influence which England exercised upon the Spanish *émigrés* may be personified in the Duke of Rivas. Condemned to death in 1824, he fled to London and from there to Malta where for five years he was on intimate terms with the members of the highest English society. Rivas had grown up in the rigid pseudo-classical period of his country, and wrote in that style at first, but at Malta he had the good fortune to make friends with John Hookham Frere, formerly British Minister in Madrid during the War of Independence, a lover of Spanish literature as he showed in his translation of the '*Poema del Cid*'. It was Frere who kindled the enthusiasm of his friend in his own literature and suggested as a subject for romantic treatment the story of the Seven Infantes of Lara. The Duke of Rivas entitled his poem '*El Moro Expósito*' and in the English dedication recognized his intellectual debt to Hookham Frere. And so, as Menéndez Pidal shows, it was an English Hispanist, lover of the traditional Castilian epic poems,

[1] R. Menéndez Pidal, *op. cit.*, p. 215.

who inspired the first genuinely romantic work of the Spanish Parnassus. Thanks to this foreigner, the ancient story of Spain's tenth century, which seemed to have crumbled away in the dust of centuries, now springs to life in full vitality and initiates a new era of literature in the peninsula. And Menéndez Pidal points out how the coincidence that the Duke had been born in Córdoba, the city which was the capital of the Moorish realm in the story of the Seven Infantes, inspired him to show imaginatively in his poem the contrast between the luxurious Moslem city of the tenth century and the austere Christian capital Burgos. This poem, which was written in the style of Walter Scott's *Marmion* or the *Lord of the Isles*, was published in Paris in 1834; its prologue by Alcalá Galiano, another exile, became for Spanish romanticism what '*Le Préface de Cromwell*' was for the French. And now the new movement began to awaken faint echoes in Spain itself, for Durán began to publish reprints of the ancient ballads, which had up to this been scorned by the poets and men of letters. Durán began his task as a result of seeing how the English were buying up at fabulous prices the rare Cancioneros and Romanceros of the past, and in 1832, when his collection was published, he added a prologue declaring that Lope de Vega and Góngora were the founders of true Spanish romanticism. The year after the publication of '*El Moro Expósito*' of the Duke of Rivas, King Ferdinand VII died, 'the tyrant of literature' as he was called, and with him died absolutism in politics and absolutism in literature.[1] The Duke of Rivas, Alcalá Galiano, Espronceda and the rest of the exiled poets returned to Spain, and romanticism, which they had taken up abroad, suddenly burst into bloom in Spain, not by gradual development as in the other countries. The repatriates made themselves masters of the intellectual life of the country without difficulty. The year after publishing '*El Moro Expósito*' the Duke of Rivas produced in Madrid the first decidedly romantic drama, '*Don Alvaro*' (1835); and in the two following years, amidst the political agitation of liberals, riots, pronunciamientos and the Carlist war, all the champions of romanticism sprang to life; a vivid cluster of poets enveloped in a halo of romance and adventure. They resembled the Provençal troubadours, whom they so admired,

[1] R. Menéndez Pidal, *op. cit.*, p. 219.

in that their lives were as interesting as their verses, but, whereas the troubadours were the slaves of some affected school of poetry which made their verses inferior to their biographies, these romantics were in pursuit of new spontaneous ideals of renewal and this gave zest to their struggle. The older generation of these romantics was represented by the Duke of Rivas, who had been gravely wounded on the battle-field during the French invasion, condemned to death and confiscation of property by Ferdinand VII, a wandering exile, who reappears in his country in time to triumph in politics and literature. The younger generation was represented by García Gutiérrez, national militia-man, who escaped from the barracks to attend the first night of his play 'El Trovador' (1836), which secured by its success the second definite victory for romanticism. The hectic rapidity of the romantic revolution is personified in Larra, who at twenty-eight years of age commits suicide, leaving behind him a reputation of the first order, or in Espronceda, who at thirty-three years of age dies worn out after a life of thriftlessness and ill-luck but of incredible activity. And even lives as short as these may leave their mark on heroic traditions; for Larra in his early years wrote a play entitled 'Fernán González', and Espronceda left an unfinished poem, 'El Pelayo', which he began at Guadalajara about 1827 and touched up again in London, with strong Byronic influences.

No event gives a more dramatic picture of the romantic movement with its clash of vivid personalities than the funeral of Larra in Madrid on 15 February 1837. Larra, the young coryphaeus of romanticism, thanks to the political revolution, was the first suicide to receive honourable burial in the Madrid cemetery, so the occasion was marked by a great number of speeches and by recitals of necrological poems. As the coffin was about to be lowered into the grave, a slender young man with long black hair, dressed in an ill-fitting borrowed suit of mourning, started to read a poem which he had improvised the night before in the garret of a basket-maker. The gentle voice and the melodious tone in which the unknown poet recited these verses, which resembled music rather than poetry, held the mourners spellbound, and when tears filled the young man's eyes at the thought of a father and a loved one's sorrow, and faintness through long fasting made his thin voice falter and stop, Zorrilla's triumph was assured. Although not yet twenty years of age he was counted among the foremost men of letters of the day.

Zorrilla himself in his autobiography attributes not only this first triumph of his, but also the success of a great part of his poems, to his inimitable talent as a reciter,[1] and he admits that when he wrote he would always arrange the pauses so that the phrases would sound well when read aloud. When he was only twenty-three he produced '*El Zapatero y el Rey*' ('The Cobbler and the King'), a play founded upon a traditional anecdote concerning King Peter the Cruel, and a few years later '*Sancho García*', one of the author's great triumphs. This play is of interest because it is based upon the epic traditions concerned with the foundation of the famous monastery of Oña. As Menéndez Pidal informs us in his analysis, monasteries in the Middle Ages were centres that attracted great hosts of pilgrims, and among them there were many minstrels, whose profession it was to satisfy public curiosity by singing of the poetical history of the monastery where the pilgrims were gathered. The foundation of Oña (from the thirteenth century) was associated with the following tragic tale told in the '*Crónica General*' of Alfonso the Wise. The widowed Countess of Castile, who was of French nationality, fell madly in love with a Moorish King, and wishing to rule Castile alone, she resolved to poison her only son, Count Sancho García. But as she was preparing the poisoned herbs, she was discovered by one of her maids, who told her lover, one of the Count's huntsmen. The Count, on being forewarned, told his mother when she offered him the goblet of poison to drink first from it herself. In vain she tried to refuse, but, in fear of her son's threats, she had to drink and fell dead at his feet. The Count, in gratitude to the huntsman's loyalty, confided to him and his descendants the guardianship of the palace by founding an institution known as the Huntsmen of Espinosa (*Monteros de Espinosa*) who were charged with watching over the sleep of the sovereign (a very ancient institution preserved by successive Kings). Later Count Sancho García, stricken with remorse for having murdered his mother, founded in memory of the victim the great monastery of Oña destined to be the family pantheon.

[1] J. Zorrilla, *Recuerdos del Tiempo Viejo*, 2nd ed., Madrid 1882–1883, Vol. 1, pp. 33, 44.

Zorrilla treated the ancient epic theme faithfully[1] in the verse tale '*El Montero de Espinosa*', but in the play '*Sancho García*' he radically changed the *dénouement* in order to fit in with nineteenth-century sentiment. A nineteenth-century poet will not allow parricide: he will, in fact, have no scruples in changing parricide into filial abnegation. And so the Count sacrifices his own reputation to that of his mother's, and though he pretends to poison her he hides her in the monastery of Oña. When taking leave of her he says: 'In Oña will you live, they will mourn over you as dead. An inscrutable mystery will surround this monastery and all the world will believe that a monument has been raised over your tomb in expiation by a parricide.' In spite of the moving scene of filial abnegation and the careful workmanship of the play the change in the *dénouement* emasculates the archaic rough-hewn majesty of the mediaeval theme. Menéndez Pidal contrasts the procedure of Zorrilla with that of the Austrian poet Hebbel who, when treating a heroic and national subject, would always hold in check his powerful imagination and respect, in the smallest detail, the archaic fiction of the 'Nibelungs' and, whereas Hebbel raises to superhuman pitch the passions which spring from the traditional theme, Zorrilla draws back horror-struck, tames them into subjection and annuls them. But Zorrilla was not the only one to do this. Generally speaking, the Spanish romantics took great liberties in modernizing the ancient themes, for they wanted, above all, to arouse dramatic interest, without paying any great attention to the traditional subjects which reached them through the decadent dramas of the eighteenth century. So far from trying to penetrate into the poetry of the ancient tales, they adapted the ancient traditions to modern tastes. A good illustration of this tendency is Zorrilla's most famous play, '*Don Juan Tenorio*' (1844), which has become so much part of Spanish life that its yearly performance in the autumn months is a family ritual connected with the feast of All Souls. But Tirso de Molina, when creating his Playboy of Seville from the traditional theme of the gallant who revels in his youthful pride and cries out: '*Qué largo me lo fiais!*' watches him move step by step inexorably to his doom without ever suggesting the possibility that a *deus ex machina* will save him in the end. Zorrilla on the other hand lived

[1] R. Menéndez Pidal, *op. cit.*, p. 225.

in the age of renunciation and abnegation, and so in the end Don Juan Tenorio, the libertine, is saved by the tears of Doña Inés.

There is one anecdote about Zorrilla which explains more than any other the master's methods of work. The impresario of the *Teatro de la Cruz* in Madrid, needing a play for the Christmas season, asked Zorrilla to write a one act drama in twenty-four hours. The master first of all tried to get Hartzenbusch to collaborate with him, but in vain. As he had no time to think out a subject he asked for a copy of Mariana's History to be brought to the theatre. Then he stuck three cards at random into three different parts of the volume 'from the period of the Goths to Philip IV', for that was the section of Spanish history that the poet considered could be dramatized. He then opened the book at the first card and read the words, which referred to the disappearance of the last King of the Goths in the battle fought on the banks of the Guadalete against the Arab invaders, and the impenetrable mystery that surrounded the destiny of the King. Mariana says: 'It is true that two hundred years later, in a certain church in Portugal, in the city of Viseo, a stone was discovered with a Latin inscription stating that "here lieth Roderick, last King of the Goths". By this it is understood that after losing the battle he fled to Portugal.' Zorrilla refused to read further: he already saw his play in his imagination. This anecdote, which Zorrilla relates in his Reminiscences, shows that for him all Mariana was history and nothing more, and it was only by chance that he happened to select epic material on this occasion. The rest of the anecdote describes Zorrilla's favourite method of working. He first of all ascertained what actors were available, but he found only the great tragic actor Carlos Latorre. There was no first actress available, so there could be no women's parts. With all those difficulties to contend with, and with so little time at his disposal, Zorrilla went back to his house, and in one sitting of twenty-four hours, with no sustenance but two coffees and a cup of chocolate, he wrote his play. He had no time to work out his subject in his imagination before putting it down on paper, and the only one point he could rely on was that, provided Carlos Latorre was given hendecasyllables to recite, he would grip the audience.

Menéndez Pidal, while believing this anecdote of Zorrilla to be in great part fictitious, considers that it was a genuine explanation of the hasty improvised nature of romantic drama. The poet made no attempt to meditate on his theme or study its possibilities, for his aim was to give free rein to his imagination. And Zorrilla was successful in '*El Puñal del Godo*' ('The Dagger of the Goth'): it is one of his best plays, with its gloomy picture of the vanquished King, who in the end becomes transfigured by a last ray of dying heroism. Zorrilla did, however, make one attempt to create a faithful historical picture of a vanished civilization in his poem '*Granada*'. He did not follow the vivid colours and incidents of the Moorish ballads and the descriptions of Pérez de Hita, but studied in detail the monuments of the city, its plain, its historians and the later foreign writers such as Washington Irving, Prescott and Garcin de Tassy. The poem owes little to the Moorish ballads, but a great deal is inspired by the frontier ballads, and the author arouses deep emotion by his delicate use of the famous *romance*—'*Ay de mi Alhama*', whose refrain, like a sad melody, echoes and re-echoes through the poem. It is but a fragment of what might have been a great romantic epic poem. Zorrilla left Spain for Mexico. He forgot the work, just as he forgot Europe itself, and at thirty-three years of age suddenly became a mute songster, and Menéndez Pidal compares this last of the romantics to Larra or Espronceda, for his creative life as a poet was no longer than theirs. For eleven years he stayed in Mexico and Cuba, and when he returned to Spain in 1866, through the influence of the great novelist Valera, he was given a special pension from the Government to enable him to write a lengthy verse paraphrase of the balladry connected with the Cid, which he published in 1882. After the death of Zorrilla, the last of the romantics, there was a change in literary taste, and epic poetry suffered an eclipse of twenty years. It was then that Joaquín Costa's command to 'double-lock the Cid's sepulchre' roused the people from their lethargy. Many in those days took the phrase to mean a total condemnation of the past and they were scandalized. Costa was an Aragonese with a strong individualistic temperament and a fiery patriotism. He was loud in his denunciation of the rhetorical appeals to the past by men unable to deal with the present, and his message was to look things sternly in the face, to cease gilding the bare present with the glories borrowed from the bygone past.[1] As Menéndez Pidal tells us, Costa had made a very deep study of the epics and the Romancero years before, in order to extract from them a political programme of the Cid, as an expression of the judicial and social aspirations of Spain.[2] He explained his phrase about double-locking the Cid's tomb by saying that he only wanted to cast the warrior Cid into oblivion, in order to resuscitate the republican Cid, the Cid who impeached the King at Santa Gadea and who to-day raises his voice in every Spaniard's heart to exact responsibility from those that govern. Again he said: 'The programme of "*Mío Cid*" has not passed yet into the pantheon of dead history, and Spain must study it seriously, if ever she is to live her own life, resume her broken traditions and acquire the stable equilibrium necessary for every people that would adapt its institutions to its temperament and genius'.[3]

After Joaquín Costa's sermon on the 'School and Larder' came a book which produced a reaction in favour of the past, namely the collection of ballads and the treatise on old ballads by Menéndez Pelayo, published in four volumes between 1899 and 1906. Just as the publication of the ancient Romancero of Durán had prepared the way for the triumph of Romanticism, and the rehabilitation of the narrative themes of antiquity, so the Romancero of Menéndez Pelayo inspired a similar movement of literary renewal, for it opened up to the general public all the treasures of ancient heroic poetry. Straightway this Romancero produced its harvest. Some figures from the Romancero made a niche for themselves in the new poetry: above all Gerineldo, the page fortunate in love, who, after inspiring an evocative poem of Manuel Machado, appears on the stage in *Poem of Love and Chivalry* by the young poets Cristóbal de Castro and Enrique López Alarcón. It is a veritable Golden Treasury of selections from the Romancero. In the same years the Catalan poet Marquina after a long and severe study of the history and psychology of the Cid produced a verse play entitled '*Las Hijas del Cid*' ('The Daughters of the Cid') in which he based his drama on the contrast between the Amazonian Elvira and the gentle

[1] S. de Madariaga, *Spain*, London, 1942, p. 81.
[2] R. Menéndez Pidal, *La Epopeya Castellana*, p. 237.
[3] J. Costa, *Mensaje de la Cámara agrícola del Alto Aragón al país*, 1898.

childlike Sol. Menéndez Pidal gives credit to Marquina for having been the first dramatist to derive his inspiration directly from the primitive '*Poema del Cid*'. Ever since the thirteenth century the heroic figure of the Campeador had only been known through adaptations that varied considerably from the original, but now when Marquina turned his eyes to the original hero he discovered a wealth of new dramatic material. Although he presents many effective scenes describing the warrior's relations with his two daughters he fails to raise the work to a climax in the great trial scene at Toledo, when the Cid obtains justice from his traitorous sons-in-law, because, according to Menéndez Pidal, he avoids the presence of the hero, as though he could not withstand his glance. As a contrast to the Marquina play we have the dramatization of another famous incident in the Romancero by Jacinto Grau in his '*Conde Alarcos*' (1917). Since 1920 every year has brought fresh works to the Spanish theatre owing their inspiration to the ballads. As Azorín says in his subtle analysis of the Romancero: 'Amongst all the ballads, we particularly love those that are short, for they are rapid visions with more than a hint of a plot. They are like a song that begins but does not end; something has come and silenced the author: something we know not what, and it may be fortunate or tragic. A deep enchantment comes from what is unfinished.' The *romance* becomes like a melodic theme in music and upon it the authors build up harmonies and decorate it with variations, or else combine it with other ballad themes. For this reason the musicians no less than the poets felt the fascination of the Epic and the Romancero, and it was in the early years of the century that Manrique de Lara composed his musical trilogy entitled 'Roderick and Jimena,' 'The Siege of Zamora', and 'Mio Cid', from which excerpts were performed by the Madrid Symphony Orchestra. Nevertheless, the most striking music drama based on ballads is '*El Retablo de Maese Pedro*' ('Master Peter's Puppet Show') by Manuel de Falla, which is based upon the famous adventures of Don Quixote in the second part of the immortal book. The play which the puppets perform for the Knight of Sorry Aspect is the story of Don Gaiferos and the Princess Melisendra from the old Carlovingian ballads. What makes this short opera so enchanting an experience for the poet and musician is that Falla has carried still further the methods he had employed with such success in '*El Amor Brujo*' and '*La Vida Breve*'; he has used themes which derive their sinews from folk-song, but he has with great humour interpreted the story, and the music seems to follow every curve and line of the literary style, and at times the listener feels as if the musical emphasis has explained some point that he had never understood when he recited the *romance* to himself.

The influence of Falla the composer may especially be felt in the greatest poet of modern Spain—the Granadine Federico García Lorca, who was murdered in the Spanish Civil War. His poems and his striking folk-dramas are steeped in the folk-lore and folk-music of the Moorish Kingdom, and this folk quality, added to his impressionable genius and subtle intuitions, make his 'Romancero Gitano' unsurpassed in its *genre*, for in addition to its modern qualities of rhythm it haunts the reader by its subtle evocation here and there of refrains from long ago.

Chapter XIII

The Essence of
Minstrelsy

In considering the epic poems and the ballads and their descent through the ages it is important to remember that they were sung to an instrument, and one of the many reasons why Menéndez Pidal has been able to go more deeply into early Spanish poetry than any one else is that he is extremely sensitive to music and realizes its importance. In explaining the irregular verse of early Spanish Epic poetry he said that a minstrel singing the 'Poem of the Cid' may have fitted the verses into a melody and a rhythm that were already given to him, but it was even possible that those irregular lines were not really sung at all, but 'accompanied by a little chant (*tonillo de recitado*) which would show a variation of accent before the break in the line, and another for the final syllables in each verse'.[1] This is the regular principle of chanting. A chant consists of two halves. It begins, as a rule, with an 'Intonation' (*Initium*) leading up to the 'reciting note' (*Tenor*) on the dominant of the mode and followed by a cadence called the '*Mediation*' (*Mediante*) at the end of the first half; the reciting note is then taken up again in the second half and leads to a final cadence: the 'Ending' (*Finalis*).[2] Minstrel and ballad singers were influenced in their performance by Church singing and by psalmody. For psalmody is a perfectly natural method. Whenever sentences are to be uttered aloud for many people to hear, in the open air or a large building, there is a natural tendency, for distinction's sake, to say the greater part on one note. It is natural and pleasing to make at the opening some short gradual ascent (intonation) to the note in question, to make at the close some gradual descent from it; and if the phrase

[1] R. Menéndez Pidal, *El Poema del Cid* (1908), Vol. 1, pp. 102-103.
[2] Grove's *Dictionary of Music* (4th ed.), art. 'Psalmody'.

is long, possibly also to make some variation of the monotone in
the middle of its course.[1] Professor Trend in an interesting paper
read before the British Musical Association analysed some of the
earliest ballad-melodies of Spain noted by Salinas before 1577,
and modern folk songs by Manuel de Falla, showing how the
metre, regarded from the musical point of view, occupied the
thoughts of the minstrels, however unconscious they may have
been of its principles.[2] Menéndez Pidal studies the whole question of the minstrels' methods in one of his most fascinating books
—'*Poesía Juglaresca y Juglares*' (1924). Some of the most important
pages describe the significance of the *juglares* or minstrels in the
early history of language and literature. When Latin began to be
forgotten by the people the *juglares* had to sing in Romance, and
as time passed they were obliged to forge a Romance tongue
which would be understood by the people. Thus the Provençal
minstrels took elements from the folk songs such as the May songs,
the *aubades*, and the *pastourelles* and inspired the troubadours,
who, in their turn sang them in praise of their ladies in the courts
of love. The Galician *juglares* followed the same example and
created their *cantos de amigo*. The road of Saint James from France
through the north of Spain to Santiago de Compostela echoed
with the songs of foreign minstrels, for the pilgrimage was made
mostly by foreigners, and it was therefore the channel by which
Romanesque architecture and Gregorian music entered Spain.
The *Pórtico de la Gloria* at Santiago Cathedral is the supreme
representation in architecture of music turned to stone, for there
we see the twenty-four elders of the Apocalypse tuning their
instruments and conversing with their fellow-minstrels prior to
their performance. Few spectacles are more thrilling to-day than
to watch the pilgrims enter the 'Gate of Glory' at the end of their
long journey, but it must have been infinitely more moving
when the pilgrims sang their song of gratitude to the twenty-four
saintly minstrels in stone tuning their instruments. For hundreds
of years it was customary for travellers to leave behind them
what Professor Trend aptly calls 'musical visiting-cards', and
in the thirteenth and fourteenth centuries these musical visiting-

[1] Id., art. 'Inflexion'.
[2] J. B. Trend, *The Performance of Music in Spain*, Proceedings of the Musical
Association, session LV, January 15, 1929.

cards were original compositions, and owing to this habit some of the earliest pieces of mediaeval harmony in Spain are to be found in Santiago.[1] The minstrels who wandered through Spain in the thirteenth century are familiar to us owing to the exquisite miniatures with which Alfonso el Sabio embellished the manuscript of the *Cantigas de Santa María* now in the monastery of the Escorial. The more elaborate miniatures give us a vivid picture of the court at a moment of great literary activity. The king is seated on his throne, holding a book in his hand and dictating a poem, making with a finger an imperious gesture to the scribes who are squatting on the ground at his feet, with quills poised in the air, listening attentively. At a short distance away are the clerics, armed with books and ready, when the occasion demands, to share their wisdom with his Majesty. Then still further away are the minstrels tuning their lutes or playing them with bow or plectrum. The minstrels are not only Christian, but also Moorish and Jewish, and the miniatures show us over thirty different classes of instruments. They include viols, citoles, and stringed instruments of various types; flutes, hautboys, bagpipes, bladder-pipes; horns, harps, dulcimers, tabors, and chime-bells. Many of the scenes in the miniatures seem oddly modern to travellers who have wandered through Spanish villages in recent years: we see the *juglar* playing in taverns with a *porrón* of wine beside him: at another he is present at a quarrel over dice, and remains unmoved while the contestants tear one another's hair: in another we see a bulging pigskin of wine that reminds us of the giant whom Sancho saw his master kill, slicing off his head as though it was a turnip. In order to understand fully the life of the minstrel in these miniatures it is necessary to move on in time to the fourteenth century (about fifty years after Alfonso the Sage) to the heyday of minstrelsy, when the Archpriest of Hita composed his poems and songs in rich profusion for the night-denying scholars, goliards, ballad singers, Moorish and Jewish dancing girls. And he was not only a minstrel with a Golden Treasury in his head, but also a master of the autobiographic style. His description of himself makes him live for ever in our mind: he was 'more than common tall, sturdy, thick-set, hairy, full-chested, bull-necked, black-eyed, with thick eyebrows, neat legs, small

[1] J. B. Trend, *The Performance of Music in Spain*, p. 60.

feet, sensuous lips, large ears and expansive nostrils'. No ascetic
was he, but a Falstaffian figure, who had such keen eyes for the
picaresque side of life that nothing escaped his notice. His lady
loves must generally have been of short stature, for he wrote one
of his most beautiful poems on short women which was very well
translated by that great ballad-lover, Longfellow:

> A pepper-corn is very small, but seasons every dinner
> More than all other condiments, although 'tis sprinkled
>   thinner,
> Just so a little woman is, if love will let you win her;
> There's not a joy in all the world you will not find
>   within her.
> And as within the little rose you find the richest dyes,
> And in a little grain of gold much price and value lies,
> As from a little balsam much odour doth arise,
> So in a little woman there's a taste of paradise.[1]

The Archpriest knew all schools of minstrelsy and could quote
from the French and the Galicians in their own language and he
could speak to the Moorish girls in vulgar Arabic. He was not
only poet but also singer and player on many instruments. He
had a subtle ear and could distinguish between all kinds of
instruments whether plucked or percussion, and he knew that
whereas plucked instruments were better suited to Arabic words,
wind instruments and viols were best for Spanish songs. He makes
a distinction between the 'Latin Guitar' and the Moorish guitar
and he explains that the former was used for accompanying
harmonically with chords, while the latter was for plucking the
tune in time with the singer. It is interesting to note that modern
guitarists employ the thrumming with chords which is called
rasguear, and the plucking method which is called *puntear*.

No minstrel was ever more popular than the Archpriest, and
after his death his popularity actually increased owing to the use
which other *juglares* made of his songs and ballads. Menéndez
Pidal gives a very interesting account of an actual performance
by a minstrel in a public square in some Castilian town at the
beginning of the fifteenth century—soon after 1410. The account

---

[1] H. W. Longfellow. The poem was published in 1833 in the *North American
Review*.

has come down to us by chance. A scribe sat copying a Spanish chronicle, when suddenly he must have heard a minstrel outside in the square, for he wrote down, on a blank leaf at the end of his manuscript, the programme of what the minstrel actually performed. The minstrel began his show by quoting a series of proverbs and moral maxims, which resembled those current in Oriental story-books. Then he gave a catalogue of various Spanish towns and the kind of people who came from them. Many of them the copyist wrote down in the margin. Then to vary his performance the minstrel cried out: 'Now watch me do a hop, skip and a jump. There's not a piebald or a chestnut horse could do the same.' With that he turned a few somersaults, stood on his hands and cut a few capers. Finally he uttered the magic words which had awakened the thrill of expectation in the people ever since the Archpriest Juan Ruiz had recited his stories in the square of Alcalá de Henares: '*Agora comencemos del libro de Arciprieste.*' 'Let us begin the Book of the Archpriest.'[1] This account is also of great interest because it explains the essential meaning of the word *juglar*. A *juglar*, according to Menéndez Pidal, meant any one whose profession it was to perform before an audience. He was not necessarily a musician: he might be a writer of ballads, an acrobat, a juggler, a sword-swallower, a hurdy-gurdy player, or a writer-cum-acrobat as in the present instance. The main duty of the *juglar* was to amuse and entertain people. If the troubadours were 'highbrows', the *juglares* were 'lowbrows', and we can understand how deeply the former despised the latter. Their scorn resembled the scorn which the modern trained composer feels for the popular theme writer, or the concert violinist for the vagrant player who scrapes the strings. The troubadour, too, did not consider himself a professional entertainer: he wrote verses in honour of his lady when inspiration spurred him on, but he would never travel the roads with a lute strung across his shoulders, halting by the way to sing for hire. The *juglar*, according to the troubadour, disgraced the knight-errantry of song by his antics: he travelled with disreputable wenches who should have been publicly whipped: he was a drunkard and base intriguer; not a word came from his

---

[1] R. Menéndez Pidal, *Poesía Juglaresca y Juglares*, Madrid, 1924, pp. 300–307, and App. III.

G

mouth that was not a foul blasphemy. Yet the troubadours did not disdain to employ the *juglares* as lute-players and even singers, for we find Gerard de Borneil travelling about with two of them from court to court. It was therefore not surprising that one should influence the other. The *juglar* was historically more ancient than the troubadour, who only came in about the eleventh century. From the seventh century we find in Europe the word *joculator*, from which sprang the French *jongleur*, the Spanish *juglar*, and the Italian *giullare*. The name lasted on until the fourteenth century when it became a term of abuse, and performers preferred the word *menestrel*. The word *juglar* remained among the people in Spain and was applied to the lonely, disreputable vagabond roaming the roads and living the picaresque life.[1]

In France and Spain in the second half of the fifteenth century no more long epic poems were written, but wandering minstrels recited the heroic ballads sprung from the epic poem source. The minstrel has already fallen in the world and his art is cruelly satirized by the court poets. Such a minstrel was Juan of Valladolid or Juan Poeta, as he was generally called, who was accused of robbing the verses of others and of roaming the world singing the warlike deeds of the past as the blind singers did. The accusations against Juan Poeta prove how low the prestige of the *juglar* had fallen. The people were beginning to sing their own ballads: life ceased to be remote and feudally exclusive. The aristocratic art of the troubadours had died, and the *juglar* with his cruder folk poems and simple melodies had begun to decline before the victorious advance of the polyphonic music of the Flemish school, which was building up an elaborate structure on the basis of the old music. The triumph of the canonic principle in music coincides with the decay of the feudal system, the growth of the communes and free cities, the use and development of the guild system. Is it not a coincidence that the stronghold of this popular, communal guild music should be in Flanders where all the foregoing social and political tendencies were more in evidence than elsewhere in Europe?

While this was happening the blind minstrel carried on obscurely and pathetically to the last glimmer the tradition of

[1] R. Menéndez Pidal, *Los Juglares*, Madrid 1924, pp. 3-7, 22-23.

Juan Poeta, and continued to sing *las viejas fazañas*, for in every country in the world blind men with their prodigious memories have always been the last repositories of national traditions. Even in modern days the blind singer may be encountered in the glens and mountains of Asturias or Avila. Menéndez Pidal on more than one occasion has described hearing one of those *juglares* recite ballads of saints and their miracles, accompanying himself on the *zanfoña* or the *rabel*, both of them instruments described in the *Book of Good Love* of the Archpriest. This blind minstrel is the last descendant of the Castilian minstrel, the kinsman of those blind French beggars, who at the end of the fourteenth century sang the last *chansons de geste* to the sound of the same instrument —the *cifoine*.[1]

---

[1] R. Menéndez Pidal, *op. cit.*

Chapter XIV

Menéndez Pidal,
Collector of Ballads

With the haunting description of the blind man chanting his ballads to the sound of his mediaeval instrument, our author brings to an end his most poetical book, and of it Professor Griswold Morley said in his review: 'In this small but solid brown volume, Sr. Menéndez Pidal has once more pushed back the frontiers of our knowledge of the Middle Ages in Spain, and reconstructed one small world of mediaeval life and letters. As in some of his previous books, Menéndez Pidal reveals here not only the brains of a great scholar, but the soul of an artist.'

Those who have criticized him merely as scholar and philologist have missed the essential part of his character. He was born a poet and a minstrel, and he has never shut his ears to the whispering call of the ghostly minstrel poets of the past, whose refrains still haunt the memories of the folk from Asturias and Galicia. When we compare the texts of ballads included in the collections of Grimm, Durán, Wolf or Menéndez Pelayo with those contained in the '*Flor Nueva de Romances Viejos*', published by our author in 1943, we find that in the latter he has fused together various versions from the great collections, and, on occasion, included variants from ancient texts neglected by the critics and from modern versions obtained from oral tradition.

In publishing these variants, Menéndez Pidal has followed the procedure of the traditional collectors of *romances*, for we encounter this fusion of many versions of a single ballad in all the ancient cancioneros: every singer or reciter in the old days as in modern times touches up and transforms every *romance* he sings. Tradition is a living thing: it is always in a state of transformation, for life is change and mutability. Cecil Sharp, the great English collector, whose personality in certain subtle respects

resembled that of our author, mentions one extremely important characteristic of the folk-singer. 'It is a well-known fact that
the folk-singer attaches far more importance to the words of his
song than to its tune; that while he is conscious of the words that
he is singing, he is more or less unconscious of the melody . . .'[1]
Cecil Sharp makes very important statements on the evolution of
folk-song which should be remembered when we study the collections made by Menéndez Pidal. 'In the evolution of folk
tunes', says Sharp, 'the principle of selection is the taste of the
community. Thus tune variations, which appeal to the community, will be perpetuated as against those which attract the
individual only. The nature of the appeal may be of two kinds.
It may be an appeal to the sense of beauty, i.e. aesthetic in
character; or it may be an appeal to the understanding, i.e.
expressive in character. Which of these will be the determining
factor in selection will depend, ultimately, upon the racial
characteristics of the community.' Cecil Sharp then sums up in
turn the three principles of *Continuity*, *Variation* and *Selection*,
ascribing to each the part it plays in the drama of the evolution of
folk-song.

Without the first, *Continuity*, no evolution can take place. Its
function is to prepare the way. It is a passive rather than an active
agent; a condition, not a cause.

The second principle, *Variation*, creates the material which
renders development possible. Variation, of itself, does not
necessarily lead to development. Change may produce growth,
or it may be sterile; or again it may lead to corruption.

The function of the third principle, *Selection*, is to ensure that
Variation shall, in certain cases, result in organic growth and
development. Of itself, Variation merely provides the building
material, the bricks and mortar. The moulding of that material,
the business of construction, the determination of the form that
the building shall take, these are the work of *Selection*. Moreover,
Variation is the product of the individual; whereas *Selection* is the
act of the community. The folk-song has derived its communal
and racial character solely through the action of the third
principle, *Selection*.

Nobody has ever put into clearer words the whole process of

---

[1] Cecil Sharp, *English Folk-Song: Some Conclusions*, Oxford, 2nd ed., 1936, p. 29.

evolution of the art of the folk than that great and generous pioneer in music, whose life quest has inspired the Renaissance of
modern English music. These words may fittingly be quoted as a
tribute to the great Spanish scholar and artist, whose life quest
has led him over the world in search of ballads, as though the
Romancero were the Magic Firebird. When Professor Ker gave
his celebrated lecture on Spanish and English ballads to the
Anglo-Spanish Society in King's College, London, in 1918, he
paid a great tribute to Menéndez Pidal's work on the Romancero
and quoted a personal story from Don Ramón which sums up the
latter's life work:

'In May of 1900,' Don Ramón writes, 'I visited the banks of the
Duero to study the geography of the Cid. It was our wedding
journey. Our researches were finished at Osma. We waited a day
longer to see the eclipse of the sun, and it happened that my wife
repeated the ballad of *Conde Sol* to a washerwoman with whom
we were speaking. The good woman told us that she knew it too,
along with others, which made up her stock of songs as she was
beating and washing clothes by the river; she consented to sing
one, and began in a sweet voice a melody "as soothing and agree-
able" to our ears as those which the historian Mariana heard
with the ballads of the Siege of Zamora. The ballad which she
sang was unknown to us, and therefore the more interesting; as it
proceeded, my wife thought she found in it a more or less historical argument, an echo of that sorrow, tribulation and sore
mischance which, according to the chronicles, was caused in
Spain by the death of Prince John, son of the Catholic Kings.
And so it proved to be, an historical ballad of the fifteenth
century, unknown to all the collections old or new in Spain. It
was necessary in the few hours remaining of our stay in Osma to
note the music and copy the ballads, the first tribute paid by
Castile to our ballad book of modern tradition, aided by the
choirmaster of the Cathedral, and getting the good woman to
repeat her songs we passed the hours, hardly sparing time for the
eclipse which was the reason of our staying there, but now had
lost its first importance.' And Sir W. P. Ker comments: 'I still
wonder whether that story sounds more like Scott or Cervantes'.[1]

To recapture the same romance of discovery let us recall the

[1] W. P. Ker, *Essays*, Vol. 2, pp. 23–24.

folk-song adventures of Cecil Sharp, who began his collection in Somerset, which led to the foundation in 1898 of the Folk Song Society. 'The Seeds of Love' was the first song he collected from a country gardener in a vicarage garden, who was called by the appropriate name of John England. This folk song inaugurated the fruitful period of folk song discovery in Great Britain. As far back as 1843 the Rev. John Broadwood had interested himself in the songs sung at harvest homes and seasonal festivals, but the organist who took them down was shocked at the flat sevenths and the modal character of the tunes, and, also, altered the cadences to fit his preconceived ideas on the minor and the major scales. Broadwood, however, published a small book, and passed on his enthusiasm to his niece, Lucy Broadwood, who became a real collector and collaborated with the music critic of *The Times*, J. A. Fuller Maitland, in *English County Songs*.[1] Then came Cecil Sharp and gave to the world a mass of English songs preserved by oral tradition among the people of the countryside, and these songs were all the more valuable because they had not been perverted by the adapter and arrangers trained on major and minor scales, but remained in their pristine modal condition. Cecil Sharp in his fascinating book *English Folk Song—Some Conclusions* (1st cdn. 1907, 2nd cdn. 1936), when looking forward to the dawn of a new musical era in England, recalled the precedent of Percy's *Reliques*, showing the magical effect that work had on English poetry. 'It not only felled at one blow the cold formalism which had characterized the poetry of the preceding age, but it led to the revival of a taste for genuine and natural poetry, which has endured to the present day.' We might compare Percy's *Reliques* with the Romancero. The *Reliques*, which were derived from a manuscript of 1650, included very old historical ballads referring to the battle of Otterburn, 1338, Thomas Cromwell, who was executed in 1540, Fair Rosamund, the mistress of Henry VII, and the murder of Mary Queen of Scots, and many ballads describing legendary heroes such as Robin Hood and King Arthur. In English ballads, however, we must note whether they have come down to us by oral tradition or by broadside. The

---

[1] The greatest treasure-house of ballads in all their varying versions is the monumental work by Professor F. J. Child, *English and Scottish Ballads* (5 vols., 1886).

English ballads settled into their own form in the sixteenth and seventeenth centuries, and it was by the winnowing powers of oral transmission that the song became part and parcel of the country's folk song. As Boehme said, 'First of all one man sings a song, and the others sing it after him, changing what they do not like.' The changing process is one by which it grows, and by which it is created. Thus a song in passing from mind to mind, and mouth to mouth, tests itself, and strengthens itself artistically. Sometimes faulty memory and an inaccurate ear caused songs to degenerate. In America, for instance, we get degenerate versions of the celebrated ballad of 'Lord Rendal'.

The ballads which have been transmitted by broadside—that is to say on a sheet printed for circulation among the populace, should be called 'popular' rather than 'folk'. Before the days of newspapers they were topical with stories of crimes and executions and they reflected the townman's point of view as against the rustic outlook of the peasant. The first broadside ballad was Skelton's poem on the battle of Flodden Field, 1513. Cecil Sharp in his book explains how the words of the folk-ballad, owing to their traditionary and communal origin, have, like its music, characteristics of their own, by means of which they may be distinguished from the 'composed' ballads of literature. He refers to the hackneyed phrase which is so frequently found at the beginning and at the end of the ballad, for peasants, like all simple people, find an especial difficulty both in making a start and in consummating a conclusion. Countless ballads, for instance, open with the line, 'As I went out one May morning', a fact that, by the way, provides the collector with a ready means of jogging a singer's memory. And Sharp describes how he would ask a singer, whose memory was exhausted, whether he had ever heard of a song beginning 'As I went out, etc.' The question always produced a flash of recognition, and very often too, a fresh ballad. The method of narration, as described by Sharp, resembles closely the Spanish: 'Much is left to the imagination of the listener; the story is sketched in a few bold strokes, with, here and there, a minute and elaborate description of some minor incident. This is one of the arts by which the ballad-maker imparts to his story a vivid sense of reality. "Yes, Sir, and it is true," is the reply that has often been made to me by a folk-singer at the conclusion of a long ballad which I have praised. Here, again, the peasant singer is like the child, and loves to think that the story which has moved him is not fictitious but true.'[1]

Very significant, too, are Sharp's remarks on the refrain in the popular ballads. 'It forms,' he says, 'almost the invariable adjunct to the ballad that has any claim to antiquity.' The ballad was originally communal in performance, and was danced as well as sung. Some writers indeed maintain that the game of ball also formed an integral part of the performance, and derive from the root 'ball' the etymology of the words 'ballet' and 'ballad'.[2] This connection between the ball game and the ballad will immediately recall the celebrated passage in the *Book of Good Love* by the minstrel Archpriest of Hita, where he tells his readers to let his book pass from hand to hand like a ball in a game played by ladies.[3] That passage would seem to corroborate Sharp's statement that the game of ball formed part of the performance of the ballad. Later on, when dance and song became separated, each taking on an independent existence, and developing along its own lines, the words ballet and ballad became differentiated, the former being applied to the dance only, and the latter to the song. But even in modern times the English peasant would say that he had learned a particular song 'off a ballet', meaning thereby a 'ballad-sheet' or broad-sheet.

Whereas Menéndez Pidal reaped a plentiful harvest in his ballad-questing, for the ballad tradition has never died out in Spain, Cecil Sharp was forced to admit that the twentieth-century collector was a hundred years too late. 'The English Ballad,' he says sadly, 'is moribund; its account is well-nigh closed.' But when he visited North America he found a living English ballad tradition in the Appalachian mountains, in the country on the borders of Virginia, Kentucky, Tennessee and North Carolina, which is a close parallel to the Spanish ballad tradition in South America and the Levant. I shall quote his description of that tradition as a fitting parallel to the lyrical description given by Menéndez Pidal of his experiences on the banks of the Duero: 'I found myself for the first time in my life in a community in which singing

---

[1] C. Sharp, *op. cit.*, p. 93.
[2] *Ibid.*
[3] Juan Ruiz, *Libro de Buen Amor*, l. 1629.

was as common and almost as universal a practice as speaking. In an ideal society every child in his earliest years would, as a matter of course, learn to sing the songs of his forefathers in the same natural and unselfconscious way in which he learns his mother tongue. And it was precisely this ideal state of things that I found existing in the mountain communities. So closely, indeed, is the practice of this particular art interwoven with the ordinary vocations of everyday life that the singers, unable to recall a song I had asked for, would often make some such remark as: "Oh, if only I were driving the cows home, I could sing it at once!" On one occasion, too, I remember that a small boy tried to edge himself into my cabin in which a man was singing to me, and when I asked him what he wanted he said: "I always like to go where there is sweet music." Of course, I let him in, and later on, when some singer failed to remember a song I had asked for, my little visitor came to the rescue and straightway sang the ballad from beginning to end in the true traditional manner, and in a way which would have shamed many a professional vocalist.'[1]

Menéndez Pidal in his '*Flor Nueva de Romances Viejos*' describes how he learned the ballads in his childhood in the traditional Asturian countryside. The singing of folk ballads and folk songs was the universal recreation of the youth when gathered together around the fires in the mountains, or when tramping through the oak forests. Later on, following the tradition of Timoneda and the scholar poets of the past, he searched high and low through Spain for variants, discovering them not only in parchments hidden away in libraries but also hearing them from the lips of nomad shepherds and stevedores on ships. Even at the most unexpected moments in his life these refrains from the past would catch his ear, as, for instance, in Monte Video, while waiting for his steamer, or on another occasion in a Gypsy cave in the Sacro Monte, in view of the magic panorama of Granada. Professor Ker when referring to these explorations of our author, which, he says, 'like Walter Scott's raids in Liddesdale, are part of the humanities', lays special stress upon the significance of the Spanish ballads preserved in the oral traditions of the Spanish

---

[1] C. Sharp, *English Folk Songs from the Southern Appalachians*, collected by Olive Dame Campbell and Cecil J. Sharp, New York, 1917, p. viii. Complete collection, 2 vols., edited by Maud Karpeles, Oxford, 1932.

Jews. They were banished in the year 1492 by the Catholic kings; and they took with them to Tangier, Constantinople, Bosnia, Salonica, Rhodes, as well as North Africa, their Spanish language and their Spanish ballads. These have been collected and recorded by the Sephardic scholars themselves in the various countries and co-ordinated by Menéndez Pidal with tireless industry. The exiled Jews never forgot the country which had driven them out: they preserved their Spanish language and the songs 'with a loyalty unexampled in any other people; fanciful, romantic, if you will, an intellectual and spiritual allegiance, an instinctive refusal to be dispossessed and disinherited'.[1] Some of the ballads that have been collected among the Spanish Jews are unknown in the Peninsula, others preserve better versions of the ballads than those known in Spain. Who to-day in Spain knows by tradition the ballad describing the complaints of Doña Jimena to the King? Yet every Jew in Tangier sings it.[2] Take the most beautiful ballad of all, the song of Count Arnaldos, which has the magic spell of 'La Belle Dame sans Merci' in its haunting lines. The mariner's son from the ghostly ship carries us away into the realms of fairy land:

> *Quien uviese tal ventura sobre las aguas del mar*
> *Como uvo el Conde Arnaldos la mañana de San Juan*

(Who had ever such adventure, holy priest, or virgin nun,
As befell the Count Arnaldos at the rising of the sun?)

Its spell springs from its vague and fragmentary character, for it awakens the sense of mystery with its phantom ship, which will carry the count away to adventures in far off climes. The sense of mystery is increased by the last riddle line:

> *Yo no digo mi canción sino a quien conmigo va*

(Would'st thou learn the great secret, in our galley thou must go').

In its fragmentary state it has always been considered the masterpiece of balladry ever since the sixteenth century, but the Sephardic Jews of Morocco sing a complete version, telling us how Count Arnaldos boards the mysterious ship and finds there,

[1] W. P. Ker, *op. cit.*
[2] R. Menéndez Pidal, *op. cit.*, p. 42.

to his amazement, his family and his retainers, who had been
searching high and low for him. And thus we obtain the explanation of the enigmatic first two lines of the ballad. In this way the
exiles have, despite the Spanish decrees, preserved the traditions
which link them to the land they so enriched by their culture.
I still remember the explorer's thrill I experienced in the summer
of 1937, when I went for an expedition through the island of
Rhodes with a coachman who was a Sephardic Jew—a most
imposing figure, with a long white beard, called Abraham.
No sooner did he hear my Spanish than he began in mellow tones
to recite me a *romance* on the Cid Campeador using quaint archaic forms of speech that were current in fifteenth-century Spain.
He and all the Sephardic brethren in the island were in great
fear, for Mussolini in his haste to copy the anti-Semitic policy of
his ally Hitler had published an edict against the Jewish communities in Italy and the colonies, and Abraham feared that,
now, after centuries of peaceful settlement he and his race would
be driven into exile again to wander as outcasts and vagabonds.
As we drove towards the Homeric town of Lindos he spoke to me
of ancient Spanish Jewish ceremonies, such as the *seradura*, with
its strange exorcism of the evil spirit by means of marjoram, resin,
and sesame oil, and he hummed snatches of *novias* (betrothal
songs), *paridas* (songs for new-born children), and *endechas* or
dirges. Listening to this bearded descendant of ancient Spain I
felt, as never before, the immense dignity and unity of the
Romancero, which is the treasure-house of the Spanish race.
Once again I experienced the same emotion; this time it was on
the occasion of a lecture-recital given by Menéndez Pidal in the
British Institute, Madrid, in the winter of 1946. The master had
brought with him a group of singers and instrumentalists to perform in traditional manner the ballads that would serve as
illustrations to his lecture on the Romancero. These singers had
been specially trained with loving care by Doña Jimena, the
daughter of Don Ramón, and other members of the family, who
have devoted themselves to the task of making the ancient songs
live. We heard the *romance* by Ambrosio de Montesinos with its
beautiful archaic melody, as transcribed by the doyen of musico-
logists, Father Higinio Anglés; then the ballad of Conde Claros
with its melody by Juan de Enzina from the *Cancionero Musical del*

Palacio; then the ballad from Osma which Pidal had collected from the washerwoman on the banks of the Duero; and lastly, to our astonishment, we heard the famous old ballad of 'Gerineldo' which has survived in a pueblo in the province of Avila, as a *baile de Tres*—a characteristic primitive ballad dance performance. And, incidentally, this form of dance was described in 1530 by Luys de Milan, as danced at the court of Germaine de Foix in Valencia.

As I listened to these traditional ballads performed by these young students of to-day, to the accompaniment of laúd, guitar, and bandurria, I began to see the little bearded master in a blurred vision. His personality seemed to shift ceaselessly from one period of time to another as though he were a fantastic wizard conjuring up for his audience scene after scene of Spain's past. I then began to understand the true significance of the Middle Ages of Spain, as personified in Spain's national hero. When, in the eleventh century, after 300 years of isolation, the ruder north of the country emancipated itself from all Moslem influence, and Spain re-entered the concert of Western nations, she was found to be more backward than her Christian neighbours, a condition to which her traditionalism contributed. The Cid made a tardy appearance on the world stage as an epic hero. He is the last hero who fully deserves the title—the last to fill the pages of national poetry. None of the neighbouring countries could show in the eleventh century an epic poetry woven around a hero of the time, whereas Spain was then living in the last heroic age of the western world and, therefore, could produce, at a relatively advanced stage of civilization, the gest of the Cid, which is so modern and revolutionary as an epic and has such exceptional value in history and poetry.[1]

As I have shown throughout my survey of the master's works, the use of archaic forms, living on in an atmosphere of traditionalism, produced similar excellent and novel results. Almost all the intellectual activity of Spain in her golden age was devoted to the development of ideas, that in the northern European Countries had attained their zenith in the Middle Ages, and assumed a fresh and unexpected value when reshaped by Spain in a more modern atmosphere. From the conception of a uni-

[1] R. Menéndez Pidal, *The Cid and his Spain*, London, 1934, pp. 472–473.

versal empire allied to the Church, from the Society of Jesus, the new mysticism of Santa Teresa and St John of the Cross, and the new scholasticism of Vitoria and Suárez that was the forerunner of modern international law, down to the chivalric novel, the ballad, the drama—all were instances of a reflorescence that was the more luxuriant in that it came at a later date. All this output of the Spanish Golden Age is not independent of the Renaissance, but it is a renaissance of a peculiar kind, profoundly mediaeval for all its modernity. Profoundly mediaeval, for though tradition had struck deeper root in Spain than elsewhere, much of the mediaeval outlook persisted in Europe in the sixteenth and seventeenth centuries, contrary to the cut and dried notion that the Renaissance brought about a complete revolution in men's outlook on life. And yet highly modern; for, if Spain cultivated mediaeval survivals, it was to fertilize them with the thought of modern times.[1] This theme, which runs through every work of Menéndez Pidal, is that which gives deep significance to his essay on 'The Spaniards in their History', which was published in 1947 as an introduction to the first volume (Prehistoric Spain) of the monumental history of Spain. He had originally intended to publish a fuller work as an epilogue to the History.

[1] R. Menéndez Pidal, *The Cid and his Spain*, p. 473.

Chapter XV

The Essay on Spain

It is instructive to compare the essay of Menéndez Pidal with some of the essays on Spain by his contemporaries. First of all, let us consider '*Psicología del Pueblo Español*' by the eminent historian Rafael Altamira which was published in 1902, and republished in 1917. Altamira describes in the preface how he wrote his book in the summer of 1898, when Spain sustained her tragic war with the United States of America. In the atmosphere of gloom, amidst the tears of some, the indignation of others, and the passive indifference of the majority he wrote feverishly in an attempt to raise the morale of his countrymen, for he hoped against hope that a movement of regeneration would come to Spain as it had come to Prussia in 1808, leading to the victorious Germany of 1870. What he longed for was a movement of regeneration which would correct national defects and inject fresh vigour into the body politic, and rescue the country from the deep decadence into which it had sunk. As a result, Altamira produced a description of the Spanish character which is a useful compendium for one reading the authors of the 1898 movement. After quoting the opinions of the eighteenth-century masters, such as Masdeu and Feijóo, he devotes attention to Ganivet, whose tragic death seemed to foreshadow the national disaster. It was Ganivet who explained the essence of the Spanish conception of justice. The Spaniard aspires to pure and absolute justice, and he insists that it should be rigorous, even implacable. But at the same time the Spaniard is always ready to pity the fallen, and he will take as much trouble to raise him up as he did to overthrow him. This characteristic, according to Ganivet, sprang from the stoicism of Seneca, and was a genuine Spanish trait. In considering the eighteenth century Altamira remarks that no

103

historian has adequately studied the causes of the decline of Spain in the last years of Charles IV, and later, when the country after the War of Independence neglected intellectual pursuits and fell into the obscurantism of Ferdinand VII's reign, thus preparing the ground for the troubled years of Isabel II. Let us not forget, he says, that Spain is the European nation which has suffered the greatest number of years of war in the nineteenth century. Up to 1896 Spain had sustained thirty-one years of war; France twenty-seven; Russia twenty-four; Italy twenty-three; England twenty-one, and Germany thirteen, but the majority of these wars were not civil but international.[1]

Altamira began to write his book in the tragic days of 1898, and in the succeeding years he analyses the various pessimistic writers who devoted their attention to the complex problems of Spanish decadence. One writer after another pointed out the defects of the Spanish character. Macías Picavea for instance in 'El Problema Nacional' described Spain as an ailing country, whose defects were immeasurably greater than her virtues, and those vices which had atrophied the organs of her national life sprang from the Caesarism, despotism, caciquism, theocracy, and Catholic intolerance which came in with the House of Austria. Macías saw no hope in the masses or in collective effort. There was only one solution: Spain would have to discover 'a man', that is to say, a genius; one of those benevolent dictators who can change the destiny of a nation. When Altamira published his book in 1902 the new literary movement of 1898 was already well under way. Azorín was already awakening the Spaniards and making them observe the world around them and discover beauties in the tiny pueblos that lie strewn like toys on the Meseta of Castile. Unamuno, with his Quixotism and his gospel of struggle and agony, was turning men's minds, not only to Tertullian and Augustine, but also to the Danish philosopher Kirkegaard: Baroja was revolutionizing the Spanish novel and creating a modern kind of picaresque narration. When Altamira published the second edition of his book in 1917 he found himself obliged to vary his text in places and add an extra chapter on actual psychological characteristics. In the new preface he refers to the great mass of literature written by the Hispanophobes as a

[1] R. Altamira, Psicología del Pueblo Español, 2nd ed., Madrid, 1917, p. 152.

result of the political passions aroused by the wars of Italy against Spanish domination, the conflict for hegemony between France and Spain, the religious wars, the struggle for independence in the Netherlands, and finally the American question in which Dutch, English and French took part. That literature makes quaint reading to-day, for in it we find Spanish psychology treated by the Hispanophobes in a special way for political reasons. This gave rise on the part of the Spaniards, the partisans of the House of Austria, and Catholics in general, to a series of counter-works defending Spanish history and the character or psychology of the people. This conflict which was acute in the eighteenth century died down in the nineteenth century, but the legendary tales of travellers and the fantastic description of Spanish life did not cease, and there arose the struggle between the Liberals and the Reactionaries, to which I referred in my description of Menéndez Pelayo. At the end of the century the dispute again became international on the occasion of the Cuban War, when Hispanophobia was exploited by the jingoist press of the United States.[1] The disaster of 1898 produced two opposite movements, according to Altamira: one that was pessimistic and tried to prove that Spaniards were lacking in the essentials necessary for adapting themselves to modern civilization: the other that reacted against the pessimistic view and turned with confidence to the task of introducing a progressive spirit into the country. Madariaga in his memorable book on Spain gives a striking description of Spain on the eve of the first World War. 'One afternoon in the month of March 1914, a youthful man with a heavy forehead, expressive eyes and an attractive, if self-conscious smile, came forward on the stage of the theatre of La Comedia in Madrid and began to speak with quiet assurance, elegant gesture and a finely modulated voice to a crowded house which listened eagerly, and now and then interrupted with vigorous ovations. He was the already famous professor of metaphysics of the University of Madrid, José Ortega y Gasset. But what he was explaining to this packed theatre was no metaphysical question; it was the grief of his generation at the sight of what their elders had done with Spain. "Our generation," he said, "has never negotiated with the topics of patriotism, and

[1] R. Altamira, *op. cit.*, 2nd ed., p. 11.

H

when it hears the word Spain it does not think of Calderón and Lepanto, it does not remember the victories of the Cross, it does not call forth the vision of a blue sky, and under it a splendour— it merely feels, and what it feels is grief." He poured scorn on what he called "official Spain". "Official Spain" consists, as it were, in ghostly parties upholding ghosts of ideas, which, backed by the shadows of newspapers, keep going Cabinets of hallucination. "The old Spain, with its governing and its governed classes is now dying," he cried. It was high time that everything in Spain was nationalized and liberalized. This memorable day,' adds Madariaga, 'was the beginning of a movement of real leadership in Spanish politics. The spring tapped by Don Francisco Giner and fed by the devoted efforts of the *Junta* or Committee for the development of Studies, had by now become a strong and clear river of intelligent opinion flowing into the troubled and muddy waters of Spanish politics.' Alas, four months after that memorable day 'an Austrian prince was killed in Sarajevo, and Europe went mad.'[1]

In the last fifty years of troubled Spanish history some of the most striking utterances by Spanish thinkers have been in the form of an essay. The *ensayo* or essay has been the most popular literary form because it embodies in concise form the dominant ideas of the moment. Sometimes it may be a *cri du cœur* or passionate appeal by a prophet to his people. Modern Spanish history has had many of these dramatic essays which in their day summed up the thoughts that seethed in the minds of the thinking minority. Before Ganivet committed suicide in the year of Spain's disaster of 1898 he poured out his soul in one of those essays—The '*Idearium Español*' (1897)[2]—following the motto he had adapted from Saint Augustine: '*Noli foras ire: in interiore Hispaniae habitat veritas.*' Altamira's work, which we have considered, is in the nature of an essay written at white heat during the tragic war and re-edited and re-issued in 1917 during the first Great War. Unamuno, the great master of the dramatic essay, has used it as a means of expressing his own philosophy, and his Quixotic self-communings. His critics tried to lay him low by calling him 'paradoxical', but paradoxes are necessary as weapons

---

[1] S. de Madariaga, *Spain*, revised edition, London, 1942, pp. 230–231.
[2] It has been very well translated into English by Rafael Nadal, London, 1947.

against routine of thought, and Unamuno's function in modern Spain has been to make men probe and sift ideas. 'My principal duty', he said once, 'is to irritate people. We must sow in men seeds of doubt, of distrust, of disquiet, and even of despair.' Indeed, if Unamuno had lived at Athens he would not have lasted as long as Socrates: he would have been made drink the hemlock on the plea that such a man was a danger to the state. Nevertheless, the essays of Unamuno are among the most significant pronouncements of the time. After Unamuno we come to Ortega y Gasset, who after his brilliant entry upon the stage on the eve of the first Great War published a series of essays which show most unmistakably the very essence of Spain's condition. First of all 'España Invertebrada' condenses in short space the philosophical history of Spanish political life. In spite of all his study of Kant and Hegel, Ortega remains for ever a man of the Mediterranean. Following the example of Plato, he illustrates his ideas by beautiful metaphors and images. His works never cease to be literature, and Gómez de Baquero called him the philosopher poet. Ortega in his essay dispassionately sets Spain in its place among the Latin nations and compares its development with that of the others. In Spain there has been nearly always a disproportion between the common people and the select minority. All that has been done is due to the people, and what the people have not been able to do, remained undone. While the history of France or England is one that has chiefly been created by minorities, the history of Spain has entirely been made by the masses. The cause of all Spain's misfortunes, according to Ortega, was the absence of strong Feudalism as in the case of France and England. The Visigoths, when they invaded Spain, had already become devitalized owing to their long contact with the Roman Empire and they no longer possessed the strong select minority that would have given vigour to Spain. Hence the Visigoths were unable to withstand the flood of Moslem invasion. The lack of the select minority made itself felt all through the Middle Ages, and the rapid unification in the fifteenth century, which made Spain into the first complete nation in Europe, was due to the lack of vital feudal elements within the country. Ortega contrasts the Spanish colonization of America with the English. Whereas the English colonization overseas was carried out by select groups who established in the countries beyond the seas their own social structure based upon the mother country, the Spanish colonization of America was carried out by the masses blindly and unconsciously. 'Our masses,' says Ortega, 'did all that was to be done: they populated, cultivated, sang, groaned and loved, but they could not give to the nations they created what they themselves did not possess; namely superior discipline, culture and progressive civilization.'[1]

The absence of the select minorities, he says, has influenced all Spanish history and prevented the country from reaching the normality of the other nations which sprang from similar stock. The absence of 'the best' has caused a blindness among the masses of the people which prevents them from distinguishing the good man from the bad, with the result that when privileged individuals do appear in Spain the masses are unable to recognize their merit, and frequently annihilate them. The periods of decadence in a country, according to Ortega, are those when the minority ruling the people—namely the aristocracy—has lost the sterling qualities which once raised it to its dominant position. Then the masses with justice rise in revolt against this corrupt and effete aristocracy, but instead of substituting in its place another and more virtuous aristocracy they generally eliminate all aristocratic impulses in the belief that society can exist without the qualities of the minority.[2] There is, continues Ortega, in the history of humanity a perpetual alternation of two contrasting periods: the period of growth when aristocracies and societies are formed; and the period of decadence when these aristocracies decline and the societies break up. The Indians called these periods by the names *Kitra* and *Kali* and one follows the other rhythmically. During the *Kali* period the régime of the castes degenerates, and the *Sudra*, that is to say, the inferior castes, dominate, because Brahma has fallen asleep. Then Vishnu assumes the terrible form of Siva and destroys the living and the twilight of the gods glows on the horizon. Finally, Brahma awakes: Vishnu as the kindly god appears, recreates the Cosmos afresh and introduces a new *Kitra* period.

Ortega y Gasset's celebrated essay '*España Invertebrada*'

[1] J. Ortega y Gasset, *España Invertebrada*, Madrid, 1925, pp. 164–165.
[2] *Ibid.*, pp. 117–118.

appeared in 1921 when Europe was struggling to recover from the
first World War and when, as Madariaga said, the whole
Iberian Peninsula was being rapidly over-run with Bolshevik
measles which had begun in Barcelona and spread to agri-
cultural Andalusia.[1] Hence the pessimistic tone of the essay and
the emphasis laid upon mob rule of the *Kali* period. In 1930 a
further prophetic essay came from the pen of Ortega y Gasset,
this time one which revealed the whole trend of European affairs.
The essay, which bears the resounding title, 'The Revolt of the
Masses', completes the doctrine sketched out in 'Invertebrate
Spain'. For many years past the prophets had announced the
revolt. 'The masses are advancing,' Hegel had said apocalyptic-
ally; 'without a new spiritual power to act as guide, our epoch
which is a revolutionary one will produce a catastrophe,' were
the fateful words of Auguste Comte. From a rock in the Engadine
Nietzsche cried: 'I see the high tide of nihilism rising.' Ortega
sums up his essay as follows: 'Owing to the perfect organization
given by the nineteenth century to life in certain respects, the
masses, who have profited thereby, no longer remember that
these benefits were the result of planning and organization, but
believe they are the products of Nature herself. Hence the absurd
state of mind revealed by these masses whose only thought is for
their personal comfort. They forget that the benefits of civilization are due to the amazing ingenuity of the inventors and may
only be maintained at the cost of constant care and effort, and
they believe that all they have to do is to shout for those benefits
peremptorily as though they were their natural and inalienable
rights. . . .'

In conclusion, Ortega writes: 'Only the determination to construct a great nation from the group of peoples of the Continent
would give new life to the pulses of Europe. . . . In my opinion
the building up of Europe into a great national State is the one
enterprise that could counter-balance a victory of the "Five
Years Plan". Communism is an extravagant moral code, but it
is nothing less than a moral code. Does it not seem more worthy
and more fruitful to oppose to that Slavonic Code a new
European Code, the inspiration towards a new programme of
life?'

[1] S. de Madariaga, *Spain*, p. 243.

It is strange to realize that this essay which contains such amazingly prophetic words on Europe's condition should have been written in 1930 on the eve of the fall of the Spanish monarchy by one of the three intellectual leaders who founded the 'Group in the Service of the Republic' to prepare the way for the arrival of 'La Niña Bonita', 'The Pretty Girl', as the republic was quaintly called by the conspirators in the nineteenth century.[1]

There is poignant significance in Menéndez Pidal's essay on 'The Spaniards in Their History' when we reflect that it was written sixteen years after the Cassandra-like prophecies of Ortega y Gasset. Those prophecies were tragically fulfilled in the stormy years of the Republic who, though she had entered as gently as a lamb amidst the blessings of the intellectuals, yet within a year began to wear a 'bitter profile'. Menéndez Pidal, however, made the *Centro de Estudios Históricos* into a meeting-place not only of Spanish humanists but a clearing-house of European ideas of scholarship. He and his followers worked patiently at their texts, withdrawing as far as possible into their ivory tower, but theirs was a pathetic Urbino, standing like a lonely beacon on a rock buffeted on all sides by the angry waves of revolution. When we look back to those years of the Republic they stand out in one's imagination as successive scenes in a ghastly drama moving inexorably towards final doom. It was a period of frantic planning and febrile scheming; for the idealists among the intellectuals imagined they could overthrow the existing order and create a new progressive Spain without leaving a vestige of the old. But all these schemes straightway crumbled owing to the forces of revolution. The whole country was in the throes of a monstrous witches' Sabbath conjured up by a host of foreign agents eager to lead the dance. The tunes and rhythms these minions of the moon played up hill and down dale throughout the country were Spanish, but so deformed and twisted by the malignant ingenuity of these minstrels of chaos that it seemed as though the spirit of Spain had been obliterated. But through the mocking cacophony I could hear the solemn booming of the *Dies Irae* announcing the approaching doom.

Menéndez Pidal's essay must be read in the light of the grim and tragic years of the Civil War. It is not a pessimistic essay

[1] S. de Madariaga, *Spain*, pp. 292–293.

written in a moment of national disaster like that of Altamira,
nor is it one written in a mood of prophecy, like that of Ortega: it
is a calm dispassionate analysis of Spain's national characteristics
written by a scientist and a humanist in a mood of detached
inquiry. It is a concise summing up by one who has followed
all the parabola of his country's history and has succeeded in out-
living all prophecies. Now and then the calm surface of his style
becomes ruffled with emotion and we expect that he will turn
aside from his stern historical course and go off in pursuit of one
of his hobbies, but he resists all such temptations and follows the
path traced out from the outset. What gives the essay particular
significance is that the author takes in the whole panorama of
Spanish history and shows how modern tendencies are due to
causes that lie embedded in the original Spanish character.
Other peoples in Europe—the Italians, for instance—possess the
virtue of moderation or soberness no less than the Spaniards, but
the latter possess it to such a degree that it has affected their
whole history and even as far back as Roman times they were
credited with this virtue which is in accordance with the doctrine
of Seneca, the Spanish philosopher *par excellence*. The Spaniard
with his doctrine of *sustine et abstine* remains even to-day an
inveterate Senecan, and this stoicism we find in the humble
reaper on the parched uplands of Castile, who endures the fierce
heat of the summer months without any refreshment but the
lukewarm water from his earthern jar. Menéndez Pidal then
shows how the physical soberness and abstemiousness of the
Spaniard appears in the scant attention he gives to material
interests and he quotes the famous instance of the Spanish
soldiers, who, at the moment of going into battle at Pavia, gave
up their pay and even handed over their personal belongings to
Pescara in order to satisfy the demands of the auxiliary German
troops. This detachment may even become a great defect of the
Spaniard leading to his notorious indifference on occasions to the
mismanagement of the vital affairs of his country. With infinite
subtlety, Menéndez Pidal analyses the fundamental traits of the
Spanish character and shows how certain characteristics may at
times be a virtuous impulse of the individual, but on other
occasions may be due to a lack of incentive. When discussing the
regionalist spirit of Spain the author takes up the cudgels against

foreign historians like Hume who have exaggerated the local particularism of the people, for he maintains that the dissimilarity of
races in the Peninsula is not perceptibly greater than that
existing, for instance, in France. The greater localism of Spain
is due to the original exclusive character of the Iberians, already
noted by the authors of antiquity long before there came to the
Peninsula even half the number of races enumerated by Hume as
causing the dispersive tendencies. In another place the author
breaks a lance with Ortega y Gasset, who, in his essay, had
referred to the lack of educated minorities in Spain. The Spanish
people, Pidal says, have not necessarily lacked leading minorities,
but those minorities have peculiar characteristics of their own
which cause their actions to appear ineffective, even null and
void. Spanish aristocracy, both that of talents and that of social
position, has never aspired to the position of a class apart, but
devotes its activities to the majority and adopts a style of unaffected simplicity based on broad human values. He also
quotes Alfieri, who travelled through Spain in 1771, as stating
that the Spanish and Portuguese peoples were the only ones in
Europe who preserved their customs intact, and possessed the
raw material for carrying out great enterprises.

When treating the problem of nationalism, Menéndez Pidal
has hard words to say of the Catalan historians who have been at
great pains to show that the Catalan people, through the course
of centuries, had always been completely and permanently
separated from the rest of the Spanish peoples. History, he says,
has thus to be de-Castilianized and therefore the wrongs done to
Catalonia do not spring from Philip IV or Philip V, but go back
to the Middle Ages, even to Count Raymond Berenguer IV, who,
they say, betrayed the Catalan cause by not taking the title of
King of Catalonia and Aragon. 'Raymond Berenguer,' says the
author ironically, 'ignorant of the fact that he would displease
the nationalists of the twentieth century, went even further than
refusing to call himself King; he actually acknowledged himself
to be a vassal of the Emperor of Toledo, Alfonso VII.'

The most striking pages in the essay are devoted to the Two
Spains, and here the author has embodied the essence of his
humanistic philosophy. These pages sum up the thoughts that

for years have continually arisen in the minds of Spanish thinkers. They are all the more significant to-day coming from the foremost scholar of the Spanish World, from one who has seen in the past so many of his ideals shattered and who yet possesses an undiminished faith in Spain's future. These pages, too, will be a revelation to those in Europe and across the seas who have shut their eyes to Spain's historical claims from the past and allowed her to be the victim, the scapegoat of world politics. Menéndez Pidal, faithful to his scientific method of investigation, studies the problem of the Two Spains back in its origins but he brings it up to the present, and the words he writes of Spain might be applied to most of the other countries of Europe, for not one is free from the dangers he enumerates: 'Larra lamented over half Spain as dead, yet the deceased rose from the tomb to continue the mortal struggle. A hundred years later, when Azaña proclaimed the death of Catholic Spain, the latter rose and it was republican Spain which fell. . . . This was the fated destiny of the two sons of Oedipus, who would not consent to reign together, and mortally wounded each other. Will this sinister craving to destroy the adversary ever cease? Evil days indeed have come before the world when extremism of a kind that leaves that of Spain far behind appears on all sides and when a ferocious cleavage such as never before existed, makes national life in common impossible in many countries owing to the exclusive tendencies which have gripped the dominant parties in the States. Mussolini called the twentieth century the era of collectivity, the century of the State; but for Italy and Germany this century lasted only a couple of decades, and although we do not yet know how the democracies will forge their victory which they share with Communism, nevertheless the individual will again win back his rights, which allow him to disagree, to rectify and invent afresh, for it is to the individual that we owe all the great deeds of history.'

And let us take leave of Menéndez Pidal the scholar, the humanist, the minstrel ballad-chaser and the patriot, cherishing in our memories his passionate appeal for the eternal single Spain that exists deep down in the soul of every Spaniard: it is not one of the half Spains facing the other that will survive as a single party with the epitaph of the other part; it will be the complete Spain for whom so many have longed, the Spain that has not amputated one of her limbs, but makes full use of all her capabilities for honest toil in order to win a place among the peoples that give the impulse to modern life.

THE SPANIARDS IN
THEIR HISTORY
by Ramón Menéndez Pidal

The Spaniards in
their History[1]

The facts of history do not repeat themselves, but Man the
Maker of History is always the same. Hence the eternally true
saying: *Quid est quod fuit? Ipsum quod futurum est*—What happened
in the past? What will happen in the future. Consequently, mankind has always been eager to know how, given its permanent
identity, each people has behaved in history. Even in the days
when our mediaeval historiography was in its infancy writers
often considered it necessary to add to the narration of events a
description of the various peoples according to their dominant
quality. For instance we find attached to the *Epitome Ovetense*[2] of
883 a chapter entitled *De proprietatibus gentium*, which signalizes
the Greeks by their wisdom, the Goths by their valour, the
Franks by their fierceness, the Gauls by their trading. Other
chronicles point out the salient vices and virtues of each human
group; the deceitfulness and wisdom of the Greeks, the violence
as well as the acuteness of the Spaniards (this observation is not
far from the truth), the fierceness as well as the steadfastness of the
Franks. These definite characteristics of different peoples with
which to a greater or lesser degree writers have concerned themselves from the earliest times, should be extensively treated in any
History, but on this occasion I shall limit myself to defining certain Spanish characteristics which I consider to be the basis of
the rest, and I shall attempt to give a general survey of those
tendencies which have most constantly operated through every
period, whether favourably or unfavourably. In this way we
shall be able to understand the peaks and depressions of Spain's
historical curve.

I shall keep two objectives before me; first I wish to show that
every quality is, as it were, two-faced; it may cause positive or

[1] The footnotes to this essay have been supplied by the translator unless other-
wise noted.

[2] This history, dating from the reign of Alfonso III in Oviedo, was the first to be
written by the Christians of the north of Spain after the Moslem invasion.

117

negative results according to the direction it takes or the circumstances in which it is developed; secondly that even the most permanent characteristics do not necessarily operate, for although they may appear in the majority of a people they do not always determine its actions, and they may even in certain circumstances be limited to a minority. Furthermore, although those characteristics survive through the centuries this does not mean that they are unchangeable. We are not dealing with any somatic or racial determinism but with historical aptitudes and habits which can, and will, vary according to the occupations and interests of life, the type of education, social relationships, and other circumstances.

Chapter I

Material and Moral Austerity

Many writers have pointed out the close connection between the character of the Spaniards and the land they inhabit. Unamuno is insistent on this point. He holds that the harsh, dry spirit of our people with its lack of the sense of compromise is intimately connected with the landscape of the central meseta, which is hard in outline, devoid of trees, boundless in horizon. The light there dazzles, the climate reaches extremes, and there are no gentler aspects of nature. But this correspondence does not apply to the climates that exist outside the two Castiles. The same physical austerity may also be found in the smiling, fertile Andalusia, and in my opinion, austerity is the basic quality of the Spanish character; it does not depend upon any Castilian geographical determinism, but is so universal that if we start from it we shall be able to understand the remaining characteristics we must now define.

The most penetrating description of the Spanish character given in ancient times was by the Gaul Trogus Pompeius.[1] He begins by saying that the Spaniard has a body adapted for abstinence and toil, for hard and rigid sobriety in all things, *dura omnibus et adstricta parsimonia*. From Trogus onward we find many references to austere simplicity, even to a glaring heedlessness of comforts prevalent in certain aspects of life in Spain. We may recall that, during the centuries when all the precious metals of the New World were flowing into the Peninsula, foreigners found our houses more modestly furnished than the

[1] Roman historian of the first century, of Gallic nationality, author of a Universal History (*Historiae Philippicae*) which has been lost, but of which there remains an Epitome written in the second century by Justin. The last book, No. 44, deals with Spain.

French, the meals very meagre, our University halls lacking in comforts (the students had to prop their notebooks on their knees); our inns very inhospitable; the public services of Madrid very inadequate, a fact that worried Philip II; in short, a way of life devoid of comfort. That is to say that all the wealth amassed by the American colonists and carried back annually in the fleets of the State was not applied by the Spaniards to the comfort and well-being of their private life or to the embellishment of their cities. Even to-day the Spaniard contents himself with little, and we continually see around us examples of that austerity allied to hard work to which Trogus referred. The humblest of all is the reaper in our fields—an astonishing specimen of *dura et adstricta parsimonia*. During the most oppressive heat of summer, without any refreshment but the lukewarm water of his earthern jar, poorly clad and poorly fed, he seems to possess nothing in the world but stoical contentment in his work.

This neglect of material necessities to which we have referred agrees with Seneca's doctrine that he who has but little is not poor, but poor is he who covets more, for the natural necessities of life are very few while those of vain ambition are inexhaustible. The Spaniard, inured to privations, believes in the doctrine of *sustine et abstine*, 'bear and forbear', and this rule of conduct sets man above all adversity. In his character there is an element of instinctive stoicism; he is a born disciple of Seneca. For this reason Spanish philosophical thinkers through the centuries have always turned to Seneca as their favourite author. A great debt certainly is owed to him, but Seneca himself, the refiner of stoicism, owed a great deal to the fact that he sprang from a Spanish family.

Due to this instinctive influence of Seneca the Spaniard can as readily endure privations as he can withstand the disturbing temptations to greed and self-indulgence, for his innate soberness inclines him towards a certain ethical austerity. This shows itself in the general tenor of his life, with its simplicity, dignity even in the humblest classes, and strong family ties. The Spanish people preserve these deep natural qualities unimpaired as a kind of human reserve, whereas other races which are more tainted by the luxuries of civilization find themselves constantly threatened by a process of wear and tear which saps their strength. It is of interest to point out some aspects of this vital austerity as an illustration of historical characteristics. We shall pay special attention to the observations made by foreign writers because they are always better qualified to note what is peculiar to a country, even though we should discount the element of superficiality that is so often to be found in travellers' impressions.

DETACHMENT

The connection between physical soberness and other qualities is clearly shown by the scant attention Spaniards give to material interests, for owing to their hermit-like abstemiousness they find the strength to resist the pressure of material necessities. To this are due the not infrequent cases of collective generosity noted by historians. The Spanish soldier is a special case in point: even though he may mutiny like any other when his pay is lacking, yet he can always rise above himself when the situation demands it. At the moment of going into battle at Pavia the Spaniards gave up their pay and even handed over their personal belongings to Pescara in order to satisfy the demands of the German auxiliaries. Another example is given by Calderón in the 'Sitio de Breda'[1] Act III, Scene 2, when the Spaniards offer their gains to the foreign troops on condition that the latter refrain from sacking the city, for thus the victory would be the nobler. Each one of those soldiers might appear as the hero in a tale of disinterested generosity. That so many together should have acted in this way is an exception to the rule that generous gestures are isolated occurrences standing out in antithesis to the collective self-interest of the mass.

It is also a natural trait in the Spaniard not to allow any calculation of gains and losses to prevail over considerations of another order. Columbus, a foreigner by birth, instead of allowing himself to be carried away by enthusiasm for his enterprise, kept postponing it while he negotiated interminably, and refused to risk the venture until he had secured for himself a dazzling series of profits and rewards. Whereas a host of Spanish explorers, despising material advantage, engaged in perilous exploits for the

[1] Calderón's comedy refers to the Dutch stronghold of Breda, captured by the Spaniards under the command of the Marquis of Spinola in 1626, after ten months' siege.

I

simple love of adventure, or with only problematic hopes of gain.

This characteristic may be observed in many aspects of private or public life, for it has always been a great quality as well as a great defect of the Spaniard to allow himself to be swayed by idealistic motives rather than by the desire for economic profit. The reduction of necessities may at one moment be a virtuous impulse in the individual, inspiring generous action, but on other occasions it may be due to a lack of incentive which produces aversion to work. This may explain both the collective abnegation displayed by the Spanish people in various circumstances, and during whole epochs of their history, as well as their notorious indifference to the mismanagement of the vital affairs of their country.

Those who, over a long period, have noted how industrial and commercial interests in Spain have been neglected explain it in various ways. In the time of the Catholic King, in 1513, Guicciardini[1] attributes it to the fact that the artisans had a *fumo di fidalgo*—pretensions to nobility—and preferred to dedicate themselves to war; a similar explanation to that given by Saavedra Fajardo[2] who referred to the 'haughty and exalted' spirit of the nation, shown even among the plebeian classes by their contempt for any occupation that was unworthy of one who was noble. At other times when the warrior spirit did not prevail, Ferdinand de la Torre,[3] describing to Henry IV in 1455 a dispute he had held with a certain Frenchman before the King of France, stated that in his opinion foreigners were more industrious and wealthy than Spaniards, because their lands were less fertile than Spain; an explanation which was repeated by the Ambassador of the Sultan of Morocco at the court of Charles II in 1690. No doubt he had heard it from Spaniards who quoted the mediaeval 'Eulogies' of Spain. This so-called abundance of Spain might in the sixteenth and seventeenth centuries have been confused with the abundance of silver and gold that arrived from America. But

[1] The Florentine historian and politician Francesco Guicciardini, 1483-1540, ambassador at the court of Ferdinand the Catholic, 1512-1513, was the author of *Diario del viaggio in Spagna*.
[2] Diego Saavedra Fajardo, 1584-1648, writer and diplomat. His *Empresas políticas o Idea de un príncipe cristiano*, 1640, is frequently quoted in the present work.
[3] Fernando de la Torre, poet and prose writer of the middle of the fifteenth century, was a native of Burgos and studied in Florence. (He was at the court of Charles VII of France, 1422-1461.)

these examples merely illustrate the essential truth that a Spaniard will always sacrifice his desire for wealth or comfort to idealistic motives of pride or glory no matter how vain they may be.

The observations given by travellers from the seventeenth to the nineteenth centuries agree with this judgment. One who visited the court of Philip III at Valladolid noted that the handicraftsmen worked disdainfully, as though merely to get out of a difficulty, and he saw some, especially the silversmiths, seated at work with their cloaks on. As soon as they had collected 200 or 300 reals they girded on their swords and strutted about like noblemen until they had spent the money, when they would return to their work. Such was the impression of another traveller who visited the Spain of Isabel II: he did not describe the Andalusian workman as lazy, but noted that as soon as he had gathered a handful of reals, he would throw his embroidered jacket over his shoulder, pick up his guitar and go off to sport among his friends or pay court to the girls, until lack of money would force him to return to work. This interruption of work was not a daily occurrence and was not caused by exhaustion necessitating long periods of rest for rebuilding energy, but by a weakening of the stimulus to work. Once his urgent material necessities had been satisfied, his attention would wander off after other incentives which appeared more attractive. The Spaniard possesses the invaluable treasure of soberness which delivers him from many embarrassing cares, but as a rule he does not make the best use of that precious quality when troubles and anxieties have really to be faced. Nevertheless this disinclination to work which has been so often noted through the centuries has, on frequent occasions, been remedied. Guicciardini himself related how a revival of industry took place under the Catholic Monarchs, and he described the looms of Valencia, Toledo, and Seville with their luxurious woven stuffs of crimson and gold, and this was confirmed by Navagero in 1526. Noteworthy, too, was the great impulse given to industry all through Spain by the efforts of Ferdinand VI and Charles III which were so successful that they roused the jealousy of the more commercial countries, as was admitted by W. Robertson in 1777. Gracián points to a special aspect of this indifference when discussing the Spanish tendency

to abandon tasks already begun. Paying a tribute to the con-
stancy in work of foreign countries, he writes: 'Impatience—that
is the defect of the Spaniards, just as Patience is the virtue of the
Belgians; the latter complete what they have begun, whereas the
Spaniards leave the task unfinished; they toil and moil until they
have mastered the difficulties, then they stop, for they do not
know how to follow up their victories.' The physical and mental
soberness of the Spaniard causes him to remain satisfied with
immediate results; consequently he is not interested in anything
that can be achieved only slowly and at a later date. He dislikes
having to pursue further what has already been attained, for this
would, in his opinion, be to confess his lack of the essential soberness. Hence he despises the quality of patience so eulogized by
Gracián, calling it unreasonable obstinacy, the failing of those
who are as slow in wits as they are in action.

Furthermore, owing to his arrogant or lazy self-confidence, he
gives no heed to the morrow: sufficient for the day is the evil
thereof; there is no need to fret about what to-morrow will bring.
The most striking examples of this lack of foresight were those
which occurred at a time when Spain's activity was at its zenith,
and though this did not prevent her triumph it seriously hampered it. It is significant to note that in so important a question as
finance, at the most critical moment of the supreme struggle of
the Counter-Reformation, Philip II was able to solve his economic difficulties only at the cost of increasing his huge debts to the
Genoese. This was because he never made allocations from one
year to the next to meet the extraordinary expenditure which continually was necessary, but lived for the day, meeting each difficulty when it presented itself, as the Venetian Ambassador noted
in 1573, among other examples of damaging lack of foresight.

Later on Spanish writers express surprise that the fifteen or sixteen millions in gold and silver which came annually from the
Indies were sufficient to flood Europe as far as Constantinople
with Castilian money, yet were not enough to prevent all the bills
of exchange from ending up in the hands of the Genoese bankers.
These latter could not be dispensed with because of the scant
attention paid by the Spaniards to banking, owing to the defect of
'impatience' we have discussed above, in this instance alleged by
Suárez de Figueroa.

Another instance often mentioned by Spanish critics is that which gives origin to the proverbial phrase explained by Tirso in '*El Celoso Prudente*': 'You are succour from Spain, useless because too late.' Cervantes in his play '*El Gallardo Español*' makes the King of Algiers assert confidently that the help the Spaniards intend to bring to Oran will arrive too late. This same conviction is the cause of the bitterness Quevedo felt in his last days (May–June 1645), when he wondered anxiously whether help would be brought in time to Rosas (town in Catalonia), for he felt that its fall was inevitable if it did not receive the necessary aid. Correas in his '*Vocabulario*' tries to diminish the reproach contained in the well-known phrase when he says: '*Socorros de España*; a complaint at the tardy arrival of help, an ordinary occurrence in great Empires; the same was said of Athens in her day.' But the proverbial phrase with its reproach was current before Spain had any extensive Empire, namely in the first half of the fifteenth century at least, for Díez de Gámez in his '*Victorial*' alludes to it when he compares the psychology of the three nations thus: 'The English remember before the event; they are prudent. The French never remember until the event is upon them; they are proud and hasty. The Castilians never remember until the event has passed; they are lazy and contemplative.' Contemplative, yes, in their bad moments, when they turn aside from action and go in quest of some vain fantasy, like the sluggish nobleman of Pérez de Ayala,[1] who renounces all enterprise as vain and futile, for

'over his head lingers the butterfly of dreams and the scorpion of laziness'.

Improvidence is double-faced; beside the contemplative kind mentioned by Díez de Gámez is the active improvidence which far from delaying action drives men into it, throwing all caution to the winds. The audacious exploration of the Amazon was carried out without the slightest preparation, and it would never have been accomplished if the explorers had insisted beforehand upon a plan guaranteeing the success of the enterprise. Indeed a great part of the American colonization and the history of Spain itself is a series of hazardous improvisations. The same may be said of the other aspects of detachment and improvidence which

[1] Ramón Pérez de Ayala, modern novelist, in *La Caída de los Limones*, 1920.

have likewise their positive side. At the very moment when Philip II's finances had failed repeatedly through lack of provident care, the same characteristically Spanish detachment drove Castile to engage in the noblest action in our history and sacrifice to the duties of imperial hegemony all her own comforts and advantages. Fernández Navarrete[1] in 1619 made pertinent references to the unusual method of governing always employed by Castile, adding that 'whereas Castile being the head ought to be the most privileged in the matter of payment of taxes and tributes yet it is she who contributes most for the defence and protection of the rest of the Kingdom. Not only does she contribute to the upkeep of the Royal House and the protection of the entire coast of Spain, but also to the garrisons in Italy, the forces in Africa, the subduing of Flanders and even to the succouring of foreign provinces and princes.' This conscientious self-denial in imperial matters wins a somewhat grudging tribute from a certain French traveller in 1612, who describes how the Castilians bore the chief burdens of war and government owing to their obedient subservience to their superiors, and their talent for command. He adds: 'It is extraordinary how being so few, they can yet win such renown in the wars in Europe. They are like the Macedonians in Greece, long-suffering, hard as well as ambitious, cruel, greedy and ostentatious: they are all-powerful in Europe and the Indies.'

APATHY AND ENERGY

A general indifference towards prosperity or adversity brings calmness to the mind, that imperturbable tranquillity so characteristic of Spain in the Golden Age. This quality, though it does not reach the extremes of stoical *apathia* is related to it as also is the doctrine of *nada te turbe* ('let nothing perturb thee') sublimated by our mystics: that Spanish calmness, 'that beautiful virtue of Castile' mentioned by Filippo Sassetti and noted by Renaissance Italy with admiration not unmixed with irony in the haughty viceroy of Naples as well as in the most wretched Spaniard, for ever penniless, but never without his serenity. This

---

[1] Pedro Fernández Navarrete, canon of Santiago Cathedral, was the author of *Conservación de Monarquías, discursos políticos dirigidos a Felipe III*, 1619; a book frequently reprinted until the nineteenth century.

quality left its mark on the Italian character and is reflected in the Hispanic word *sussiego* which denotes that virtue of a tranquil mind, and grave serenity.

This tranquillity of spirit was the virtue so praised in Charles V, for he was as unassuming in the hour of triumph as he was un-dismayed in adversity. His only gesture at Madrid when he learnt the great news of the battle of Pavia was to retire to his oratory to give thanks to God for having thus manifested His justice, but as the victory was at the cost of Christian blood he allowed no rejoicings at court. He was worthy to rule as Emperor and give impulse to the serene efficiency of the Spaniards who were eager to complete the greatness of their sixteenth century.

But this imperturbable serenity has its double aspect, for as well as calm serenity at the moment of energetic action, there is the calmness of apathy. In that phlegmatic Madrid society created by Philip II's ministers, who were nicknamed 'Ministers of Eternity', a young German baron wrote despairingly in 1599 of the slowness and delays of the Spanish officials in negotiating, for this slowness made him lose days and days, and similar com-ment was made by another *Monsieur sans-délai*, victim of the 'Come back to-morrow' system described by Larra[1] in 1833, and as common a feature to-day as in the past.

Then when decadence had become a reality, when mis-fortunes multiplied, another state of mind grew up related to this calmness—the Spanish 'doesn't matter', 'what's it matter?' This attitude, too, has a double facet, for it is a cross between the indifferent and the devil-may-care. Francisco Santos[2] in his book '*El No Importa de España*', written during years of national disaster (1668), described only the negative aspects. He witnesses everywhere Spaniards adopting the devil-may-care attitude to justify their own faults. Out of flattery he finds praiseworthy the indifference of Philip IV, but even then it is to show that when the king receives news of some disaster his only reaction is to order the celebration of the Forty Hours in the royal chapel. He is the lazy, apathetic king very much in tune with the rest of the easy going Spaniards listed by Francisco Santos. Santos did not live

[1] Mariano José de Larra (1809–1837), author of plays, novels and many news-paper articles dealing with customs, political and literary criticism.

[2] The author of many books, especially dealing with customs, such as *Día y Noche de Madrid*, 1663, *El No Importa de España*, 1668, etc.

on into the more hopeful times when he might have noticed that when a Spaniard feels the urge to engage in an enterprise which he considers of great moment, his very devil-may-care attitude enables him to recover unimpaired all his energies, with the result that even the severest reverses will not dishearten him.

Spaniards are always torn between two extremes: when they are eager to reach a decision they display inexhaustible vigour, but they show scant interest in the activities of everyday. They can endure the greatest hardship in any perilous and protracted expedition, but they are unable to withstand the monotony of daily toil. On the one hand they are high-spirited; that is their devil-may-care attitude: on the other hand they are dispirited, when their attitude is 'I don't give a damn'. Strong to face the worst, slack to procure the best, if in some respects theirs is the *apathia* of the stoics, in others it is mere commonplace apathy.

In its stoical aspect the apathy of Spaniards does not mean that they are merely impassive: rather does it mean acceptance of destiny which may even produce in them an attitude towards life of satisfaction and contentment. An English traveller who visited the Peninsula in 1830 wrote as follows: 'The happiness displayed by the people of all classes in spite of their misfortunes, privations, and grinding poverty is scarcely believable. Not a complaint comes from any of them, and they possess an innate dignity which prevents them from lamenting their fate even in private, and perhaps in this alone are they reserved.' Similar tributes are repeated by other foreign observers, and at this point we again recall Seneca, who held that contented poverty was not poverty, and there is no doubt that this sentiment predominates to a striking degree in the Spanish people.

The imperturbable, contented, 'what's it matter?' attitude united to soberness has created a belief in the mind of the Spaniards that they are able to endure greater hardships than other peoples and that this quality enables them to perform deeds that would be impossible to others. In the eleventh century the '*Historia Silense*'[1] states that the long-drawn-out war against the advancing force of the Saracens could only be waged by the hardened Knights of Spain, not by the self-indulgent peers of

---

[1] The so-called *Historia Silense* is a history of Spain written about 1118, probably in León, by an anonymous monk.

Charlemagne who retired from Saragossa longing to refresh themselves in the baths of Aachen. And in the thirteenth century Archbishop Roderick of Toledo[1] relates proudly though sadly that the crusaders from beyond the mountains, disgusted by a temporary scarcity of provisions which was soon after remedied, returned to their country, leaving the Spaniards to wage alone the gigantic battle of *Navas de Tolosa*. Afterwards every account of our wars or explorations describes episodes of amazing endurance against fatigue and fasting, of fearlessness in the face of death. It is this robust physical and spiritual constitution, with its inexhaustible reserves of energy, which explains the greater part of our history from the transcendental deeds performed in the unremitting war against Islam, as related by the historians mentioned above, to the countless enterprises in the old and new world at the beginning of the Modern Age. The Spaniards needed no more than the short space of fifty years to discover the lands and oceans forming an entire hemisphere of our planet; to explore, subdue and civilize immense territories, subjecting thousands of tribes and vast barbarian empires. Any other people less hardened to privations and risks would have needed five centuries, for they would have found it necessary to plan out their enterprises so as to reduce to the minimum the discomforts and the unfavourable contingencies. Two hundred years it took Rome to dominate the barbarian tribes of Spain alone.

HUMANITARIANISM AND BROTHERHOOD

Soberness is a quality that is highly equalitarian. When material it is a precious boon possessed by the humble no less than by the powerful; when mental it has no need of accidental or secondary distinctions. Thus the Spaniard is by nature inclined to stoical thought as refined by Seneca: man's only value is the soul which makes the servant equal to the master.

Owing to its innate stoicism no people is more intimately conscious of the Christian doctrine establishing the equality of all human beings in the sight of God the Creator and Redeemer, and

---

[1] Rodrigo Jiménez de Rada, Archbishop of Toledo, author of the most widely known history of mediaeval Spain, *De Rebus Hispaniae*, finished in 1243. He took part in the battle of *las Navas de Tolosa*, 1212, the most memorable battle in the Reconquest when a great invading army of 'Almohades' from Africa was conquered.

it is to this quality that Spain owes her historical position in the colonization of America. Columbus suggested to the Catholic Monarchs the enslavement of the Indians as though this were the most natural proposal in the world; it was an economic proposition at so much a head. Father Las Casas,[1] though an apologist of the discoverer, attacked him harshly for making profit out of slaves, and at the same time recalled the words used by Queen Isabel when she indignantly denounced the transaction: 'By what authority does the Admiral venture thus to dispose of my vassals?' The queen always considered the Indians her vassals as she did the Castilians, and afterwards the Catholic King invoked the equality of all races as the fundamental principle of colonization in the celebrated Injunction on the just dominion of Spain in the Indies, an injunction that was drawn up for the expedition of Pedro Arias de Avila,[2] and which began by explaining to the Indians how God created Adam, 'from whom you and we and all men in the world are descended'. This sense of human brotherhood was felt by every Spanish colonizer, with the consequence that whereas the English or the Dutch did not fuse their blood with that of the nations whom they colonized, but considered themselves a race apart, and did not strive to attract the native into the family of European civilization, the Spaniards, on the other hand, from the earliest days of the discovery, pursued an active policy of crossbreeding and at the same time devoted themselves to giving the natives both religious and cultural education. In the internal affairs of Spain this humanitarian spirit shows itself in a strong tendency towards levelling social categories and classes. He who feels great would consider his greatness diminished if it was founded on vanity. Trogus Pompeius notes that Viriathus, in spite of his famous deeds, and his repeated victories over the consular armies, did not change his former habits whether in dress, arms or food, so that any plain soldier seemed richer than the general. Trajan was praised a

[1] Fray Bartolomé de Las Casas, native of Seville (1474–1566), Dominican, Bishop of Chiapas in Guatemala 1544; consecrated his life to the defence of the Indians against the abuses of the Spanish colonists. He wrote the *Historia de las Indias* up to 1520 and a *Brevísima relación de la destrucción de las Indias*, 1552.

[2] Pedro Arias de Avila (or Pedrarias Davila), appointed governor of Tierra-Firme (the coasts of Panama, Colombia, and Venezuela) in 1514, was ordered to address to the Indians a *Requerimiento* in which was stated the claim of the King of Spain to dominate and evangelize the lands recently discovered.

hundred times by Pliny for his modesty and temperate habits. Theodosius, sober in behaviour as he was in his appetite, and humble in his self-imposed penance at Thessalonica, according to Saint Augustine 'despised all human glory'. And this humble sober-mindedness continued to be the typical and unvarying quality. The greatest praise which Hernando del Pulgar[1] could give to his distinguished men, cardinals, grand masters and noblemen was to say: 'He was a genuine man, a hater of appearances,' or else: 'He was a true man and never made show of what he possessed or what he was doing.' The historians take special pains to praise in their heroes their unaffected familiarity with their subordinates and their own behaviour as true and genuine men.

Along with this simple familiarity in high born men we find in the lower classes, even in the poor, the essence of dignity and noble bearing. We all know the type of Spanish beggar who resembles a nobleman come down in the world. A Frenchman who visited Spain at the beginning of the seventeenth century was astonished to hear even a poor squire of no consequence boast of his noble stock, saying: 'I am as much a noble as the king, aye, and nobler, for he is half Flemish.' As a consequence of all this we find the same observation constantly repeated by historians; in the time of Philip IV, Saavedra Fajardo noted that the distinction between nobles and people was less marked in Spain than in Germany; in the time of Charles III, Cadalso,[2] and in the time of Isabel II Balmes,[3] both make the same observation, namely that there is no country in the world where there is more levelling of classes than in Spain. In Spain, Balmes added, a man of the humblest class in society will stop in the road the highest magnate in the land. We Spaniards, he goes on, lack the aristocratic aloofness of the English: people of high category, when we meet them,

<hr />

[1] Ambassador and chronicler of the Catholic Monarchs, author of a series of twenty-four personal portraits of the fifteenth century, *Claros Varones de Castilla*, printed in Toledo 1486, and of a *Crónica de los Reyes Católicos*.

[2] José de Cadalso (1741–1782), cavalry officer killed in the siege of Gibraltar; lyric and dramatic poet and author of prose works. The work here quoted is entitled *Cartas Marruecas*, which the author pretends to have been written by a Morrocan traveller, Gazel, criticizing Spanish customs of his time. They were published posthumously in 1789.

[3] Jaime Balmes (1810–1848), Catalan priest, author of important philosophical works. The quotations are mostly from his newspaper articles of 1840–1846, collected by him and entitled *Escritos Políticos*, Madrid, 1847.

bid us drop the ceremonious form of address straightway: if they are slow in doing so, we use the familiar form without asking permission, in this way making the conversation informal. About the same time Théophile Gautier pointed out that Spain was the true home of equality where a beggar lights his cigarette butt from the cigar of a great lord, and the latter lets him do so without any trace of condescension; the marchioness steps smiling over the ragged bodies of the beggars who sleep on her threshold, and when she is on a journey she has no hesitation in drinking out of the same glass as her coachman. What a contrast with the English who used to have their letters served on a tray and pick them up with silver tongs!

Many remarkable instances of this sense of human brother-hood among the different classes in society might be quoted from Spanish history and they can be found even in remote days though we lack general descriptions of the kind here noted. Very early in the tenth century the villeins began to enter into the order of chivalry at the invitation of the Counts of Castile, Garci Fernández and Sancho García. In this democratic procedure Castile was in advance of the kingdoms of León and Aragon, as in another reform of capital importance, the abolition of serfdom.

TRADITIONALISM AND MISONEISM

To material soberness, then, corresponds moderation in aspirations and aims. Given this, the Spaniard, satisfied with what he has always possessed, does not feel the craving for new satisfactions. But this refers only to the cultural field, for in adventurous enterprises the Spaniard has always been pre-eminent. Hazardous adventures in far off lands have always made a powerful appeal to him as we may see from the picaresque novels which describe this tendency in everyday life, while the exploration of America gives us plenty of historical examples. On the other hand the Spaniard is not interested in obtaining general cultural knowledge of foreign countries, hence he is not a lover of travel for travel's sake. In cultural matters new theories instead of rousing his interest rather put him on his guard, and he is inclined to distrust them. Thus among the fundamental mean-ings of the Latin word *novitas*, the French take as the predominating one the positive value given to *haute nouveauté* and *nouveautés*, while the Spaniard allows the depreciatory meaning to dominate in the common phrase *sin novedad* which, when applied to any situation implies in any change that may occur a possible turn for the worse. This negative value given to the word develops in other languages too, but not to the same degree as in Spanish where the depreciatory sense suggests a note of severe warning, and this precisely in the period of greatest material activity. Guevara in the first pages of his *Marcus Aurelius* warns his readers against the many dangers that spring from novelties, and states that in his opinion it is best to set oneself against all changes. Thus admonishing the President of Granada in 1531, he said: 'Do not attempt to introduce new things, for novelties bring in their train anxieties for those who sponsor them and beget troubles among the people.' Even when giving a cold lexical definition Covarrubias feels it necessary to add a note of warning: '*Novedad*, something new and unaccustomed. It is wont to be dangerous because it means changing what has been sanctioned by ancient usage.'

For the Spaniard, therefore, it is safer to cling to what is ancient, for this is in accordance with the sober and austere style of life. But this soberness implies a negative element which bans all progress in the name of the misoneism recommended by Guevara.

A greater or less degree of traditionalism can never be an infallible touchstone for testing the genuine qualities of a people. A people may be very traditionalist and yet at the same time evolutionist, as for instance the English. A country's traditions may become deeply permeated by new progressive ideas, while innovations may imply retrogression and decline. Traditionalism should not be given all the blame for the backwardness of the Spanish people. In fact to the traditionalist spirit we owe the best that Spain has produced, the tardy fruits of its culture to which I shall refer later on. Traditionalism in itself is a positive force, the only system suited to a strong personality. Misoneism is the negative side of traditionalism, for it means the rejection of all that is new, and it has in certain periods of Spanish history hindered the nation's progress when to it is added the general apathy of the people. Where soberness of aims may be most clearly seen in relation to the dangers of misoneistic traditionalism is, to quote an example, in the field of scientific studies which continually aim at enlarging their scope progressively. Often in our writers do we meet the declaration that all sciences which do not teach man to live healthily and honestly are of no consequence, and there is no doubt that the Spaniards' indifference to pure science, which in their opinion is superfluous, is due to the innate tendencies inherited from Seneca of which we have already spoken. Seneca disapproved of philosophical and grammatical discussions that were too theoretical, for he considered that they did not help to perfect the moral nature of man or give him that wisdom which leads to the Highest Good; 'to wish to know more than is necessary is a kind of intemperance,' it is to fail in the quality of *sobrietas* or soberness: *plus scire velle quam sit satis, imtemperantiae genus est.* The same comforting thought may be derived by Spaniards from the words of Saint Paul, if applied loosely to profane science: 'Do not wish to know more than is necessary, but know with moderation,' *sapere ad sobrietatem*. This meagreness of men's aspirations was not perceptible in mediaeval periods of splendour (Arab-Spanish science; Toledan translations; Alfonso X). But from the beginning of the Modern Age the difference was very marked between Spain and the other peoples who gave impetus to knowledge. The writers of the golden centuries (without taking their authority from the doctrine of Seneca, though he was a very familiar author to them) considered it a special virtue of their own to avoid busying themselves in what they called the vain discussions of the humanists and grammarians, so popular in Europe, in order to concentrate their attention upon the 'necessary' sciences, namely theology, dialectic, law, medicine, in which, they boasted arrogantly, Spain was superior to all other nations; and they were right as regards certain branches of those sciences. Later on, when the decadence began, misoneism developed, and there was a well-known maxim which stated that to say *novedad* or novelty was the same as to say *no verdad*, no verity. Hence the aversion or at least the indifference to all progress which lay like a dead weight over the nation. Whenever it was possible to conquer this spirit of neglect we find an immediate advance in scientific work, always in bitter opposition to the reactionary tendencies.

LATE AND EARLY FRUITS

The most successful products of the Spanish genius have been created as a result of the constant effort to give life and perfection to individual qualities sprung from traditional roots, but ripened at a late season. Such fruits are esteemed for their rarity; being no longer found in other countries they introduce elements whose efficacy has been missed.

The best examples are to be discovered in the Renaissance, the period which was in other countries radically modernist, but in Spain made a truce with traditionalism, thus avoiding as far as was possible a break with the Middle Ages. This break was practically complete in other countries but Spain remained staunchly loyal to the great truths and beauties of the Middle Ages and strove to revive them, adapting them to the new spirit of the Renaissance. The Spanish Monarchy from Ferdinand the Catholic for the two ensuing centuries is conceived as a Renaissance state which still supports the mediaeval doctrine of universal Catholicism. The imperial idea of Charles V was based upon a similar combination of principles. Saint Ignatius keeping vigil in Montserrat[1] gave life to the metaphorical idea of 'spiritual knighthood' so dear to the Middle Ages, but he also gave a new meaning to asceticism in his foundation of the great religious order of modern times. Other examples were the restoration of scholastic philosophy which had such a long flowering under Vitoria, Soto, Maldonado, and Suárez and afterwards extended its vast influence over other Catholic countries; the development of contrapuntal technique on traditional foundations in the fifteenth and sixteenth centuries with masters like the Andalusian Ramos de Pareja, the Toledan Diego Ortiz, Antonio de Cabezón and Francisco de Salinas from Burgos, Tomás Luis de Vitoria from Avila, all of whom had great influence in Italy and Germany; finally mysticism, the *Romancero*, the books of chivalry, the drama, all are further examples of late ripening fruits, the slow evolution of some mediaeval type, which were very much appreciated outside Spain and exercised admitted influence. All those

---

[1] St Ignatius watched over his arms the night of the 24th to the 25th March, 1522, in front of the altar of Our Lady of Montserrat, in order to become a Knight of Christ, thus imitating the ceremony of watching the arms which used to be performed by the aspirant knight on the eve of his installation.

achievements were accomplished with a broad sweep, and continuous effort truly national in character. At a later date we have the War of Independence when Spain, in defence of her traditional institutions, made a concerted nationalist movement which was admired by all, and which was instrumental in giving back to revolutionary Europe a restorative monarchical spirit.

When we contrast the broad continuous policy on traditionalist lines backed by the majority of the nation, with the programme of innovations put forward by a minority group of reformers, we find that the latter seems unstable and unsubstantial by comparison. Even the most successful individual enterprises fail for lack of some one to carry them on, and once this happens it is necessary to start afresh from the very beginning. Owing to envy, that distinctive element of the Spanish character, which I shall discuss presently, no one is willing to attach any value to the work of others, for it seems that to give any credit to another means to curtail one's own. Thus masters do not found schools, and in consequence their teaching does not reach its possible perfection, or pave the way for higher development by later masters. This is the reason why Spain is a country of forerunners, who lead the way only to become forgotten, once their innovation reaches another country, readier to receive and develop it. Examples of these early fruits, as we might call them, which never ripen to their full may be found even in the Renaissance itself. Take the case of the Grand Master of the Order of St John, Fernández de Heredia. It was he who gave the earliest impulse to Greek scholarship by, among other remarkable works, his Aragonese translation, about 1385, of the first text of Plutarch known to the West (it was soon to be translated in its turn from Aragonese into Italian). But this precocious enthusiasm did not find any support and it remains as a pathetic isolated example. Feijóo noted various examples of forgotten precursors such as Antonio Agustín in medal-coining and Fray Pedro Ponce in the art of deaf and dumb language.

As a result of all this lack of continued effort the vital evolution of Spain, both in intellectual culture as well as in political action, has produced its moments of intensity only at long intervals; in fact it represents a curve with peak points widely spaced out, its sound waves are long and their deep low tone is less often heard than that of other great peoples. The peak points are few and far between and the sound only occasionally becomes sharper and more perceptible.

Chapter II

Idealism

Among the special characteristics of the Spanish peoples handed down to us by ancient authors, Livy relates that when the Iberians north of the Ebro were forced by Cato to disarm, many committed suicide, for owing to their fierce pride they held that life without arms was of no value. Strabo,[1] giving examples of ferocity, describes how, in the Cantabrian wars, mothers killed their children rather than allow them to fall into the power of their enemies. A youth, whose father and brothers were chained up as prisoners, killed them all at the father's orders. He also relates how a woman killed her fellow captives. Belonging to a civilization already in decline, Strabo sees in this only the barbarian side, but he points out other examples where scorn of death is the result of noble unselfishness: the famous Iberian *devotio*, namely the consecrated loyalty to a chief and the promise made to sacrifice one's life for him, or the case of the crucified Cantabrian prisoners who sang victory hymns on the cross. Trogus Pompeius notes as a special characteristic of the Spaniards that their minds are as well prepared for death as their bodies are for abstinence and toil (*corpora ad inediam laboremque, animi ad mortem parati*). Frequently indeed they have been known to die under torture rather than reveal a secret, preferring to keep silence than to save their life. Tacitus, a century later than Trogus, gives a particular instance; namely that of the rural Arevacan[2] from Tiermes who died under torture, shouting his refusal to reveal the names of certain conspirators. Life is not the

---

[1] A Greek geographer who lived at the end of the first century B.C.

[2] *Arévacos*, a Celtiberian tribe living in the actual province of Soria. Its capital was Numantia.

supreme boon. The ancient Spaniard sacrificed his life with patriotic enthusiasm, as in the case of the Cantabrians on the cross and the Numantians in their collective suicide. They sacrificed their life in order to accomplish the high duties of loyalty, not only individual but also national and international, as in the case of the sacrifice by the Saguntines. In these and other cases we do not know definitely what religious, political or social principles were responsible for this attitude of preferring death to other penalties, especially to the loss of liberty. But in all these instances we see traces of something akin to stoical doctrine. Seneca exhorts men to suicide as a liberation. Death is not to be feared; it is the end of all evils and the beginning of true freedom in eternity.

FAME

Both in the dimness of primitive times and in the clear light of modern days we find the truth of the saying of Trogus: *animi ad mortem parati*. Death is accepted as the beginning of survival in another higher life.

On the threshold of the great Spanish historic age Jorge Manrique[1] reveals calmly and serenely an attitude to death which draws distinctions between three lives; first of all temporal life which perishes; then the life of fame which is more enduring and more glorious than the life of the body; lastly eternal life, which is the crowning of the other two. Now these two lives after death are as consciously felt by every Spaniard to-day as in the past, and so intense is his awareness that it contrasts with the attitude of neighbouring races. With regard to the second life, that of fame, it is significant how the ideology of the Spanish soldier differed from that of the Italian in the early quarrels that took place between the leaders of both peoples, who served under Alfonso V of Aragon. We have accounts of one of these arguments which took place before the Magnanimous King in 1420. The Spaniards reproached the Italians for their slackness in fighting, and for the fact that so few died in their battles; whereat the great

---

[1] Jorge Manrique (1440–1478), knight of the Order of Santiago, engaged in the political struggles at the beginning of the reign of the Catholic Monarchs. His greatest poetical work is the elegy, *Coplas por la muerte de su padre*, 1467, very famous even to-day in Spain.

condottiere Braccio da Montone[1] replied, rebuking the Spaniards for their loutish fierceness: 'You think it more honourable to
allow yourselves to be cut to pieces by the enemy than to escape
with your lives and reserve yourselves for the day of revenge.'

Let us not consider those words as those of a typical condottiere
devoid of warlike and patriotic spirit. The French, who abounded
in both, yet noted the same tendency when they refused to fight
the troops of the Great Captain, saying: 'Those mad Spaniards
value a little honour more than a thousand lives and are incapable of enjoying this life.' This judgement shows how closely
related Spanish idealism is to the sober austerity which we considered as the basis of the Spanish character. The tendency to set
little value upon the pleasures of life, whether accompanied or
not by noble aspirations, persists as a fundamental trait, with the
result that the second life praised by Jorge Manrique, that of
fame and honour, is not in Spain reserved merely for the illustrious hero, but is the stimulus for all men. Every knight aspires
as Don Juan Manuel[2] did to win the guerdon of fame, for then
mankind will say of him: 'The man died, but not his name'
(*murió el hombre, mas no su nombre*); a motto which later became
the heraldic device, *Muera el hombre y viva el nombre* (let the man
die, but the name survive). This happened not only in those centuries when great national enterprises gave a high, coherent purpose to the wills of all. Quevedo in his Epistle to the Count-Duke
Olivares[3] lamented the disappearance of the ancient valour:

> The luminous freedom of the spirit that refused to pro-
>   long life a day
> Once Death with honour showed the way.

But valour had not entirely perished. Even in periods of decline
there are many unknown heroes who will face with unbowed
heads death with honour on the altar of their ideals, and, as

---

[1] Braccio da Montone (1368–1424), lord of Perugia and a great part of Umbria.
Ruled Rome for seventy days in 1417; in 1420 commanded the militia of Queen
Joan of Naples (1414–1435) who adopted as successor Alfonso V the Magnanimous,
King of Aragon.

[2] Grandson of King Ferdinand III, the most powerful noble in Castile, author of
the book of exemplary tales, *El Conde Lucanor*, written about 1330.

[3] Conde Duque de Olivares, famous minister of Philip IV from 1621 to 1643,
was pictured several times by Velázquez. The epistle of Quevedo was written in
1624.

Trogus said, men ready for death may be found even when they have lost all hope in the result of their self-sacrifice, as for instance in cases where war is waged against hopeless odds to the death of the last man.

This persistent longing for a second life and survival through honourable fame which absorbs the Spaniard reaches its purest and most complete fulfilment in religion.

RELIGION

A motto frequently used by the soldiers of the Counter-Reformation was: 'Give your life for honour, and give both, honour and life, for God.' By these words we see how the three lives which had been relatively appraised by Jorge Manrique were at that time present in the mind of every Spaniard and similarly appraised. All knew that in the end it was for God that the soldier sacrificed his life. Tansillo[1] in the three sonnets he wrote in memory of the huge heap of unburied bones lying on the Dalmatian shore—the bones of the 3,000 defenders of Castelnovo[2] in 1539—celebrates the glory won on earth by those heroes of Iberia, but he adds that they won the supreme crown because they had sold dearly their perishable lives in order to buy eternal life. This third life to which religion guides mankind surpasses all the joys of earthly life, and it not infrequently happens that in the midst of this life's troubles the longing for death grows to a high pitch of exaltation, for to die will be to cross the threshold to a higher existence. This was how it appeared to Doctor Villalobos[3] when he wrote: 'Come now, gentle death, and give me freedom.' This thought of death, which is thirst for immortality, is the profound concern of the Spanish people and has been noted in its various aspects by our writers, but here it concerns us only as the ultimate basis of religion and in so far as the latter influences civil life.

---

[1] Luigi Tansillo (1510–1568), poet who served under the Viceroy of Naples, Don Pedro de Toledo, and fought against the Turks. Author of a famous poem, *Le lagrime di S. Pietro*, 1539.

[2] Castelnovo in the Bocche di Cattaro in Yugoslavia was a Turkish military base. Captured by the Venetians and the Spaniards in 1538, it was defended by the Spaniards and recaptured by Barbarossa, 10 August, 1539.

[3] Francisco de Villalobos, 1473–1549, doctor at the court of Charles V. The poem quoted was written by him on the occasion of the death of the Empress Isabel in Toledo, 1539.

When considering the general effects produced by deeply-rooted religious feeling we must note that it is the most powerful force for correcting the Spanish individual's disinclination to make concessions to the common welfare. A Spaniard usually does not trouble himself with duties or generosities of a social character beyond those inspired by charity towards his neighbour, and these he generally performs, not owing to his direct love for God and his neighbour, but rather owing to his desire to reap his merited reward in the life to come. As a result, therefore, the only people charged with giving effect to the charitable impulses of the individual in the direction of social welfare were the religious institutions. They, as was natural, interested themselves above all in the charitable aspect of their mission, but neglected other more worldly aspects, as has frequently been noted in the sphere of education. Owing to the policy of granting this exclusive credit to the religious institutions their number multiplied out of all proportion, and so likewise did the numbers of clerics and friars, a fact which was deplored by the political pamphleteers of the seventeenth century. Canon Fernández Navarrete devoted six Discourses to the evils caused to the monarchy by the excessive number of religious foundations and the multitude of secular priests. Saavedra Fajardo also referred to 'the devout prodigality' which impoverishes the people and its ruler owing to the excessive number of pious legacies. This excess continued in the following centuries; Jovellanos, for instance, points out as a grave economic evil the mortmain due to the 'countless foundations of convents, colleges, brotherhoods, guardianships, chaplaincies, anniversaries which sprang from the generosity of wealthy souls at their hour of agony'. It is clear that this excess could not be easily remedied, for this deep-rooted habit of devoting private charity to religious objects is also due to the definite distrust which every benefactor feels towards charitable organizations run by laymen, for they are sure to be as inefficient in social questions as he is himself, and thus he has no alternative but to place all his confidence in religious bodies.

This beneficial action exercised by Spanish religious sentiment in overcoming the lack of a collective spirit extended its influence also by giving a moral tone to civic behaviour. But here, too, we must note certain deficiencies. The Spaniard, owing to his customary disregard for ultimate perfection, is inclined to pay scant heed to strictly ethical standards. Content with natural moderation and simplicity of behaviour, he has no scruples about breaking the moral law more or less. When the decline was beginning in the golden centuries we find Simon Contarini, the Venetian ambassador at the court of the very pious monarch Philip III, noting one blatant contradiction in the Spaniards: 'They are,' he says, 'essentially Catholic in religion but by no means moral in their conduct.' Even if we discount this dogmatic assertion, it is quite true that we do at certain moments of political life meet this contradiction. It is disquieting that at times of great religious fervour, as, for instance, in the reactionary movements of Ferdinand VII in 1814 and 1823, the Spanish people, while experiencing a revival of patriotism through religion, did not follow its dictates of mercy and cease ruthlessly suppressing their political opponents, nor did they learn from it the principles of integrity which would guide them in administering the State.

Leaving aside the power religion has over the individual, its influence in public life appears as paramount on many vital occasions in Spanish history. At the beginning, the Councils of Toledo intervened under the Visigothic monarchy, guiding and moderating wisely the actions of the State, elaborating an admirable system of laws, and inspiring the government with noble politico-juridical principles, which are in contrast to the crude barbarity of the other Germanic kingdoms. But at the end of this period when there was a decline, the ecclesiastical element found itself so directly entangled in party struggles that when the catastrophe came both State and Church fell victims, one disappearing altogether and the other submitting to the Mozarabic domination.

The pure unfettered religious spirit which had been preserved in the north gave impetus and national aims to the Reconquest. Without its strength of purpose Spain would have given up in despair all resistance and would have become denationalized. In the end it would have become Islamized as did all the other provinces of the Roman Empire in the east and south of the Mediterranean. In the period from the eighth to the tenth centuries Islam appeared so immensely superior in power and culture to the West that it was amazing that Spain did not succumb as did

Syria and Egypt when they were Arabized, in spite of their more advanced Hellenistic culture; and as did Libya, Africa and Mauritania, likewise Arabized. What gave Spain her exceptional strength of collective resistance and enabled her to last through three long centuries of great peril was her policy of fusing into one single ideal the recovery of the Gothic states for the fatherland and the redemption of the enslaved churches for the glory of Christianity. This fusion of ideals was solemnly declared as a national aim in the *Epítome Ovetense* of the ninth century.

The Spanish religious spirit reached its zenith in the sixteenth and seventeenth centuries. Then it could count on a ruling minority which included men of highest worth in the nation, theologians who were able to intervene decisively in the Council of Trent and serve as leaders of learning in the European universities; mystical writers, ascetics and scripturists who were of the greatest produced by any country; poets who succeeded in interesting the whole people in the deepest problems of grace and free-will, in the most recondite questions of scholasticism as well as in the most subtle allegories of religious history. This great growth of religion had a political aspect that was of cardinal importance, namely, that it arose in a moment of national adversity. The Renaissance strengthened the spirit of nationality in the modern states and caused each of them to look exclusively to their own interests without any consideration for the spirit of Catholic unity upheld by the Middle Ages but now cracking and splitting asunder. Spain was the only country that carried on its inveterate mediaeval purpose and identified its own national aims with the universal aims of Christianity, taking them as her own from the reign of Ferdinand the Catholic, who, as Gracián said, 'knew how to join earth to heaven'. What Ferdinand began was afterwards developed by Spain in the magnificent outburst of enthusiasm of the Counter-Reformation when she devoted her entire life and energies to urging on in Europe the Catholic movement of reconstruction.

Once the bond of unity was broken there entered the new Renaissance doctrine of Reason of State. Every prince who was a reader of Tacitus and Machiavelli believed the interests of his State to be superior to all moral reasons, but Spain did not believe that there was any contradiction between her interests and religious precepts. The Christianization of the Reason of State which had been theoretically initiated in Italy by Botero[1] as a work of the Counter-Reformation, was afterwards a subject of general interest in Spain in the works of López Bravo, Saavedra Fajardo, Blázquez Mayoralgo and Gracián. All contradict Machiavelli yet all select one of the heroes of the Florentine secretary, namely Ferdinand the Catholic, as the 'great oracle of the Reason of State'. Thus, although in these treatises (as in Botero) we find various quasi-Machiavellian maxims peering out here and there from the purest doctrine of Christian and pagan authors, yet the evangelical law is essentially maintained. All those treatises were written when Philip IV was called 'the Great', in order to hide the beginning of decline which was already making itself felt. The fact is that even beneath the indolent Catholicism of 'the Great', Spain continued firm in her determination to join earth and heaven and clung desperately to the religious ideal she had created.

Although not on the same great scale, the superimposition of the religious ideal on political life could still be observed at a later date in many cases, and when we come to the War of Independence this superimposition becomes of the highest significance, for it contributed effectively to the strength and unity of the country. Afterwards, when in Spain national unity ceased to be identified with Catholic unity, this identification still remained as the essential aim of a great section of the Spanish people.

---

[1] Giovanni Botero (1533–1617), secretary to Cardinal St Charles Borromeo in Milan. His chief work, *Della Ragion di Stato*, was published in Venice 1589.

Chapter III

Individualism

THE INDIVIDUAL AND THE COMMUNITY

The Spaniard is inclined not to feel a sense of solidarity with the community except in so far as it will bring him immediate advantages, for he will always neglect indirect or future benefits. Hence he is rather indifferent to the welfare of the community or its problems, but in compensation he possesses a lively perception of his own individual case as well as that of his neighbour. This over-valuation of the individual has direct bearing upon the two cardinal principles of communal life: justice which regulates it and selection which divides it into hierarchies.

JUSTICE

Spanish literature in its most popular and most representative types has always betrayed an interest in juridical questions. The national drama continually brings the idea of justice to bear upon the most powerful dramatic situations, especially when justice is carried out, not according to the letter of the law, but for the benefit of individual cases; we come across terrible sentences in consequence of monstrous outrages; judgements like that of Solomon in which free will, outside all written law, enables the equitable decision to emerge triumphant from the difficulties that beset it; or again we find the solemn justification of rebellion against a tyrant, or of the formal illegality of a just sentence (*El Mejor Alcalde, el Rey*[1]; *Audiencias del Rey Pedro*; *Fuenteovejuna*; *Peribáñez, El Alcalde de Zalamea*).

Mediaeval epic poetry had created various scenes dealing with questions of law and justice which became famous and were used repeatedly up to modern times, as for instance, the challenge

[1] *El Mejor Alcalde, el Rey*, etc., plays by Lope de Vega and Calderón.

of Zamora,[1] the Oath at Santa Gadea,[2] the Cortes of Toledo.[3] These scenes were genuinely Spanish, for they did not adapt themselves in any way to the literary pattern brought into fashion by the celebrated and masterly French Epic. In fact, they broke this model and dramatized poetically conflicts of public and private law in which respect for justice prevails over military force or over the passion of vengeance which was then so strong. The *Romancero*, too, is so packed with legal saws and instances that Joaquín Costa[4] gathered them together and produced therefrom a complete corpus of legal usage. Some of those literary themes certainly sprang from historical fact; as, for instance, the oath at Santa Gadea which resembles another significant one in the history of the Kingdom of Aragon, namely, the Compromise of Caspe[5]—an arbitral decision which prevented a war of dynastic succession.

In history every period of prosperity is marked by a strengthening of justice and the opposite is the case in periods of decline. This contrast is abundantly clear in the most radical of the changes that have been registered in Spanish history. A transformation such as that which took place in the entire national life when, after the disastrous period of Henry IV, the Catholic Monarchs came to the throne, can only be explained by regarding it as a reinstauration of justice. In those days it was a long and wearisome task to secure the proper functioning of justice, and almost all the first seven years of the new reign were devoted to it. Most of the time was spent in curbing the knights who had be-

---

[1] *El Reto de Zamora* (The Challenge of Zamora), an epic story dealing with the treacherous murder of King Sancho II in 1072, and the duel or judicial challenge which ensued in order to prove whether the Council of Zamora was innocent or culpable of the murder of the king.

[2] The oath at S. Gadea, a famous scene in the epic poem when Alfonso VI swears that he was not guilty of the murder of his brother Sancho II.

[3] The Cortes of Toledo, principal scene in the *Poema del Cid* where the Infantes of Carrión are tried for having abandoned shamefully their wives, the daughters of the Cid.

[4] Joaquín Costa (1846–1911), Aragonese jurist, sociologist and politician. The works quoted here are: *Concepto del derecho en la poesía popular española; Oligarquía y caciquismo*, 1901; *Reconstitución y europeización de España.*

[5] When the King of Aragon, Martin I, died in 1410 there were six claimants to the throne; in order to prevent strife between the partisans of the three parliaments of Aragon, Catalonia and Valencia, each parliament named three delegates or *compromisarios* (one of them was S. Vincent Ferrer from Valencia) who met at Caspe (March–June 1412). Ferdinand, the Infante of Castile, was elected and crowned at Saragossa two months later.

come highway robbers, and other petty tyrants whose hands were against all men. After those seven years came a long period when there were less disturbances, but there still existed the need for strict control in order to preserve law and order. The transformation which had taken place was clearly visible in all public administration and the chroniclers note it. Before this period not only civil but even criminal justice was for sale. Every judge would repeat one of the favourite aphorisms of Henry IV, namely that the corpse of an executed criminal is worth nothing, and so it is preferable to free criminals from the gallows for money. Afterwards as a contrast to the corrupt maxim of Henry IV we have the case of the noble-born highwayman from Medina, who, to save his life, undertook to pay over forthwith 40,000 doubloons for the war against the Moors. The Catholic Queen, however, rejected the offer and had him executed, but refused to confiscate his goods according to the criminal code of the day, 'that people might not think that she had ordered justice to be done because she coveted his possessions'.

Thus the Crown, even though it was already firmly implanted in the minds of the people, yet wished more and more to rely upon public opinion and promote a spirit of confidence and optimism. This the Catholic Monarchs did achieve decisively, and every one praised what Vespasiano da Bistici[1] calls the *inviolabile giustizia* of Ferdinand whereby he satisfied both rich and poor, and the severe and inflexible sense of duty of Isabel when she expressed pleasure at seeing every one in his right place: 'men-at-arms in the field, bishops in their pontificals, robbers on the gallows'. This inexorable and incorruptible justice brought about a golden age which was perpetually remembered in successive centuries as the most prosperous era of the nation.

This devotion to just government, once it was established and practised with truly religious zeal, continued under the great succeeding monarchs throughout the whole sixteenth century, its special note being its refusal to give heed to personal considerations. It was not only in the autos-da-fé where, in the sacred interests of religion, a Marquis de Poza was degraded, or where Doña Ana Enríquez, the daughter of the Marquis de Alcañices

[1] Vespasiano da Bistici (1421–1498), famous Florentine bookseller who was associated with all the men of letters of his day, among them Spaniards. His principal work is *Vite di uomini illustri.*

appeared in the *sambenito* (penitential gown) and was condemned to prison amidst general commiseration, for all were
moved by her great beauty and noble bearing. Many scions of the
noblest houses suffered exile or prison for common offences, even
when the accused was the Duke of Alba, the Count of Tendilla,
the Duke of Osuna or the Count of Paredes.

This stern integrity prevailed in the early years of the seventeenth century and in Philip III's reign a counsellor and almoner
of the King of France observed in his travels through Spain that
the laws were, without distinction of classes, better observed
there than in France, where all was permitted to the nobles, even
crime, whereas in Spain a duke's son suffered the full rigour of
the law, and in the case of gentlemen who fought a duel, the
penalty was to have a hand nailed to a pillory in the plaza, no
matter how richly dressed they were. In the same period
Pinheiro da Veiga[1] at the Court of Valladolid observed that it
was the memory of Philip II, a true priest of justice, that caused
justice and its ministers to be not only feared and respected, but
even adored in Castile.

This deep concern with legality affected the very foundations
of the State which had expanded owing to the recent advances in
geographical discovery. In the reign of Charles V lawyers de-
bated for years the legal problem of how to incorporate into
western civilization a vast number of peoples who were living in a
state of nature. At the very moment when the ancient notion of
European history-laden Empire was dying out, there arose the
Spanish empire, without history, the first one of modern times
not anchored to Roman and mediaeval law, but eager to discover
new standards of natural and international law. Hence the opposition which existed between the humanitarian cleric Las Casas
and the humanist scholar Ginés de Sepúlveda,[2] both of them in-
human, for the former made all colonization impossible, and the
latter permitted it to flourish under tyranny. This chaotic and

---

[1] Tomé Pinheiro da Veiga (1571–1656), native of Coimbra, resided in Valladolid
when Philip III had his court there and wrote a diary of his stay (April–June 1605)
under the title *Fastiginia o fastos geniaes*.
[2] Juan Ginés de Sepúlveda (1490–1574), humanist, chronicler of Charles V.
His work, *Democrates sive de justis belli causis apud indos*, upholding the right in law of
the Spaniards to make war on the Indians and subjugate them, attacks Las Casas
who held that it was lawful only to negotiate peacefully and from equal to equal
with the chiefs of the Indians. The polemics on the right of domination over the
Indians took place chiefly between the years 1542–1551.

misleading position was remedied by the great theologians and jurists such as Francisco de Vitoria, Diego Covarrubias and Domingo de Soto, who raised the whole controversy to a higher and more serene level of doctrine, this enabling the necessary guardianship to be applied to primitive peoples. At the same time, with a spirit of impartiality, they dispelled the two ideas which had been the mainstay of the mediaeval empire, by denying that ascendancy over the whole world was possessed either by the Pope, who had made the celebrated Donation, or by the Emperor, who at the moment reigned in Spain. Here we had the unusual occurrence of a State undertaking to discuss with itself the legality of its own dominion. From this lofty spirit of justice sprang the exemplary Laws of the Indies, which are a model of modern methods of colonization never surpassed; their noble spirit may be summed up in the ordinance of Philip II which directed that any injuries and ill treatment inflicted by Spaniards on the Indians should be more heavily punished than if those crimes had been committed against Spaniards, and he declared that they were to be considered crimes against the State.

EQUITY AND ARBITRARINESS

This radiant sense of justice which is reflected in the above examples is united to feelings of moderation inspired by the anxiety to temper the rigidity of the abstract law to the individual case.

It is worthy of note in the works of Saint Isidore, the Conciliary Canons and the *Fuero Juzgo*, how much the principle of *aequitas* and *pietas* prevails as a means of reducing the severity of punishments. And by extending the notion that the general written law is unjust in many concrete cases, primitive Castile revolted even against the *Fuero Juzgo* when considered as an inviolable law, and decided to submit to judges who would judge according to their own idea of the equitable principles required by each individual case. It is in this way that Castile comes into being in an impulse of individualism over against the Kingdom of León. It is due to freedom of will, equity and compassion that the idea of pardon is given such a prominent place in our Spanish penal code. A French writer, Monsieur Legendre, although a fervent Catholic, considers that the traditional collective pardon given

on Good Friday is contrary to the duty which society has of
punishing the guilty. From early days it has been observed how
easily the Spaniard is moved to pity and sympathy for the man
who pays the penalty: he may even take the side of the criminal
and help him to escape, as Don Quixote did with the galley
slaves. In fact all look upon one who has come within the range of
the law more as a victim of misfortune than as a dangerous
criminal. This is another instance of how the interests of the
individual are set before those of the community.

This tendency may, sometimes, lead to dangerous extremes.
The unvarying justice of the great periods, which was considered
superior to that prevailing in other countries, disappears in
periods of decline and gives way to an inferior state of affairs,
likewise noted in comparison with foreign countries. At such a
time the Spaniard does not recognize the common good of
society except in very special circumstances. He refuses to bear in
mind that the individual cannot avoid the repercussions caused
by the vicissitudes of the community. This individualism then is
far removed from that of the Anglo-Saxon, who for ever looks to
social justice as the necessary support for the interests of each
individual. And since a society which has degenerated in such a
way is nothing but the sum total of individuals, the laws governing that society will also disintegrate into a series of individual
cases, and the peculiar circumstances of each case will be considered exceptions to the general rule. The result will be a
general lack of respect for the law, whether because it is considered inequitable as regards the case in point, or because of the
unconscious contempt for the public good felt by the individual.
'Laws', it is said, 'are only made for the pleasure of breaking
them'; a degrading pleasure indeed and one which is principally
enjoyed by rulers themselves in a degenerate age, when any
authority, be he high or low, thinks that his dignity suffers if he
submits to the rules followed by the common citizens, and starting
from this maxim believes that he will lose his main chance if he
does not exercise the abusive prerogatives to which his public
office lends itself. Caciquism[1] or the petty-boss system organized

---

[1] *Cacique*, a word derived from the Indians of Cuba and very frequently used in
the fifteenth century to describe a person who uses undue political influence in a
locality or region; *caciquismo*, a word admitted into the Spanish Academy Dictionary
in 1884, signifies the grave defects of the parliamentary system in Spain. The

the most shameless illegality under the motto: 'Go as far as injustice for your friend and refuse justice to your enemy' (*Al amigo hasta lo injusto, y al enemigo ni lo justo*). Similar arbitrary methods, though on a less systematic scale, have been frequently noted throughout Spanish history, as the Duke of Maura has shown conclusively.

The total lack of civic spirit in the depressed periods of history is shown clearly by the falsification of votes and the jerrymandering of elections. This evil does not date from the period of caciquism, when such arbitrary practices aroused great anxiety among the foremost thinkers and politicians, but from the Middle Ages when the kings and grandees brought pressure to bear upon the cities in the matter of the appointment of Procurators to the Cortes. In those days and as late as the seventeenth century they made a practice of bribing these Procurators, inducing them to be generous at public expense and to impose burdens upon the people. In the constitutional period, however, it is clear that the Spanish people never succeeded in making its will felt through universal suffrage and had no belief in it.

Amongst the other means of expression it preferred the *Pronunciamiento* as a regular institution. In the first third of the nineteenth century *Pronunciamientos* begin to be the order of the day and the necessary instrument for the constitutionalists who had no legal means of defending the introduction of suffrage. When later there were both Constitution and suffrage, Progressives and Moderates alike launched their *Pronunciamientos*, from Espartero and Narváez[1] to Prim. Generals, who, in addition, were deputies to the Cortes, wished to express the opinion of their own party, not in the Cortes or in elections, but by force of arms. On the other hand when the politicians of the Restoration came into power, they showed no greater belief in suffrage, but adapted it to their own convenience and corrupted it by means of caciquism. And the Spanish people remained indifferent in face of this falsification of their vote, not only because they lacked civic

---

arbitrary behaviour of the caciques perverts the elections and the application of the law. This national problem culminated in the publication of Costa's book '*Oligarquía y caciquismo*', 1901, and when Maura, who was Minister of the Interior in 1902, published what he called *Descuaje de* (or Disintegration of) *caciquismo*.

[1] General Baldomero Espartero, victor in the first Carlist war 1839, and later his opponent General Ramón María Narváez were alternately the masters of Spanish politics between 1837 and 1868.

sense, but also because they were given a kind of universal franchise which did not arouse their interest. It is strange that nobody suggested as a remedy for this state of affairs the possibility of adapting to Spanish needs foreign methods of franchise, in a way which would suit the extremely individualistic nature of the Spaniard, always inclined to disregard collective interests unless they are concerned with immediate objectives of daily life.

GOODWILL AND ENVIOUSNESS

One special characteristic of the opposition between justice and arbitrariness is that existing between selective appreciation and envy. Generous esteem of others might be personified in Cervantes, in whose mind all the reverses of life, all the unjust buffetings of chance arouse no resentful or rancorous thought but rather inexhaustible optimism and benevolent irony, the unfailing abnegation of Don Quixote, the kindly roguishness of Sancho, who is prepared to find good people even in hell.

This benevolent appreciation of the world has as its opposite the attitude of envious disparagement, which is lack of clear vision, an intellectual blindness rendering a man incapable of seeing merits in any one but himself. In most cases it degenerates into envy which is aversion to the excellent qualities of others and a reaction excited by the painful realization of one's own inferiority.

It is due to an excess of individualism and a deficiency in social values that envy is so widespread in Spain. Gracián calls it *malignidad hispana* (Spanish maliciousness) and he indicates the master qualities (*primores*) which will enable the Great Man to attenuate the attacks of this malevolent spirit. To the passion of envy Count Gondomar, an acute observer, attributed in 1606 strong literary repercussions, for he believed that the reason why no historical reports were being written was due to 'the envy and rivalry existing between Spaniards who believed that each one deprived himself of whatever praise or merit he allowed to his neighbour'. An infinite number of discourses and discussions on this passion by Spanish and Ibero-american authors could be collected. Foreign authors, too, have continually noted its prevalence and have pointed out the truth of the famous caricature of the three greased poles in the fair, each with its prize at the top.

L

The first is a French pole, and the competitor who climbs up does so amid the encouraging applause of the audience: the second is an English one, and the public watches the climber in silent rapt attention: the last is Spanish, but here the spectators yell at the man who tries to climb up and one even pulls him by the legs to prevent him from reaching the top.

The life story of every celebrated Spaniard has to note these envious obstructions, and the first separate biography in Spanish literature, that of the Cid, gives repeatedly details of this perpetual struggle between generosity and malevolence. The Cid is an object of envy to the grandees at court, to his own relations, to the King himself. But although driven into exile on several occasions he steadfastly refuses to harbour thoughts of resentment or revenge, and behaves with great magnanimity. He never weakens in his resolve not to use the right granted to him by the *fuero de los hijosdalgo* (privilege of nobility), whereby it was lawful for him to make war on the king who had exiled him, but uses his arms in the national war and offers his conquests to the ungrateful king. This generous behaviour is confirmed by history and idealized by poets as a characteristic Spanish trait, and it contrasts with the usual behaviour attributed by the ancient epic poetry of all peoples to the exiled vassal who is for ever at war with his king.

The reverse of the generosity of the Cid, namely the envy of the king which was denounced by the ancient biographer, is of great significance. Although Alfonso VI was a king of eminent qualities and in the first period of his reign won brilliant successes, nevertheless he exemplifies the essentially Spanish saying of Calderón:

No man so hapless lives but has one to envy him;
No man so full of honours but has one he envies more.

Alfonso the fortunate envies the Cid but will not make use of his services, and this rebuff it was which decided the fate of the monarch, for in the second part of his life he lingered for twenty-three consecutive years in misfortune, meeting with defeat after defeat at the hands of the Almorávides,[1] while the Cid whom he

---

[1] Almorávides, a name taken by a nomadic Berber tribe of the Sahara which built up an eastern African empire (1042–1147). In 1086 they invaded Moslem Spain, routing Alfonso VI in the battles of Zalaca or Sagrajas, 1086, Jaén, 1092,

had exiled went from triumph to triumph against those same
invaders from Africa. Alfonso VI had the advantage of having
inherited a kingdom which was on the ascendant grade as a
result of the exploits of his predecessors to the throne, but nevertheless his fortunes declined when, prompted by envy, he gave
way to his impulse and exiled the hero. The opposite course was
followed by the Catholic Monarchs. They came to the throne
after several decadent reigns, especially the last one, but far from
rebuffing the famous hero, they endeavoured constantly to discover unknown heroes, and, as a result of their efforts, Spain's
fortunes, which had been at their nadir, soared to their zenith; a
country which had been reduced to a heap of ruins became the
most powerful state in Europe.

FROM HENRY IV TO THE CATHOLIC MONARCHS

Alonso de Palencia, the first to stress the change which occurred
at the death of Henry IV and the succession of Ferdinand and
Isabel, compares the transformation to the sun suddenly piercing
the clouds after a long storm. According to Modesto Lafuente[1]
the social anarchy of the previous period disappeared 'as though
by enchantment', and the corpse-like nation became a robust
healthy body. But this transformation did not occur with such
suddenness; there was no such magic resurrection when the
Catholic sovereigns mounted the throne. What happened was
that a period of patient reconstruction ensued in which the most
important part was, as we said before, the restoration of justice.

Justice, however, by itself would explain public well-being,
but not great prosperity. We must specify another decisive
peculiarity in the methods of governing adopted by those sovereigns, one which among all the qualities attributed to them was
the principal cause of their extraordinary success, namely the
spirit of selection, which after all is another form of justice.

We have denied that the transformation which took place at
the coming of Ferdinand and Isabel was sudden, but neither was
it very slow. It took place among those very generations which

---

Consuegra, 1097, and Ucles 1108. The Cid drove back in confusion a great army
of Almorávides at the gates of Valencia and destroyed another big army at the
battle of Cuarte, 1094.

[1] Author of a *Historia general de España* in thirty volumes, 1850–1859.

had lived amid the corruption of Henry IV's reign. This means that among those generations there existed certain healthy elements which afterwards co-operated towards the rise to prosperity. On the one hand there were the resolute people who grouped themselves together into 'brotherhoods' to chastise lawlessness, first in Castile, then in Biscay, Galicia and Aragon; on the other hand there were certain grandees who gathered together in plotting bands, insisting on reform both in the government and social habits. Nevertheless, all those valuable elements proved ineffective since they were passed over and could take no part in the direction of national life. Those worthy grandees who gathered in Burgos in 1464 put forward as the cause of misgovernment the fact that public charges were 'sold to the highest bidder', and that they were always held by 'inefficient persons of little learning'. Many other witnesses of those days refer to this faulty method of selection: Gómez Manrique[1] says that it was the order of the day in a kingdom which was in decline and handed over to covetous self-seekers, where the fool is appointed mayor and the best candidates are passed over:

> The best are of less worth,
> Mark what a government:
> That the good should be governed
> By those who are not so!
> The wise should flee away
> When madmen rule the day,
> For when the blind are leaders
> Woe to those who follow after!

From this country where fools, madmen and degenerates ruled, from among those nobles who served only to deceive the people with false promises, sprang those who shortly afterwards were to devote themselves to enterprises of high renown and lead the nation from its lowest depths to the highest peak of its historical destiny. The only explanation for this radical and relatively rapid change lies in the scrupulous system of selection mentioned above, which enabled the rulers to extract from a spoiled mixture the uncontaminated leaven. Had they not at the height of their power

---

[1] Gómez Manrique (1413–91), Castilian noble, uncle of Jorge Manrique. The poem referred to is entitled *Querella de la gobernación* and was written during the youth of the poet in the reign of Henry IV (1454–1474).

persevered in this method of careful selection, those in the country who wished for reform might have succeeded in grouping themselves effectively and managed to establish a government. But though it would have been an improvement on conditions under Henry IV, it would not have given rise to the astonishingly rapid prosperity which actually did take place.

FERDINAND AND ISABEL TOGETHER

It would be necessary to search contemporary documents for details concerning this selective work, for the historians have not investigated the question. Only one ancient chronicler, Galíndez de Carvajal,[1] drew attention to the great importance of the subject and gave general information on it. Galíndez attributes to both monarchs the rules which were adopted, but one suspects that this was due to the fact that Isabel had ordered her chroniclers not to speak of her alone but to employ always the double expression 'the King and Queen', and Hernando del Pulgar,[2] who was wearied by the usage of this rigid formula, made fun of it by entitling an imaginary chapter of his history as follows: 'On such and such a day the King and Queen gave birth to a daughter'. In one case, at least, as we shall see, certain procedure which Galíndez attributed to both monarchs is by another author (and an Aragonese to boot) attributed to Isabel only; and by the way, we should note that Castiglione[3] limits his encomiums to the Queen alone. Nevertheless, in support of Galíndez we should remember that Machiavelli praises Ferdinand for his subtle discernment of men, and it is well known that this great king distinguished himself by his power of selecting the assistants he needed for carrying out his own system of government. We may thus reach the conclusion that the skill in selection was more the quality of Isabel and was applied by her scrupulously and religiously to all questions in life. The necessity for selection was a rule of conduct for her both in trifling as well as in important matters. Ferdinand, whose distinctive quality was his amazing

---

[1] Lorenzo Galíndez de Carvajal (1472–1532), jurist and historian, author of *Anales del reinado de los Reyes Católicos*.

[2] See note 1, p. 131.

[3] Baldassare Castiglione wrote a famous book *Il Cortigiano* between the years 1507 and 1513. He was Nuncio of Pope Clement VII at the court of Charles V in 1524 and died in Toledo, 1529.

clearness of vision in political matters, a quality which made him the first king in Christendom, was without doubt selective in all that concerned his political tasks, but in other matters he did not pay much attention to the worth or worthlessness of people, as we shall see. He admitted his inferiority in this point, and even in his great international undertakings made use of Isabel's wisdom, and she would point out to him the right man for the task. Castiglione was correct in saying that the principal dowry that Ferdinand had received in his marriage was not the kingdom of Castile but the talent of the Queen.

By this we do not intend to bring up once again the puerile problem which obsessed so many in the past and still does to-day, namely, which of the two monarchs was the greater, for the distribution of personal characteristics in this exceptional married couple was very complex. From our point of view it is evident that Ferdinand took part in the work of selection, and even in cases where his actual share was negligible, there was positive value in the fact that he trusted in the Queen's opinion and accepted it.

CHARACTERISTICS OF ISABEL'S SELECTION

When we discover details left by contemporary witnesses of the selective care taken by the Catholic Monarchs in appointments we find one detail of general character which presents the Queen to us in a predominant rôle. Count Baldassare Castiglione in the third book of 'Il Cortigiano' tells us of 'the divine manner of governing' of the Catholic Queen, saying that her will alone was equivalent to an order preventing any one from doing anything which might offend her, for all knew that her sense of justice was as ready to chastise as her sense of generosity was to reward, and he adds that all this depended upon 'the marvellous talent she possessed for discovering and selecting the most suitable men for the tasks she imposed upon them'. This sharp judgement of men which she constantly practised was lasting in its effects, for when Castiglione wrote more than twelve years after the death of the Catholic Queen he adds: 'In our days, all the celebrated men in Spain, no matter for what reason they were famous, were creations of Queen Isabel.'

All the life of this Queen was a perpetual process of selection carried out meticulously and scrupulously from childhood, when she managed to procure for herself, against the will of Henry IV, detailed information about her English, French and Aragonese suitors, and decided by herself alone to marry Ferdinand. And in this first selection she discovered truly the one person with whom she was able to share both actions and thoughts. Passing on now to more precise details, in the first place Galíndez de Carvajal tells us that the Catholic Monarchs, in dealing with questions of government, 'were more inclined to appoint prudent people suitable for their service, even though they were of middle rank, rather than those of noble houses'; that is to say, they avoided ancient deep-seated privileges and broadened the possibilities of election, thus building up an aristocracy of talent against the aristocracy of birth. This note by Galíndez can be illustrated by many examples. We may recall the case of Cisneros. This stubborn, cross-grained friar was, against his will, appointed by Isabel Archbishop of Toledo, but his appointment was against the wishes of Ferdinand, who wished the mitre to be given to his natural son the Archbishop of Saragossa. In spite of this Isabel decided that the see of Toledo should cease to be the exclusive patrimony of the noble clerics as it had been in the past. Had this decision not been taken Cisneros would not have been more than a friar of no importance, hidden away in some convent, and the princely funds of the archdiocese of Toledo would not have been applied to the conquest of Oran, the first step made by Spain in Africa, nor to the University of Alcalá, to the Polyglot Bible, which was the first application of modern philology to the text of the Scriptures, and to many other enterprises. Another important example may be given to illustrate the point made by Galíndez, namely the fact that the monarchs appointed to the Royal Council, the Chancery of Valladolid and the various special governmental commissions learned jurists, 'people midway between the great and the small, whose profession was to study law', as Diego Hurtado de Mendoza said. In other countries there was a general tendency to admit the middle class to take regular part in the government, but nowhere was this tendency so decisively marked as under the Catholic Sovereigns.

The most subtle stroke in this matter of selection, one that makes it no less difficult than profitable, is that the election or rejection be independent of services or disservices rendered. Galíndez notes that when any one asked for a post in justice, government or war, and pointed out the services he had rendered, or as it was said, 'his adhesion to authority', he received the answer that services were rewarded in other ways, as indeed they were, but that in matters of government it was necessary to consider only the business in hand and see to it that posts were efficiently held. 'Hence many were called from their homes who had no notion that they would be appointed, and this was the reason why those monarchs were well served, and their vassals were inclined to virtue.' Here we may recall how Ferdinand, through the wise though risky advice of the Queen, appointed as leader of the Aragonese expedition in Naples Gonzalo de Córdoba, the future Great Captain, who was a younger son of an Andalusian house, and could not claim to have performed great services, in fact none at all for the Crown of Aragon. To this we should add that they did not by any means count only upon their supporters, but took special care to use the services of former adversaries, as in the case of the Marquis of Cadiz, Rodrigo Ponce de León, who, though a staunch partisan of La Beltraneja[1] and the King of Portugal, yet, through the instrumentality of the Queen, was attracted and received with marked favour by both sovereigns. It was they who made him give up the fierce war which he and the Duke of Medinasidonia had been waging fruitlessly to their own destruction, and succeeded in persuading both to co-operate in the conquest of Granada, vying with each other in great exploits. In short, owing to the influence of the sovereigns, a period of noble rivalry succeeded one of hatred and envy.

The same insistence in making use of former enemies was shown by Isabel in her treatment of Carrillo, the Archbishop of Toledo. Although she was very jealous of her own royal dignity, yet she endured the slights she received from him, and out of magnanimity tried her best to placate (in vain, it is true) the ire of that prelate, who though stubborn and valiant was of limited

---

[1] La Beltraneja, nick-name given to Juana, the daughter of Henry IV, born in 1462, on the suspicion that she was not the daughter of the king but of Don Beltran de la Cueva. Henry IV declared the illegitimacy of Juana and recognized Isabel the Catholic as heiress to the throne in 1468; but in 1470 he named Juana. The wars of succession caused by this proclamation ended with the Battle of Toro, 1476, in which the King of Portugal, who had married Juana and upheld her rights, was defeated.

intelligence. Even the most adverse circumstances never confused the subtle judgement of the Queen in searching out and
making use of profitable material. Columbus, who had failed in
his schemes with various sovereigns, and who could not convince
any one, owing to his deficient knowledge of cosmography, and
his exorbitant ambition, found in Isabel one who appreciated in
him the extraordinary man of action, who was able to endure the
untold risks of an unique adventure.

With the patient tenacity of genius ('she was very hardworking
herself and very firm in her purpose') she kept a sharp look-out on
all sides for people to fill both high as well as humble posts. Fray
Juan de Santa María relates that once a piece of paper fell from
the Queen's hands; on it she had written in her own handwriting
the following reminder: 'The office of common crier must be
given to so-and-so, for he has the bigger voice.' Doubtless she was
determined to prevent some piece of petty jobbery.

This constant attention which the monarchs gave to every
detail was aided by a regular information service which they set
up. According to Galíndez 'they had persons of their own close
confidence, who travelled through the country finding out how it
was governed and how justice was administered, and what was
said about the ministers. These confidential agents brought back
to the monarchs special reports on what they noticed, and reme-
dies were found as dictated by necessity.' This diligent watchful-
ness is another essential point. Thanks to their continued perseverance in the task of selecting the holders of office, the Catholic
sovereigns managed to change the downward course which the
workings of envy had given to the nation during the preceding
reigns. The problem was, in each struggle which arose between
the selfish thoughtless man and the man with genuine civic sense,
to help the victory of the latter. In the fratricidal scene of
Montiel,[1] Rocaberti, by merely helping to turn over the two
brothers in their mortal struggle, when they fell to the ground,
had done enough to set up a new dynasty. In the hubbub of the
days of Henry IV the best men in the realm fought under hopeless conditions and were only a helpless minority. By a change in
the relative positions, it was possible for them to become a vic-

[1] Montiel in the province of Ciudad Real, was the place where in 1369 King
Peter the Cruel was killed in a hand-to-hand struggle with his bastard brother,
Henry. The dynasty of Trastamara begins with the latter.

torious majority. There was no attempt to create new personnel, nor was there any waiting for a new generation educated on new principles. Cisneros, the Marquis of Cadiz, the Great Captain, all were men whose characters had been formed in the society of Henry IV. Thus, from the lowest pitch of decline to the highest peak of prosperity of a people there is only one step, but a step that is truly difficult to make, as difficult, in fact, as it is to pull out of the quagmire of selfish personal aggrandisement and tread the firm ground of honour and duty. It is difficult to continue day after day constantly and inflexibly overcoming covetousness and ambition, scrutinizing and testing the great or small capacities of each candidate to discover the best place in which to put him, so that he may develop those capacities; and once that is done to protect him against the attacks of the envious, as Isabel had to do with the utmost diligence when her protégés were the victims of malicious slander. She would as willingly defend the Great Captain when he was in difficulties after Barletta,[1] as she would the poor town-crier with the bigger voice when he was about to be passed over.

A period of prosperity is not the mysterious result of a series of fortuitous circumstances. The plethora of great men at certain periods and the scarcity at others has been explained by the saying that nature has her alternating periods of fertile harvesting and restful fallow (W. Pinder). But this metaphor does not explain matters, for in this case we are not dealing with mysterious natural forces, but with historical causes and circumstances which may favour or retard the blossoming forth of the very best human capacities which lie beneath the surface of everyday life. These causes and circumstances indeed may at one moment select and encourage the growth of those capacities, at another moment they may destroy them. In the case of the Catholic Monarchs, in addition to considering the fermentation produced by the ideas of the Renaissance, which were spreading through Spain during all the fifteenth century, we must consider as the decisive element Isabel's genius for selecting the right man for the right job.

[1] Barletta, an Italian city in the province of Bari on the Adriatic, where in the war between the French and the Spanish for the kingdom of Naples the Great Captain was besieged for nine months (July 1502–April 1503). Afterwards he won the great battles of Cerignola and Garigliano.

Castiglione has a phrase which is most revealing in this connection: '*A' nostri tempi tutti gli uomini grandi di Spagna e famosi in qualsivoglia cosa, sono creati dalla regina Isabella.*'

The prosperity of Spain was not a product of natural forces plentifully disseminated, but was the result of pure human will, which spread through an uninterrupted series of effects. Every man chosen became in his turn an agent of selection, and this spread like a drop of oil on paper. The very names we have quoted bring back the memory of the courage inspired by the Great Captain in his followers; his speeches to his troops with their admiring references to the heroes of antiquity made all long to emulate those glorious exploits. Cisneros, too, is a proof of how strong is the power of attraction or repulsion wielded by the 'select' individual over the man of positive or of negative sign, as in the case of Nebrija. Nebrija had quarrelled with him over a difference of opinion with regard to the Polyglot Bible. Nevertheless, Cisneros welcomed him generously to Alcalá when he heard that he had been deprived of his chair at Salamanca, and persecuted by the Inquisition. He assigned to him a professorship worth 60,000 *maravedís* with 100 *fanegas* of bread, telling him 'to lecture or teach whatever subject he wished, and if he did not wish to lecture not to do so, for he did not give him this appointment to make him work, but as a reward for all that Spain owed him'. The reverse side of the medal appears when we note the mutual antipathy between Cisneros and the Archbishop of Santiago, Alonso de Fonseca, the second of those of that name, a man self-willed in everything, who actually excommunicated Cisneros. When Fonseca in 1506 passed on the Archbishopric to his son Alonso de Fonseca, the third of the name, with the consent of Ferdinand the Catholic, Cisneros censured the king for violating in such an outrageous manner all selective principles, saying: 'Sir, it seems that Your Highness has made of the archbishopric of Santiago a family inheritance, and I would fain know whether women are excluded from it.' The complaint did not cancel the arbitrary act but at least it produced great remorse in the king's conscience, and this itself was a guarantee against further errors. In a word, in spite of such blemishes, the 'divine manner of ruling' attributed to Isabel by Castiglione, and the practice of incorruptible justice and vigorous selection, created an atmosphere of optimism among the people, for each individual felt that he was allowed to give the best of himself; there was a general *afición a la virtud* (love of virtue), as Galíndez said, and the continual insistence on incorruptible justice produced a society which was well ordered according to its human possibilities, and in which all the first values in the nation were enabled to flourish.

Furthermore, the selective system is held firm by a keystone. Isabel did not make her chief appointments in haphazard fashion when the necessity arose, but prepared them carefully beforehand. Antonio Agustín relates that 'Queen Isabel had a book locked in a casket of which she alone had the key, and in that book she kept a list of names of the people who deserved to be appointed to bishoprics, councils, judgeships, governorships and other posts, and she received previous information against the occurrence of a vacancy.' Galíndez, as usual, attributes this practice to both sovereigns, saying that 'in order to be prepared when the time came for making appointments they had a book containing lists of the ablest and most deserving candidates for vacant posts, and the same for bishoprics and ecclesiastical dignities.' Every distrustful and envious governor, too, has his book but he imagines that, as there is always a surplus of office-seekers, he will have no difficulty in selecting, and so he notes down in the book only the people who are disloyal or to be avoided, so that he may reject them if they do apply for posts.

DECLINE OF ISABEL'S SELECTIVE SYSTEM

This Book of Capabilities must have seemed to the people to be an effective system, for the Cortes of Valladolid of 1537 begged Charles V to follow the example of his grandparents and gather together secret information concerning the qualities and merits of candidates for office, and they added: 'Such a book is all the more necessary as Your Majesty has more kingdoms and dominions.' Charles granted the petition and Juan Ginés de Sepúlveda relates how conscientiously the Emperor considered the matter of his appointments, what aversion he felt to men whose reputation was unfounded, and how he would prefer to appoint unknown persons about whom he had received good reports. By thus continuing the selective system Charles has been praised by historians as a ruler who knew how to find his collaborators and make the best use of their talents.

Philip II continued to use the Book with its list of eligible candidates for office, but nevertheless this great king, owing to his enormous power of work and his distrustful character, kept all to himself and gave scant trust to those he had appointed, so that on occasions he would favour men of mediocre talent or none at all. The reports by ambassadors or historians show us that Philip, though he made up for it by his good qualities and his lofty ideals, yet had in his nature a touch of the envy to which we referred before. According to these reports, Philip at times appointed president of some Council or mission an insignificant or foolish individual, and placed under him others of genuine merit, who would prevent any grave blunders being made. Thus, as the president was of no account whatever, the king's supreme directing hand could be all the more apparent to all and would meet with no obstacle. But this unfortunate system was applied even in the case of the Great Armada. The incapable Duke of Medinasidonia, although he insisted that he was utterly inexperienced in nautical matters, had to accept command over the greatest naval force that was ever mustered, at the supremely decisive moment for the Spanish empire and the Catholic Counter-Reformation. Under the useless Captain General were appointed expert commanders and admirals, whose advice, it was believed, would be followed by the prudent, docile Medinasidonia, but naturally such advisers were powerless to prevent the continuous vacillations and the countless obvious mistakes which led to the great disaster. Thus all the abnegation and sacrifice shown by the nation in this vital enterprise was frustrated more than by any other cause by a wrong appointment made by the king under the stress of envy.

The nomination of that grandee as commander of the 'Invincible Armada' is a proof that times had changed from the days when it was possible to appoint an unassuming younger son to the Naples enterprise or a humble friar to the archbishopric of Toledo. Among the experienced commanders who had been chosen to assist the incompetent chief, Philip did not try to select one who might become a future hero. He preferred that the God of armies should grant the triumph of his cause to a well-known incompetent, for there was no danger that glory would turn his head: this, doubtless, was what Philip felt in his mind, according to the interpretation of a sharp-witted Italian, who added that the king suffered from *la infirmità della sospetta* (suspicion sickness) for he showed himself in all things *assai sospettoso*. But the fatal shipwreck of the Great Armada produced irreparable confusion in the Spanish people, for, believing that they were the chosen people, they had to ask themselves: 'Why does this disaster come upon us? *Si Dominus nobiscum est, ubi sunt mirabilia ejus?*' Thus a deep depression fell upon all with fatal results thereafter. And so among all the causes of the decline of the Spanish Empire which have been so carefully studied and discussed, history must set as the very first and principal one the abandonment of Isabel's selective system, so clearly shown in the case of Medinasidonia.

The high qualities of Philip II and the greatness of his political vision kept the Empire in the crescent stage, but it was evident that the wane would soon follow. The Book of Capabilities, which was the symbol of efficient government, was given up by Philip III, or rather by his favourite. Bermudez de Pedraza in 1620, when noting great injustice in the allotment of privileges, misses the register book in the office of the royal secretaries. That is to say, when the decline began to be clear to all, simultaneously the desire for a selective system had ceased to exist. Henceforth it is not the most suitable candidate who will receive the post but the one who is the luckiest office-seeker. The evolution is absolutely clear. The Catholic kings created and organized for the first time a complete training-school for candidates for office, and they spread their net far and wide throughout their kingdom. Charles V continued this system of selecting, grouping and encouraging the best men for service. Philip II inherited this rich legacy of human talent, but at times he employed men of no account, and when he did make use of the many illustrious personalities around him he cut their wings and refused to allow them any initiative, for he was suspicious of what they would do in their hour of triumph. Philip III, unintelligent and apathetic, drove away the select men and chose as his favourite one of inferior capacity, and through him lost, as Quevedo says, the inheritance of doughty men which his father had bequeathed to him, wherefore the whole government crumbled away.

When the forceful government of the Prudent King ceased there followed an uncontrollable burst of envious plotting. After Philip III had been reigning seven years, the Venetian ambassador Simon Contarini, when describing the Spanish court, observes that there is no rivalry for public office, but only for private gain, and he ends: 'There is nought here save prejudice and passion; no nation suffers more from mutual jealousy.' Once more envy is the order of the day and there is complete lack of selective efficiency. It is the period of Rodrigo Calderón, when office-selling was rampant. Contarini himself notes that the favourite, the Duke of Lerma, accepts bribes and keeps far from the Court the best brains of Spain. This judgement itself is a full explanation of the decline, and it coincides with that of Quevedo and is confirmed by the evidence which Pinheiro da Veiga, resident in Valladolid, gathered here and there from various sources during those years. He says: 'The Duke of Medinasidonia is to be appointed commander of the fleet; he will do with it what he did with our expedition to England (in effect Medinasidonia repeated his mishaps in his new command); and another who has never seen the sea nor India is to be named Viceroy there; and others who have never seen action are to be made members of the War Council. They believe that to be a count, marquis, or grandee is to be omniscient. . . . Empires were successful as long as they went in search of men and brought them in from the deserts to govern. If this were the method used in Spain there would be no lack of men to fill the posts nor would so many be forgotten.' As time went on the lack of selectivity increased, the downward slope became steeper. How complete it was under Philip IV we know from the striking records of Don Juan Palafox y Mendoza[1] who relates how he saw everywhere '*tantos hombres sin emplear, tantos empleos sin hombres*' (so many men without posts, so many posts without men). These lines do but condense in concise form the thoughts contained in the words of Pinheiro da Veiga quoted above, which refer to the reign of Philip III.

[1] Juan de Palafox y Mendoza (1600–1659), a writer of many historical and religious works, was Bishop of Puebla de los Angeles in Mexico.

THE HISTORICAL CONCEPT OF SELECTION
AND ENVY

In forming a general concept of the history of Spain the depression reached under the Austrian monarchy has been taken as the main viewpoint, and, as we shall see, there are authors who believe that characteristics similar to those of that decline are visible before and after the Austrian period. One should then speak not of a decline, but of a congenital infirmity which has always menaced the Spanish people. This comparison with human pathology, like all similes, can both clarify and confuse at the same time. Applying it to the subject before us, instead of saying that Spain irreparably lacks something possessed by all peoples of normal health, we should say that Spain is, among the great peoples who have played a part in history, the one where selectivity is exercised with the greatest difficulty. Enviousness, together with the isolation in which Spain tends to live, will not allow her to see in the unity of other nations the qualities necessary for success. The power of selection is blunted by the egoism of individuals and groups. The difficulty does not lie in the qualities of the mass of the people, but in the ruling minorities, for to them and not to the mass belong the subtle tasks of selection. It is a defect of the minority and for this reason less constant in its effects.

No doubt the periods of depression due to faults of selection occur much too frequently in Spanish history. But they are not continuous, and it must be the historian's special care to bring into relief those intervals when justice and efficient selection were the rule, in other words, the periods of prosperity both political and social. An examination of these, pointing out the effects of the special individualism we have been discussing, should take the place of the uniform notion of congenital deficiency. Alternations of selective prosperity, such as reached its height under Charles III, and complete depreciation of human values, such as touched its lowest depths under Ferdinand VII, are constantly repeated in Spanish history, though not always in such violent contrast. But no inquiry into the causes, based on documentary evidence, has been made; nor has use been made, for historical purposes, of the great writers, from Feijóo to Larra, who most concerned themselves with problems arising from this lack of selection. As regards cultural life, though similar alternations of abundance and scarcity in first rate men is evident, again there is no study of the causes of these fluctuations, which do not coincide with those of political life. The highpoints of literary and artistic life—the most complex product of periods of selection—generally occur at the end of such periods and the beginning of periods of political and social decline.

The simile we quoted concerning the congenital infirmity of the Spanish people has foundations of fact in the notorious disproportion we can observe between the rise and fall in these alternations. The depression may appear to continue without a break, for its predominance is natural. Selection needs constant care in order that full profit may be drawn from the free development of any talent possessed by the individual; care also is needed in order to guess who will be the unknown hero; and care, too, is necessary if only to save the tender bud that will produce the flower that men desire. Every inferior being called upon to rule over any aspect of the life of a community easily and necessarily enters into relationship with other inferior beings, who are always in the majority, and he finds himself immediately surrounded by a powerful group. The oil stain in each negative selection spreads with far greater rapidity than in the case of a positive one. Gradually the best men find fewer points of support in other select people, for the disorganization of society secludes these and sets them aside instead of grouping them together and strengthening them: 'Where the blind lead the way, woe to those who come behind.' This being so, the gradual disappearance of vigour, intellect and virtue in a period of decline is not always due to the degeneration of the mass of the people which produces too few talented individuals, but to lack of judgement in the ruling classes, because the failure to make adequate selection repels the most talented and renders them useless. Certainly if the action of envy and the consequent weakening of the best elements continues for a long time there is bound to be a decline in the number of births of well-endowed individuals. But the contrary is also true, that selection causes an increase of vitality, and the persistence of selective action may even bring into predominance as a majority a type different to the one which had always prevailed

M

when matters ran their own way and there was no selection.

Just as we noticed in the case of the alternation between justice and arbitrariness, so on this other alternative between selection and envy (a mere variant of the former) is based all the mechanism of rise and decline, and it is this mechanism which can explain the heights and depressions of our vital curve better than the other themes which generally absorb the attention of historians. It is not necessary to devote attention to the well-intentioned programmes drawn up after 1898, to the undertakings which range from urgent national reconstruction to grandiose plans for the future. All that is important is to see whether behind these attempts there is an efficient, just and selective action, or whether time is being wasted in attending merely to unconditional supporters at a moment when the country, which is passing through a lean period, cannot, even with all its resources, manage to carry out its functions with regularity. We have shown as a remarkable example how great results were achieved in a short period of time by the tenacious work of Isabel and Ferdinand. Spaniards of different ideologies often look back to the period of the Catholic monarchs with longing regret as an incomparable epoch, unique in Spanish history, a golden age that the nation enjoyed through some inexplicable design of Providence. We have indicated that the primary explanation of this success is the perfect system of selection adopted by those monarchs, and we consider this is a suggestive case to set against the opposite conception of congenital deficiency. A similar selective policy has brought at other moments in the past and may bring in the future, the same blossoming forth of full collective capacity, and it is of secondary importance, in the study of causes, whether the historical scene on which this total capacity develops is of greater or smaller dimensions.

WAS THERE A LACK OF SELECT MINORITIES?

The short duration of the selective moments in modern Spain makes the depression in its historical curve seem continuous, and causes the belief that there is a permanent congenital defect which authorities from Costa and Macías Picavea[1] onwards

---

[1] Ricardo Macías Picavea (1847–1899), novelist and sociologist, and one of the early writers to reflect the deep political anxiety in the future of Spain in his work *El Problema Nacional*, 1891.

attribute to the lack of an *élite*, a chosen minority who could direct the life of the country. In Spain, it is said, everything is done by the people; the people, deprived of a ruling minority, without any pre-established plan; the strong individualism rooted in the mass of the people brings with it the pride of the inferior who will not allow himself to be directed by his superior. It is certainly true that many Spanish activities whether in the political or the cultural sphere have a special mark which is called popular, but as this designation lends itself to a false interpretation, it should be avoided or at least explained.

The people as a mere collective mass, without any guidance, is incapable of taking any initiative. We cannot to-day continue to believe in the romantic theory that the people is the author of many things such as the four lines of a folk poem, the notes of the simplest melody, the drafting of a law or a treaty: all these are never the work of the people but of an individual, a chosen one, who emerges from the common herd. Even the most primitive manifestation of the folk cannot be produced without the leavening of a minority.

What can be said is that the Spanish people does not necessarily lack leading minorities but that those minorities have peculiar characteristics of their own which cause their actions to appear ineffective, even null and void. Spanish aristocracy, both that of talents and that of social position, does not aspire to the position of a class apart, above the level of the common herd, nor does it aspire to carry out eventually a personal policy of its own within a small minority group; rather does it devote all its activities to the majority: thus it adopts a style of unaffected simplicity based upon broad human values. This does not mean that a work which is directed to the majority of the citizens may not be select, profound and suggestive. Cervantes wrote *Don Quixote* to be read by the entire Spanish people, high and low; surely nobody will place him second when such a masterpiece is compared with another excellent work, the '*Soledades*' of Góngora, which was written for a small coterie of men of letters.

When a leader wishes to create a work for the general majority he does not claim absolute authority to the exclusion of all others. He does not even neglect the co-operation of those he leads, for he recognizes that the latter may possess greater powers of initiative than he has. According to the Spanish legend, the

Cid ordered his troops not to break their ranks, but when Pedro Bermudez did break them, the Cid helped him and backed up the wild initiative which led to victory. In the Roman legend Manlius Torquatus, when his son returned triumphant from single combat, ordered him to be beheaded because he had broken ranks contrary to the commands of his father. Such harshness is repugnant to a Spaniard. Pulgar in his book 'Claros Varones' justifies it only by saying that the Romans must have been very undisciplined when they needed to have such a cruel example before them.

In any work destined to sway majorities, in addition to this sharing of leadership which counts on the help of the directed, we find also a fragmentation of leadership among a large number of directors. This is very characteristic of Spanish individualism which often tends to split up into little operative groups. When we consider the conduct of war, which most rigorously calls for command, Spain has given us as a model two special types—the guerrilla fighter and the conquistador. Both represent the organization created by the individual against an enemy far superior in numbers. The guerrilla fighter is engaged against armies that are superior in resources and technique; the conquistador against an enemy superior in numbers but inferior in arms. The guerrilla fighters became famous when the Peninsula was invaded by the troops of Napoleon and the name guerrilla spread through Europe and was used in various languages to describe the tactics employed by other countries when they found themselves in a situation resembling the Spanish War of Independence. The conquistador, on the other hand, has remained a peculiarity of Spain, for neither English nor Dutch colonists evolved this special type which implies the diffuse collaboration of the whole nation in a work of expansion and civilization. While the colonization of Anglo-Saxon America was the work of commercial companies and Puritan expatriates, namely small groups which sought well-nigh uninhabited lands where they might carry on their industry and serve God according to their own consciences, the colonization of Hispano-America was a genuinely national work at the service of God and King, propagating the Gospel to a number of primitive peoples and incorporating them in the millenary culture of Europe.

Spanish colonization is the best model for minorities who exercise powers of direction which will call majorities into action. The religious-cultural design was initially conceived by Isabel even before the discovery of the New World was completed. To this plan which was of the highest universalist idealism was added afterwards the contribution of the jurists and theologians who were considered the greatest in Europe. With them collaborated high administrative and commercial enterprises such as the Council of the Indies and the *Casa de Contratación* (Board of Trade). Finally the work was carried out by a host of conquistadores and explorers among whom such men as Balboa, Magellan, Elcano and Orellana, investigators of the geographical secrets of the planet, may well figure, though belonging to a different sphere of human activities, beside the great investigators of the universe such as Copernicus, Tycho Brahe or Kepler.

There is no other nation which can show similar collective movements that should be called, not popular, but national. The people produced its guerrilla fighters and conquistadores because, in spite of its individualism, it was capable of becoming inspired by great collective ideals. The full national scope of its reactions is often not appreciated, but even in cases where such movements appear to be amorphous we may recognize in them a superior guiding inspiration. The Gaul Trogus Pompeius, who is always a valuable starting-point for the observation of Hispanic traits, judges adversely, as devoid of high direction, the anti-Roman resistance in the Iberian Peninsula, and notes that during the various centuries of struggle, the Spaniards had only one great commander, Viriathus. But to this we should add that the Gauls themselves had only one, less of a strategist and less victorious, Vercingetorix, and when he fell all his people were conquered; whilst the Spaniards, before and after Viriathus, prolonged the war for 200 years under the leadership of many chiefs who were anonymous or quasi-anonymous. Their weakness was more than anything else due to their lack of cohesion, but they maintained for two centuries the spirit of national independence, a thing that no other province of the Roman Empire did. Certainly the Iberian guerrillas had no ideological organization as the conquistadores and explorers had later, but they had no lack of patriotism, and this spirit gave to their fragmentary actions a certain vague unity which could always become effective at determined moments. In periods that are better documented we find that the resistance during the 300 most difficult years when weak Christian Spain faced the far superior power of Islam, although it was diffuse and languid in its direction, yet counted many kings and captains, who far from being anonymous, enjoyed illustrious fame, such as Pelayo,[1] Alfonso the Catholic, Sancho Abarca, Fernán González, Ramiro II, Vifredo el Velloso, all of whom symbolize the collective consciousness of duty towards universal Christianity. In the centuries following the Reconquest we find examples of a diffuse and chaotic frontier activity, but already there begins the predominance of great kings and heroes, conquistadores and campeadores, all agreeing in pacts whereby they shared their efforts against Islam and cooperated one with the other in times of difficulty.

MAJORITIES AND MINORITIES

In all historical epochs there is certainly no lack of excellent leaders of the masses. What often is lacking, however, is agreement among them, and the efficient daily co-ordination of effort which unites the wills of all, thus ensuring the greatest benefit. Minorities, both those of capacity and those of command, organize themselves only with great difficulty and do not usually show the generous cohesion, the selective justice and the other virtues of leadership, and by allowing the vice of envy to run riot in their hearts they destroy any chances of success. The contrary takes place in the common run of people where the individual often gives proof of positive virtues. The most salient of all is the keen sense of personal dignity which lends lustre to a man's whole life. We can perceive this quality even in the poorest classes, in the most humiliating situations, and this fact has been noted by all foreign observers from Lucius Marineus Siculus[2] onwards. Spanish literature has celebrated this virtue in many a noble

---

[1] Pelayo, first king of Asturias in the eighth century; the other personalities mentioned are the primitive kings and counts of Asturias, Navarre, León, Castile and Catalonia.

[2] Lucio Marineo Siculo (1460?-1533?), Sicilian humanist, settled in Spain 1484 as tutor to the young nobles. Wrote *De rebus Hispaniae memorabilibus*, 1530, *Epistolarum libri decem et septem*, 1914.

poem, and it has also satirized the excesses due to its deep influence. Above all, literature has dramatized the impulse that
causes a man to defend his personal dignity when it has been
injured. When this concept of honour is examined in its most
typical literary expression we find that even Menéndez Pelayo
and Unamuno, who possessed such deep understanding of the
national character, considered it not as a virtue, as we have presented it here, but as a disordered and unhealthy pride, a peevish
fear of public opinion, productive of deeply immoral tragedies as
a solution. But this is to misrepresent a certain poetic stylization
(very Spanish indeed in its exaggeration), taking it as the normal
or fundamental form. The most implacable and monstrous vindi-
cations of the offences against honour that have been the theme
of Spanish literature sprang from the individual considering himself as the trustee and the responsible champion of the essential
values in collective life. Individual honour is one part of the social
structure of the entire community and the tragedies which it
inspires represent a point of contact between the individual and
consciousness of social solidarity. But these tragedies are not, as
has always been believed, a morbid exaggeration of passion
peculiar to the Spanish baroque epoch. On another occasion I
have examined mediaeval subjects quite as Calderonian as those
of Calderón and I was able to prove that the exalted passion for
honour must be set among the enduring characteristics of Spain.
We must here add that the jealous sentiment of honour has not
been dramatized in the Spanish theatre merely with reference to
the class of the nobility, as other literatures have done, but it has
also been represented as the element giving dignity to the plebeian and rustic class of the Spanish nation in the seventeenth
century. We may finally conclude that in contrast to eminent
minorities, the gregarious majority possesses to a greater degree
the good qualities of its class, and exercises them even when its
leaders are found wanting. It is strange to note that when
Quevedo in 1609 considered that all the virtues that shone in a
Cisneros, a Cortés, and in those who created the greatness of the
nation were extinguished, he nevertheless praised the Spanish
people for preserving intact their virtues, their discipline, their
loyalty to their princes, their religious obedience to the laws, their
love for their generals and captains to the generous disregard for

their own lives. At a very different period we find this trait noted by Vittorio Alfieri who travelled through Spain in 1771. He considered that the Spanish and the Portuguese peoples were the only ones in Europe who preserved their customs intact, and although their high exploits always failed owing to their innumerable blunders (that is to say, owing to the mistakes of the group that rules), yet he believed that both peoples possessed the raw material for carrying out great enterprises, especially military ones, for they were gifted to a high degree with all the necessary qualities, namely, valour, perseverance, honour, moderation, obedience, patience, and high mindedness. This comparison between minorities and majorities is repeated many times by modern observers.

And so, far from putting down the weakness of Spain to the indocile nature of the people which is unable to follow the lead of its select minority, we must attribute it to the discord and want of harmony existing among the members of that select minority, to their deficiencies which split up and disperse all sense of leadership and direction. The war against Napoleon was the most remarkable example of this. Spain, abandoned by all her leaders, then displayed the most spontaneous national spirit of unity and firmly struck out for her independence, even though she was divided under fragmentary leadership, and in addition torn within by two opposing ideologies.

In conclusion Spanish individualism can harmonize with high collective ideals, and when this is the case, the people, the majority, produces in great profusion its ruling minorities. Castile exercises hegemony over her brother peoples in the Peninsula, because in individualistic Spain, Castile preserves in its popular masses a more efficient individualism. The Catholic King considered what he called *desconcierto* or predominance of the individual an essential element in the life of Castile and one which differentiated it from Aragon. And Castile with its predominance of the individual was able to furnish this loose leadership, characteristic of the majority movements which are so much in keeping with the nature of all the Hispanic peoples.

Chapter IV

Centralization and Regionalism

The individualism felt by a whole region, that is to say local individualism as an obstacle against fully concerted action between various regions, has predominated to such an extent on occasions that it lends itself to erroneous interpretation historically when localism is considered the essential and absolute element in the life of the Spanish people. Once again we find ourselves inclining to consider as unique one of the two active opposing tendencies. Both tendencies we shall treat when we come to explain the various historical periods. Here, nevertheless, we shall proceed to show that the centralizing tendency was always in the ascendant, at one moment as the only vital force in periods of increase and prosperity, at another having at its side as an inferior force the localist sentiment in periods of decline.

EXCESS OF LOCALISM

It is clear that there is in Spain an especial weakness in the spirit of association. The benefits to be derived from co-operation are less clearly felt than the advantages of separate individual action, even though this, in the long run, shows less results. Communal life comes to be regarded as something hampering owing to the restrictions it imposes upon the individual, for every one wishes to work at his ease without having to take account of his neighbour. This weakens the relationship between the different provinces as has been noted at various periods by foreign observers. A French traveller, Bartolomé Joly, was surprised in 1604 at the localism prevalent in the minds of Aragonese, Valencians, Catalans, Biscayans, Galicians, and Portuguese, for their habitual entertainment was to tell one another their defects, and he even found that those from Old Castile felt contempt for those from New Castile. The same observation was made by Richard Ford half-way through the nineteenth century; he encountered in Spain a shy and diffident local spirit, where the link between the peasantry was even more exclusive than among the Irish of Tipperary or the Scots. Théophile Gautier, when he heard in the Puerta del Sol descriptions of certain atrocities of the Carlist War related with complete indifference, and the reason given for this indifference being that 'the incident happened in Old Castile and there was no need to worry about it,' finds in this answer the summary of the contemporary Spanish situation and the key to many things that had appeared incomprehensible when seen from France.

But it is not so easy to interpret the localist spirit. The Spaniard who visits the great cities of America is astonished to find that the Spanish colony have built a magnificent Club, be it Galician, Asturian, Riojan or Catalan, but not one all-including Spanish Club. It is easy to draw the conclusion that the higher concept of one Spain is lacking, but in reality what has happened is that those Spanish emigrants do not feel foreign in the New Spain which they inhabit, nor do they feel inclined to evoke their fatherland, and so they find that the most immediate and intimate method of expressing their love for old Spain is to concentrate all their patriotism on their particular locality. Nevertheless love for one's homeland which is bound up with the unfading recollections of infancy remains a mean and poor thing if experience and the generous ideas of youth do not enlarge it so as to include the Fatherland itself; just as patriotism degenerates and becomes a limitation to man's spirit if his greater maturity does not lead him to share it with the universal fatherland, namely with every other country from which he receives some beneficial inspiration towards a higher life, and it cannot be denied that the Spaniard allows his local patriotism to prevail excessively. The fact of having been born in the same province creates among Spaniards a sense of companionship and an obligation to help one another which is as great as or even greater than that among relatives, and this causes them to become rigidly exclusive in their dealings with others.

This local particularism, as Théophile Gautier said, explains

CENTRALIZATION AND REGIONALISM   179

a good part of Spanish history, and there are authors like Martin
Hume, in his History of the Spanish People, who continually
insist upon this characteristic, both in its causes and in its effects.
According to Hume, regionalism is due to ethnological variety
which is maintained by the mountainous nature of the country.
Spain in fact is, owing to its geography, a country of divisions, for
its enormous mountain barriers separate one province from
another. In this soil the basis is represented by the Iberians,
brothers of the Berbers, two peoples equally individualistic.
Afterwards came the Celts, Afro-Semites, Carthaginians, Greeks,
Romans, French, Goths, and the mixed hordes of Islam, leaving
relics of population hidden away in the countless valleys of the
Peninsula. Adopting the same geographical method Herculano
explained the formation of the mediaeval kingdoms as due to the
difficulty of communication across the high mountains, but not
even the lofty mountains have as much decisive power to isolate
as is attributed to them, nor in Spain do they limit the regions
which were most influenced by the spirit of autonomy. The great
mountains that run from north to south of Catalonia are very
much towards the east of the country but not on the boundary
with Aragon; the hundred tunnels of the northern railway do not
separate Castile from León, but León from Asturias; the Portuguese frontier, too, is not decided by mountain ranges. And with
regard to the racial question, apart from the fact that the so-
called brotherhood of Iberians and Berbers is untenable in view
of the radical differences of language existing between one and
the other, and the similar divergence of abilities, the dissimilarity
of races in the Peninsula is not perceptibly greater than that
existing, for instance, in France. The greater localism of Spain
does not depend upon a multitude of ethnico-geographical reasons, but on the contrary, on a uniform psychological condition;
it depends upon the original exclusive character of the Iberians,
already noted by the authors of antiquity long before there came
to the Peninsula even the half of the races enumerated by Hume
as causing the dispersive tendencies. The fact that the ethnico-
geographical characteristics of the Peninsula do not imply any
special tendency towards splitting up into fragments is shown by
the variety of dialects in Spain which is much less than that of
France or Italy.

Also it is incorrect to hold that local sentiment was so strong and deep-seated that it was able to prevent the creation of all national Spanish feeling up to recent times. It is commonly held that this idea of one Spain only began to grow up in modern times, an opinion which apparently derives from the widely-read prologue which Lafuente wrote for his History. When speaking of the title chosen by the successors of the Catholic monarchs, he writes: 'King of Spain, a term long-wished for but one which we were not able to pronounce in all the centuries of history we have traversed up to this point'. Lafuente speaks only of the royal title, but not even in this limited sense is his observation correct, for he forgets that the title *Hispaniae rex* was used in the eleventh and twelfth centuries not only within the Peninsula, but outside, even by the great international power of those days, the Roman Curia.

THE CONCEPT OF SPAIN IN ANTIQUITY

In the first century B.C. Strabo made observations concerning Spanish individualism similar to those made by modern writers. He noted that the Iberians possessed greater local pride than the Greeks and this prevented them from uniting together in a powerful confederation. If they had been able to link together their forces, the greater part of Iberia would not have been subdued by Carthaginians, Celts and Romans. Thus Strabo, while noting the weakness of collective spirit in the Iberians, yet recognizes its existence as a factor in assuring the independence of the Iberian community. Livy on his side considers *Hispania* as an entity and speaks frequently of the *Hispani* in general, without deeming it necessary to state whether they come from this or that tribe. Later Florus, an African historian who lived at Tarragona, uses the very expressive phrase *Hispania universa* to describe a human collectivity and like Strabo blames Spain for not recognizing its own strength until it had been conquered by Rome after a struggle lasting 200 years. He thus implies a common interest neglected, a nation with an imperfect sense of nationality.

Within the Roman administrative organization Spain, though divided into various provinces, was always considered as a higher entity uniting the provincial divisions. And under the splendour of the Empire, when for the first time we can observe the full cultural development of Romanized Spain, we note that it forms a unity similar in its distribution of forces and values to what modern Spain became at another Imperial moment, namely in the time of its greatest unity during the golden ages of its literature. So too in antiquity the central part of the country, as afterwards Castile, represented the cohesive nucleus, *Celtiberia robur Hispaniae*. Then, too, this Celtiberian centre, together with Baetica, produced all the great representative men in letters and in politics, just as in the sixteenth and seventeenth centuries the greatest number of them came from Aragon, the two Castiles and Andalusia. The similarity between the 'intellectual map' (as Feijóo would say) of Roman Spain and Austrian Spain is surprising: and such similarity between the two most brilliant moments of unified Spain shows that this spiritual unity was governed by certain organic principles, by certain vital energies which endured in action and in strength.

Roman Spain, shortly before the dissolution of the Empire, appeared already with a precise national significance in the first Universal History composed by a Christian, that of Paulus Orosius.[1] This Galician disciple of Saint Augustine possessed to a special degree the sense of patriotism. Spain for him was still a province of the Empire within which Divine Providence had unified the world, but, in spite of this, the Province rises proudly in opposition to the City, affirming an historical destiny of its own, within the Empire, and claiming for the wars it had waged against Rome greater accord with the eternal laws of justice than that shown by the conquering metropolis. Orosius pointed to the Goths in Spain as the people ready to play a part which would restore the providential unity of the Christian world.

GOTHIC UNITY AND ITS DESTRUCTION

Immediately after Orosius, the Roman Empire of the west was dismembered into various Germanic Kingdoms. An important factor in the strengthening of the weakening unity of the Iberian people was the fact that at the time of the invasions the

---

[1] Paulo Orosio, native of Bracara, to-day Braga, travelled to Africa and Palestine, visited S. Augustine at Hippo in 414 and 416 and S. Jerome in Bethlehem in 415. He wrote the first universal history of Christianity. His work *Historiarum adversus paganos libri septem* was written in the years 416–417.

last emperors handed over the pacification of Spain to the Visigoths, who were the most Romanized of the Germans, entirely
convinced that the Roman idea of the State as the arbiter of good
and justice for the whole community was one that was superior to
the dominant particularism of the rest of the barbarian governments. Those Goths, although they were Arians and consequently adverse to the Catholicism of the Hispano-Romans, yet
unified politically the entire peninsula, and some years later
unified it spiritually by becoming converted to Catholicism. The
strength of national sentiment which the Gothic unification
aroused even in the period of the heterodox monarchs may be
seen in the case of the rebellion of Saint Hermenegildo against his
Arian father which was censured even by the Catholic clergy
that had to suffer persecution at the hands of the public authorities. This national sentiment achieves enthusiastic literary
expression in the writings of Saint Isidore: over all the wide
world, from its oriental boundaries in India to the extreme west,
holy Mother Spain is the fairest and happiest land, incomparable
in its natural riches, the fatherland of famous princes. After a
first union with the conquering fortress of Romulus, she has now
celebrated a new betrothal with the glorious and flourishing
nation of the Goths.

The idea of a united Roman-Gothic Spain which was so
nobly portrayed by Orosius, and so eloquently exalted by Saint
Isidore, never ceased to be present to the spirits of men during the
following centuries, for both those authors were widely read all
through the Middle Ages. Nevertheless, this idea did become
obscured. After the prosperous period of Leovigildo[1] and Saint
Isidore, the Gothic Kingdom declined into an anarchical contest
between different parties, and the party struggle obscured
national sentiment. One of the parties called to its help the Moslems and when these turned from allies to invaders all possibility
of cohesion and unity in the face of national danger faded away.
The result was chaos and every man for himself. The sons of
Vitiza[2] contented themselves with retaining possession of their
3,000 patrimonial estates under a guarantee from the invaders;

[1] Leovigildo reigned between 573–586 and brought the Gothic kingdom to its
highest power and political unity. He was the last Arian king. In 579–584 his,
eldest son Hermenegildo, on being converted to Catholicism, rebelled against him,
but was defeated and killed in prison, 585.
[2] Penultimate Gothic king of Spain, 702–708.

Teodomir secured another special pact at Orihuela; various principal lords cleverly managed to preserve their property, their religion and their laws and paid no attention to the rest of the country. As late as in the eleventh century an Aragonese lord boasted that he as well as his ancestors had lived independent of the caliphs of Córdoba and the Kings of Aragon, *quia libertas nostra antiqua est*. When Spain was faced with ruin, these powerful barons, saturated with individualism, had no other thought in life but to preserve unimpaired their utmost freedom. The characteristic Iberian unsociability had broken out everywhere like a plague, which, when strength diminishes, invades the whole body. One centre of resistance organized itself to carry on the combat, namely Asturias, but it fought on weakly in isolation. Nobody was interested in the plight of his neighbour. The Mozarab in Toledo who, full of sorrow, wrote an extensive chronicle for the year 754 does not say a word about Pelayo or Alfonso I; perhaps he did not even know about them or he did not consider their audacious wars and raids of importance.

THE MEDIAEVAL KINGDOMS

Thus began a long period of disintegration, truly a long one, because the formation of many new states on the ruins of the Visigothic Kingdom was favoured by the tendency to disintegration brought by the feudal epoch to all Europe. We should note, however, that Iberian individualism did not organize itself within the régime of vassalage which was the basis of feudalism, but in the form of independent kingdoms. By the side of the primitive Asturian-Neogothic kingdom there rose the kingdom of Pamplona in 905, the kingdoms of Castile and Aragon in 1035 and that of Portugal in 1143. The ancient Astur-Leonese kingdom possessed over the others a vague, though significant imperial superiority, a weak Spanish substitute for the equally weak bond of vassalage which linked up the European feudal system.

It has been pointed out as a great misfortune for Spain that it never had feudalism, that is to say, a strong, enterprising nobility. But if it did not have a number of feudal states, it had a variety of kingdoms which were able in a freer way to develop their personality and spread their influence far and wide through the Mediterranean, through Africa and the Atlantic, as an apprenticeship and trial for the greatness achieved when those kingdoms became reunited in the sixteenth century. There were no powerful barons, but there were a number of kings at the same time, who directed in rivalry enterprises of a kind that no feudal duke could ever have dreamt of. The division into kingdoms retarded the main enterprise, the Reconquest, but in exchange it caused the various expansive actions outside the Peninsula. Among the Islamized Spaniards the Taifa Kingdoms of the eleventh to the thirteenth centuries show development similar to that of the five Christian Kingdoms. Just as the latter were in opposition to European feudalism, so the Taifa kings, even to a greater degree, fought against the spirit of Islam, both by their tributary system and by their regarding the kingdom as their personal property to be divided among their heirs, as did the Christians of the north. Thus Spain, as always, was in disagreement with the two worlds that crossed one another's path on her soil. At the fall of the Caliphate of Córdoba the Islamized Iberianism caused the creation of more than twenty little kingdoms, which later were reduced to a smaller number owing to successive reincorporations. In vain the great African empires of the Almorávides and the Almóhades crossed in turn the Straits and reimposed Islam in El Andalús and re-established political unity there. As soon as the African invasions lost their impetus, then inevitably the Taifa kingdoms rose again.

And when we follow the parallel between Christian and Islamic disintegration we must likewise admit as regards the Taifa kingdoms a certain advantage, while recognizing the great weakness which the division of territory brought to Moslem power. Each petty king wished to surpass his neighbour by reason of the plentiful library which he had managed to gather together, or the number of distinguished poets and men of science he had been able to attract to his court. Thanks to this many-sided impulse Spanish Islam produced a brilliant cultural display before its extinction. Shortly before Jaime I and Saint Ferdinand destroyed these Moorish seigniories, the benefits of this disintegration were celebrated in the 'Eulogy of Spanish Islam' which was written by El Secundi[1] about 1200 in praise of the magnificence

---

[1] El Secundi, Andalusian-Arab, man of letters, died in 1231. He was called Secundi from his birthplace Secunda, a small Roman village situated opposite Córdoba on the left bank of the Guadalquivir.

of the ancient petty kingdoms of Seville, Almería, Toledo, Valencia and Denia. 'All the kings of the Taifas,' he says, 'rivalled one another in their longing for culture: every day was for them a feast and they gathered round them all branches of knowledge.' And this cultural rivalry was of transcendental importance, for it was by absorbing and utilizing the science created by these Moorish kingdoms for centuries that Alfonso X merited the epithet of 'the Learned' in Western Christendom.

THE IDEA OF SPAIN IN THE MIDDLE AGES

But the destruction of the Gothic kingdom, followed by the long-drawn out period of disintegration, did not blot out of men's minds the idea of unity, but only obscured it. It banished the idea from political life, but not from men's aspirations. For the mediaeval kingdoms never broke Gothic unity in an arbitrary manner but tried to patch it up and save it from destruction. They came into being naturally and spontaneously as guerrilla fighters of Iberian individualism, who began the struggle against the Islam colossus when it was at its zenith of power. These kingdoms served no local patriotism. Localism has as its chief basis a linguistic difference, but none of those kingdoms, except that of Portugal, founded its power upon a language basis. León, Castilla, Navarra and Aragon were all bilingual. All sprang into being as a first step towards reintegration, the only one possible in view of the superior power of the Moslem. For this reason the long existence of these kingdoms did not blot out the idea of Hispanic unity which remained stronger than the temporary division.

Very soon after the Moslem invasion, the Asturian kings proclaimed themselves kinsmen and heirs to the Gothic kings. In 883 Alfonso III, when writing the first history of the small kingdom of Oviedo, calls it the History of the Goths, proclaiming by this title the uninterrupted continuity of the Gothic monarchy and declaring expressly that the small kingdom of Pelayo was the salvation of Spain, *salus Hispaniae*, for it would not cease to fight 'day and night until divine predestination decreed the total expulsion of the Saracens'. It is noteworthy that the Kingdom of Asturias, in spite of its insignificant size, insisted that the soil of Spain should not be divided among the Christians of old and the

N

Moorish invaders, though this seemed the likely course, considering the overwhelming power of the Caliphates of Damascus and Córdoba; and in view of the relative strengths of the two antagonists, such an enterprise did actually entail many centuries of struggle. Asturias would not be contented with less than the firm determination that Islam should not remain installed in Spain in perpetuity. Thus the Moslem invasion, instead of achieving its purpose whereby the small Christian territories of the north, feeling themselves estranged from the rest of Spain which was solidly Islamized, would abandon the old concept of Saint Isidore, actually strengthened that concept by inspiring the northern kingdoms with a religious ideal as well as with the patriotic resolve to recover the national territory. This political idea by the very fact that it was of immense difficulty and of slow achievement, was a deeply formative one, and influenced men through centuries. The fact that this idea of total reconquest was conceived and expressed as an Hispanic idea shows that there was a very deeply-rooted national feeling in the country. No similar idea was conceived or attempted by any of the other provinces of the ancient Roman Empire in the west or the west which had fallen as a prey to the Moslems; with the exception of Spain not one of them reacted, when Islam began the gigantic struggle against Christendom for the domination of the world.

Asturias thus served as initiator and teacher in this ideal of resistance and total restoration, which, as centuries passed, became less disproportionate and unattainable. The various kingdoms which rose later all proclaimed the same resolve which implied unity of origin and destiny. All recognized in the total re-conquest a *united Hispanic enterprise*, and by means of special treaties they fixed the districts which each one of them had to conquer, or else they all made alliances in order to beat back fresh invasions from Africa, even though those invasions only threatened one of the kingdoms, Castile. Secondly, the various kingdoms also recognized up to the twelfth century a certain *political unity* as the heirs to the Asturian Gothic kings whereby the kings of León took the title of Emperor, or to be more explicit, Emperor of all Spain, *Imperator totius Hispaniae*, and as such they were recognized by the King of Navarre, the King of Aragon, the Count of Barcelona and by many of the Taifa kings. The kings of Navarre

and Aragon, Sancho Ramírez and Pedro I, rushed to defend
the imperial throne of Toledo when Alfonso VI was attacked
by the Almorávides. Then, too, the most popular of heroes,
the one celebrated in heroic poetry, gave new strength to the
neo-Gothic idea of unity, for in the moment of trial when the
war effort of the 'Emperor of all Spain' gave way before the
invasion of the Almorávides, Roderick de Vivar proposed by his
unaided efforts to restore the whole of the Gothic kingdom which
had been destroyed about four centuries before. The restoration
was longed for by all, and it was said: 'If a Roderick it was who
lost Spain, another Roderick will restore it.' This threat, according to Ben Bassam, filled the Moslems with dread, for the total
liberation of Spain was no longer a fantastic dream of Spanish
faith as it had been two centuries before for the Asturian people.
Besides, as a third unifying element, all the kingdoms felt themselves included within a kind of *cultural unity* based upon a long
political and religious tradition common to all Roman and
Gothic Spain. All, for instance, at the beginning, were ruled
according to the Visigothic code, and it was only in the eleventh
century that this was supplanted by laws of local custom amongst
which we discover likewise close relationships and reciprocal
influences between one kingdom and another. Finally, all the
kingdoms became every day more closely associated and reached
a *dynastic unity*, for from the eleventh century onwards their kings
descended from a common stock owing to the frequent matri-
monial alliances. And these dynastic relationships, in addition to
implying close intimacy in the government of the various kingdoms, were an inspiration to still closer union. The attempt to
link Castile and Aragon through the disastrous marriage of
Alfonso the Battler[1] was followed by the effective union of Aragon
and Barcelona, and later by that of Castile and León, both the
result of marriages. Later the 'Compromise of Caspe' meant a

---

[1] Alfonso the Battler, King of Aragon (1104–1134), married the Queen of Castile,
Urraca, in 1109; but owing to quarrels between the two the marriage did not result
in the political union of Castile and Aragon. The union of Aragon and Barcelona
was effected by the marriage of Petronila with Ramon Berenguer IV in 1137. The
kingdoms of Castile and León united in the person of Ferdinand III the Saint who
inherited both kingdoms owing to the marriage of his mother, Berenguela of
Castile, with the King of León, Alfonso IX, in 1197. The Compromise of Caspe in
1412 enthroned in Aragon the Castilian dynasty. The marriage of Ferdinand and
Isabel brought about the unity of Aragon and Castile in 1474.

strengthening of dynastic unity. It was through marriage also that the union of Castile and Aragon took place, and the desire for complete unification was rounded off by the various Portuguese marriages which the Catholic monarchs arranged with so great insistence though with such unfortunate results.

The proposal to recover all the soil of the fatherland, which never ceased to appeal to the mass of the people, was felt to have been accomplished in the thirteenth century, and both the people and the kings considered the great work terminated, and were convinced that it had been the united enterprise of all Spain. Among Galician poets and Castilian chroniclers we find a very expressive popular phrase: 'Ferdinand III and Alfonso X won Spain from sea to sea', that is to say from the sea of Asturias to the sea of Seville and Carthagena. Simultaneously James I completed the part of the reconquest that had been entrusted to Aragon, and after this was done, on the occasion of a rising of Moors in Murcia, he rushed to the help of Alfonso X, proclaiming that he and his Catalans wished to win the high renown of *saving Spain*, as the king himself declares in his own chronicle. The total liberation of the fatherland was carried out as a task in common by all the Spaniards.

With the completion of the Reconquest coincides the renaissance of historical studies on Spain, considered as a unity in spite of its division into various kingdoms. In this sense were written the works of the Bishop of Tuy,[1] 'El Tudense', who was a Leonese, and the Archbishop of Toledo, 'El Toledano', who was a Castilianized son of Navarre. Both wrote in the reign of Ferdinand III. The Archbishop of Toledo, Jiménez de Rada, owing to his far greater erudition and his gifts of clarity and style, was more widely read and had greater influence. His work *'De Rebus Hispaniae'* begins by taking as the foundation of Spain's population the government of Tubal and Hercules. It follows the long centuries of unity in Romano-Gothic times and ends with a eulogy of Spain imitating that by Saint Isidore, but followed by what is an important innovation, namely a poetic lament for the destruction of Spain, in which it is announced that its restoration

---

[1] The History of Lucas, Bishop of Tuy, was finished in 1236. The history *De Rebus Hispaniae* was finished by the Archbishop of Toledo, Jiménez de Rada, in 1243 and the *Estoria de España*, begun by Alfonso X, was finished in the reign of his son, Sancho IV in 1289.

has begun in Asturias and has been continued by the other king-doms. The dynastic unity of those kingdoms is the basic principle of the second part of the work in which the nucleus is the kingdom of León-Castile.

Within these general lines Alfonso X created his great '*Estoria de España*', a more extensive work than that of El Tole-dano and richer in narrative. In the prologue he announces as the main theme of his work *the Spaniards* and with a laconic phrase (which is an improvement on the title '*De Rebus Hispaniae*') he says that he is going to relate *El fecho de España* (the Emprise of Spain) and the harm that came to her through being split up into kingdoms (*por partir los regnos*) for it retarded the task of win-ning back what had been seized by the Moors. But he then adds, '*la ayuntó Dios*', that is to say, God linked together the chief king-doms. He then goes on to relate how now all the land from the 'sea of Santander to that of Cadiz' has been won, and he ends by relating how Saint Ferdinand left all Spain conquered at his death, and Granada a tributary kingdom which wept for him as its lord and protector. In this way the History culminates in the idea that the Reconquest has been completed. This was virtually the case, though this vassalage of Granada, which satisfied Saint Ferdinand at his death, became for his successors an opiate dulling the concept of their duty, which was to combat Islam. This neglect brought on them the censure of the Aragonese King James II. Finally, we must distinguish above all, in this concep-tion of history, the fact that the division into separate kingdoms was looked upon as a temporary evil which God would remedy. This is an essential political thought necessary to explain the con-stant tendency towards unification which goes on peacefully through all the later Middle Ages. And this condemnation of separatism and sub-division as being abnormal and harmful was not held by historians and statesmen alone, but by the mass of the people. The 'jongleurs' in their epic songs declaimed against the partition of the kingdoms made by Ferdinand I, saying that the Goths of old made a pact among themselves that never should the Empire of Spain be divided, but that it should all be under one lord. This minstrel poem was of such weight and authority that we find it written in prose in the '*Estoria de España*' itself. Thus in opposition to sporadic localism, the concept of Spanish unity,

which was expressed for the first time in the ancient chronicle of
Alfonso III, reaches its perfection and highest divulgation in the
Latin pages of El Toledano and in the Spanish prose of Alfonso
X. These two works served as a guide to all subsequent historians
whether from Castile or from Aragon, Navarre or Portugal, and
this was the constant reading matter of scholars and masses for
five centuries. In spiritual accord with them was every man who
felt the inspiration of the past as a spur to the present.

POLITICAL UNITY

The disintegrating period in which five kingdoms were
formed finishes with the last partition by inheritance which
occurred in 1157. The attempt by Alfonso X to form a kingdom
apart with Jaén, destined for the Infante Alfonso de la Cerda,
was a temporary expedient which failed as soon as it was made.
On the other hand the unifying impulse which had been in oper-
ation since the marriage of Ferdinand I and from the wars of
Sancho II and the Cid continually asserts itself until final unity
is achieved by the Catholic monarchs. The unity which then
took place was not an aspiration limited to the upper spheres of
the government; it was, we insist, entirely popular. The Aragonese marriage of Isabel in opposition to a foreign marriage was a
natural desire of the whole people, and even the children sang of
it in their games, as the Parish Priest of Los Palacios, Andrés
Bernáldez, tells us.

When political unity was achieved, an attempt was made to
secure greater internal unity to the advantage of the central
government. Castile was the first, under Charles V, to succumb
in its attempt to impose the authority of the Cortes on the King;
Aragon followed suit, defending the function of its 'Justiciar'
against Philip II. The Renaissance had given to the monarchy a
turn which was incompatible with the severe limitations of the
Middle Ages. Theorists and ministers continued to combat these
traditional limitations in the reigns of Philip III and his son. The
Count-Duke Olivares proposed to Philip IV, as the most effective
means of making himself a true king of Spain, to reduce the
various kingdoms 'to the same style and laws as Castile so that
there might be no difference'. But this extremist policy was no
longer possible owing to the great decline of the very royalty in

whose name it was proposed to unify the various kingdoms, and those apathetic kings were unable to obtain any privileges comparable to those secured by the early Austrian monarchs. On the contrary, local feeling arose as in all periods of great depression. The general decline, the disappearance of the spirit and the ancient virtue which had created the empire, led to very grave secessionist movements all over the country, such as the emancipation of Portugal and the rebellion of Catalonia in addition to two big risings, chaotic affairs but which showed how wide in extent was the evil, that of the Duke of Medinasidonia who was suspected of plotting with Portugal to raise the standard of revolt in Andalusia, relying on the general discontent in that province (1641), and years afterwards a similar attempt by the Duke of Hijar in Aragon, whose adherents, according to Philip IV, seemed to be 'rather madmen than traitors' (1648). In so far as the change of dynasty, at the opening of the eighteenth century, checked the extreme national weakness and brought with it an increase of vitality, the unitary principle was strengthened both in government action and in the ideological sphere.

LOCAL PRIVILEGES
FUEROS, FEUDALISM AND CANTONALISM

The spirit of localism breaks out afresh as an element in the first Carlist war. In this case it is necessary to read the comments of a Catalan writer, Balmes, who in 1843–1847 repeatedly contradicted the opinion which was widely held, especially abroad, that Spain was under the domination of a provincialist spirit, a 'federal spirit', which was opposed to the centralist administration imposed by the monarchy. This is inaccurate, said Balmes: the Spanish people does not cherish federal tendencies opposed to the 'total monarchy' which has been governing and unifying them for three centuries. A proof of this is that all the provinces rose up against Napoleon uttering the cry of 'long live the king' with one accord, spontaneously, without any previous agreement. For this reason it is naïve to believe that the Carlist war was fought in the name of the ancient 'fueros' or charters, for neither the Basques, nor the Catalans, nor the Valencians, nor the Aragonese of to-day know what they signified. Apart from this, the provincialist or federalist movement is upheld and encouraged by some foreign countries that are interested in keeping Spain weak. Starting from these arguments of Balmes we must note that the centrifugal force prevalent in the middle of the nineteenth century cannot claim a traditional link with that which inspired the defenders of Lanuza.[1] It was something fresh and spontaneous that had sprung up as a consequence of the confusion and weakness, both moral and material, which had come upon the country; but there was no doubt that the Carlist monarchy was for unification but not uniformity. The claim for charter rights is an accessory, a parasite on the political and religious principles which the Carlists upheld and which were professed with equal passion by Carlists from regions where there was never any question of demanding special charter privileges. This new tendency, more or less centrifugal, though beaten back when it first appeared, yet reappears at every moment of great national weakness. It is also helped by a far off echo of romantic idealism, springing from the desire of each region that its own special genius should assert and express itself freely and naturally without the interference of the central state. It was in this sense, and as a spokesman for the widest liberalism in politics, that Pí y Margall theorized on the federal principle. Yet, after the revolution of 1868, when the second Carlist war broke out in the north and the Republic was proclaimed, Pí y Margall[2] as president proved how complete was the failure of the federal idea, for he himself had to struggle against the degeneration of that idea into the anarchical cantonalism which broke out in the south of the Peninsula.

NATIONALISM

The reappearance of federalist ideas which has taken place in contemporary times was due to the confusion which arose in Spain after the disaster of 1898. We may add to this an important economic cause, namely, the loss of the colonies which disturbed the commerce of Catalonia and caused serious hardship to that

---

[1] Juan de Lanuza, Chief Justiciar of Aragon, who, basing himself upon the *fueros* or traditional laws and customs of Aragon, tried to resist with arms the decisions of Philip II. He was beheaded in Saragossa on 20 December 1591.

[2] Author of *El principio federativo* (1872) and of *Las Nacionalidades* (1876). He was president of the Federal Republic in 1873 when Malaga, Seville, Cadiz, Carthagena and Valencia rebelled and declared themselves independent cantons.

region. Also the foreign influence to which Balmes referred came to aid the Iberian particularist spirit: the 'small nation politics' which is practised by the big nations for their own benefit; the doctrine of self-determination of countries which has progressed since the first world war.

Catalan federalism among the extremists takes the form of nationalism, and artificially exaggerates the differences which represent the Catalan people, through the course of centuries, as completely and permanently separated from the rest of the Spanish peoples. In order to prove this, History had to be treated from a national standpoint, as was done with great learning by Rovira Virgili[1] among others. But this historical method meets with many difficulties: one has to sever carefully all the strongest ties that link Catalan history and the general history of Spain, and when this is impossible, it is necessary to show how unjust and harmful the ties were. History has to be de-Castilianized. Then we find that the wrongs done to Catalonia do not spring from Philip V or Philip IV but go back to earlier centuries when the dynastic unity of the peninsular kingdoms was strengthened. Thus the Compromise of Caspe, the most famous and exemplary political event of the fifteenth century, is condemned, as though those saintly and learned jurists, who studied and settled the question of succession, were a band of iniquitous judges. Other nationalists go three centuries further back and head the list of historical injustices against Catalonia with Count Raymond Berenguer IV, saying that when he married the Aragonese child-queen he made too many concessions, for he ought to have taken the title of King of Catalonia and Aragon. But those who make this reproach forget one difficulty, namely, that Catalonia then had no clear existence, even in name, for Catalans and Catalonia do not appear in official documents until thirty or forty years later. They also forget that taking the title of king did not depend then, nor afterwards, upon personal whim. Nevertheless, Raymond Berenguer, ignorant of the fact that he would displease the nationalists of the twentieth century, went even further than refusing to call himself king; he actually acknowledged himself to be a vassal of the Emperor of Toledo, Alfonso VII. This fact was published by Zurita, always punctili-

---

[1] *Historia Nacional de Catalunya*, six volumes, 1922–1931.

ous as an historian, but is omitted by the nationalist Catalan historians, who when they have to speak of the Emperor and the Count-Prince of Aragon use anachronisms and bombastic terminology. They speak of *els dos sobirans* (the two sovereigns), he of the 'Castilian State' and he of the 'Catalan-Aragonese State', and they call 'Catalan-Aragonese Confederation' what was always simply called Kingdom of Aragon. But leaving aside questions of nomenclature, we must not think that the history of Catalonia has been a huge mistake for the past eight centuries, but that the nationalists have written it mistakenly for the past forty years. It is they who misunderstand Catalonia, not Raymond Berenguer IV, nor the signers of the Compromise of Caspe. It is the separatists who fight against History by insisting on living alone, *Nosaltres sols*, when Catalonia never wished to live alone, but always united in a bilingual community with Aragon or with Castile.

THE LINGUISTIC QUESTION

In modern days, in the secessionist movements the greatest importance is given to diversity of language. While culture moves every day nearer to universal uniformity, greater value is given to the individual characteristics of many minor cultures based upon languages, whose historical development may be said to be incomplete, in comparison to the great cultural languages. The lively scientific and literary interest awakened in modern days in languages that were less studied before has acted as a support to the political interest taken in 'small nations'. But those whose interest is political do not appreciate how different is the part played by the great dominating languages to that played by those that have less substance, owing to the lack of so intense or original a culture or so continuous and unbroken a development. Flemish, Esthonian, Irish, Catalan come to represent political aspirations, and languages such as Basque which never were expressions of culture make desperate attempts to be so and achieve self-sufficiency. In short, there is a tendency to reduce the great cultural languages to the same historic level as the small ones, or even those which had no previous cultural existence.

In this connection we should note with regard to Spain that its superabundant Iberian individualism did not produce greater diversity of languages nor did this diversity operate in determining the historical disintegration which we have to record. If we take as a point of comparison a country so unified as France, we find far greater linguistic variety in each one of the regions, whether Breton, Basque, Gascon, Languedoc, Catalan, Franco-Provençal, French, Picard, as compared with Spanish Basque, Catalan, Gallego-Portuguese, Asturian, Leonese, Castilian and Upper-Aragonese. Abundant local variants comparable in number to those which are found all over the country in France and Italy can only be discovered in Asturias, Upper-Aragon, and in North Catalonia. So that Spain for all its individualistic traits is exceptional in being of great linguistic uniformity: it is in fact the Romanic country in which the diversity of dialects is least in relation to the extent of its territory.

There was one great unifying movement, namely the expansion of the Reconquest from north to south, which influenced both the linguistic elements and the general character of the people in a way that contradicts the theory of the disassociation caused by mountains and valleys. It all confirms the view that the causes of localism are not ethnological, psychological or linguistic differences, but rather the reverse, namely the uniformity of character, which is universally individualistic, in fact the Iberianism which Strabo describes as finding a difficulty in the very notion of solidarity.

Secondly, the differences of language had no influence on the process of subdivision which took place in the Middle Ages when this obeyed truly historical necessities. Language did not determine the formation of the kingdoms and counties in those days, and it was not taken into account. The Asturo-Leonese Kingdom was from the eighth century onwards a bilingual kingdom, for Galicia, which had no independent life, was always linked to it, and within this kingdom was established a series of administrative regions which were always bilingual likewise: namely, Asturias, El Bierzo, Sanabria. The three spoke Galician in their western and Leonese in their eastern divisions. The Kingdom of Navarre, from its beginning in the tenth century, used indifferently two spoken languages, Basque, and the Navarre dialect, which is akin to Castilian. For their written language only Latin and the Romance dialect were used, for Basque did not begin to be written at all until the sixteenth century. The capital, Pamplona, has spoken Castilian from mediaeval times. Even Castile itself was, from its origins, in the tenth century, a bilingual county or kingdom, for incorporated in its territory were both Alava and Biscay, already bilingual. Throughout practically all Alava, and the western half of Biscay up to the City of Bilbao itself and including it, the language spoken from time immemorial has been Castilian. The same may be said of the Kingdom of Aragon; from its beginning in the eleventh century it was bilingual owing to its county of Ribagorza, in whose eastern half Catalan is spoken, and the bilingualism of the kingdom asserted itself when in the twelfth century it was united to the great county of Barcelona. The county from that time onwards ceased to lead an isolated life and formed a single state with Aragon. As Rovira Virgili shows, the court or curia of the single monarch was a mixture of Aragonese and Catalan nobles, and the Cortes of the Kingdom was a mixed body frequently. The Kingdom of Valencia, finally, from its reconquest in the thirteenth century was bilingual and spoke both Catalan and Aragonese. Thus, during the many centuries when the centrifugal force of localism was on the increase, owing to the need for consolidating national life, we find bilingualism extending all over the country.

Consequently bilingualism, which has increased its effects owing to constant life in common, is to-day more intimate and more penetrating a force than in the Middle Ages. Castilian, as the language of authority, after having assimilated both the Leonese and Aragonese dialects, struck ever deeper roots as a cultural language in Catalan, Galician and Basque territory. Its greater activity as a literary medium of expression attracted not only the Basques, who always kept it as their written language, but also the others, for the literary use of Galician had practically ceased from the fifteenth century, and Catalan had noticeably diminished from the sixteenth century until in the nineteenth century the Romantic movement caused a rebirth of local cultures. Milá y Fontanals[1] in a lecture to the University of Barcelona reminded his audience of the enthusiasm for Calderón and

---

[1] Milá y Fontanals (1818–1884), Professor in the University of Barcelona, was the historian of Catalan as well as Castilian culture during the nineteenth century. One of the greatest authorities on mediaeval Castilian and Catalan literature.

the classical Spanish theatre shown in Catalonia, and he described how the plays were performed in cities and towns, and the sonorous, high-sounding verses were repeated with majestic emphasis by simple workmen. He concluded as follows: 'The Castilian language has been for us the language of a brother who has sat at our hearth and whose dreams we have mingled with our own.' And literary prestige makes itself felt not only in the exclusively learned productions of art, but also in the popular forms of wider appeal such as the traditional ballads so well known all through Catalonia and Galicia, either in Castilian versions sprinkled with Catalanisms or Galleguisms or else in Catalan and Galician versions full of Castilianisms. All this goes to prove how deep is the influence that cultural hegemony has over all social levels, over both learned and illiterate. The *Romancero*, which owes its beauty to its Castilian element as well as to its Catalan or Galician variants, comes to be a kind of everlasting plebiscite on behalf of the natural hispanic need for that intimate bilingualism which the autonomists reject as though it had been imposed by the arbitrary and intolerable tyranny of a central authority. This plebiscite of the *Romancero* is so alien to any centralism that the voting began from the early years of the fifteenth century at least, that is to say, long before the time when, through the union of Aragon and Castile, the latter could possibly have exercised any political pressure on Catalonia. Already about 1420 the traditional Castilian ballad, mixed with other Catalan poetical compositions, figured among the delightful literary curiosities which a Mallorcan student in Italy used to quote in order to evoke his distant Spanish fatherland. The nationalist, who is in revolt against these great facts of history, attempts to shake off the dull weight of history and subject his native tongue to a violent de-Castilianizing treatment. He would suppress the natural and universal linguistic phenomenon of borrowings and loans between two adjacent languages, mutual loans, though the less vigorous of the two is the greater debtor. Sometimes the nationalists, wishing to avoid a commonplace Castilian term of everyday usage, would select an uncommon expression which occasionally turned out to be itself a Castilianism in disguise. On other occasions they would invent a string of undigested neologisms. The whole plan was to pad out artificially

the 'differentiating facts', do violence to nature, use the language
as an instrument of political spite when it should be one of
fraternal mutual comprehension, and poison the natural love
that one has for the maternal tongue by inoculating the virus of
envy. And the trouble is that the exaggerations of nationalism
are often answered by the exaggeration of the defenders of
centralization who even go as far as to forbid the reasonable and
necessary use of the local language.

To sum up, the historical development of local languages and
independent kingdoms in the past does not warrant us in believing that a difference of language is a natural cause of autonomy,
nor that the intimate and popular bilingualism which has been
practised by long tradition should be rejected as something
imposed by the central power.

A TEMPORARY SUCCESS OF NATIONALISM

Nevertheless the ideas of the nationalists based on linguistics
came to full fruition during the Second Republic. First of all
approval was given to the Catalan Statute; then to the Basque
Statute; and later the Galician Statute was to follow. There was a
veritable craze for disintegration and a wish to build up a new
structure for Spain, as if one were to break a jar against the wall
in order to make a number of vessels with the potsherds. No
anomaly of history was too far-fetched in order to separate what
the centuries had always recognized as united. The Basques of
the three Basque provinces, for example, even separated from
their neighbours the Basques of Navarre, and wished to live alone
though they had always lived in brotherly union with Castile.
They invoked the claims of a language and a culture of their own.
But, we may ask ourselves, what is Basque culture if not insepar-
ably linked to Castilian for the glory of both? Basque did not
begin to be written until the sixteenth century, and then only in
exceedingly limited matters. If Saint Ignatius had not thought in
Castilian more than in Basque he would never have been able to
create his 'Spiritual Exercises', nor would he have been the
universal Ignatius, but an obscure Iñigo, hidden away in his
native mountains: if Elcano had not possessed a Castilian name
and had not piloted a ship with a Castilian name at the service of
ideals forged under Castilian hegemony, he would not have

planned any maritime enterprise but that of fishing in the Bay of Biscay. In the same way we cannot even imagine the great Catalan or Galician heroes without setting them against the background of the kingdom of Aragon or Castile, any more than we can imagine the history of Castile or Aragon without those figures. Finally, during the Second as well as the First Republic, the tendency to subdivision appeared as the offshoot of the Republican ideology and, as in the days of Pí Margall, that tendency brought serious troubles to the Government, even to the point that severe measures had to be taken in Barcelona.

THE HISTORICAL THEORY OF UNITY AS AN ACCIDENTAL FORM

This contemporary federalism had like its predecessor a historical theory which is worth examining, as it is more fully developed than the former. It was most completely described in a speech delivered at Valencia during the Civil War in 1937 by the then rector of the University of Barcelona, the learned ethnologist, P. Bosch Gimpera. He examined the ethnological elements that inhabited the Peninsula, the fusion of even the most antagonistic elements through the effect of long periods of life in common, the events that had been shared together, and the part taken by the various peoples in the creation of determined spiritual values. He agreed that all this 'created a feeling of solidarity and a culture in common'; but as there exist underneath certain differences among the various elements that have fused together, while rejecting separatism, he defended the federalist policy of Pí Margall and Prat de la Riva which triumphed with the second republic. This difference of elements it is held, was not understood by historians, for up to to-day official and orthodox history, the Castilianizing history, is the history of the State, and the State is only an artificial *superstructure* imposed on the authentic Spain, that is to say, the Spain composed of primitive peoples. The superstructure which was imposed on those people by the Romans, the Goths, the Caliphate of Córdoba, the Austrian and Bourbon monarchies, was an artificial form which, though at times beneficial, in the long run was injurious, because it interrupted the flowering of the primitive stock, which is the essence of Spain. The Federalists wished to give life to this indigenous and genuine element of Spain, for they believed that unitarism limits itself to the superstructure.

This term *superstructure* (which, by the way, we find in Karl Marx) obliges us to consider its opposite: the indigenous basis which stubbornly reacts against the higher organization. This is bound to be an *infrastructure* which cannot represent what is eternally natural and authentic, but always something that is inferior to the superstructure, for though the latter at the beginning may have been artificial or imposed (it hardly ever was), yet it has been transformed by the work of centuries into an essential and authentic element. Let us take, for instance, in the case of Romanization, the first superstructure, its most artificial aspect, namely the expansion of Latin, which imposed itself and completely supplanted the various native languages. In the Latin implanted in the soil of the Peninsula and in the Romance language which succeeded it, all that survived as a poor *infra structure* were a few scanty relics of primitive languages. As a result, to-day it is only possible for us to think and live within the linguistic patterns given to us by the Roman elements, and the primitive Iberian tongue contributes but an occasional word or phrase mixed with the general Latin basis. The same is true of the principle of Hispanic unity. If Rome perfected and established it, thus perfected it incorporated itself in the Iberian spirit, once it had been confirmed by centuries of Gothic monarchy, the rule of the Caliphate and the years of unified monarchy ever since the fifteenth century. The mediaeval subdivisions and the brief modern revolts against the unity of the state belong to the *infra structure* with its tendency to subdivide and split up. Though in the Middle Ages this saved the country from disaster, later on it became a destructive force even though it operated inconsistently and as a passing phase.

It is now supposed that all action directed against the super structure was due to an outburst of primitive native forces in revolt against the artificial deformation which had been imposed upon them. Thus, for instance, the mediaeval kingdoms were the result of pre-Roman nuclei which could not be dominated and which rose up in revolt. But the true story is that the structure of pre-Roman Spain is all but unknown to us, and even where we do possess some knowledge of it, we have to leave it aside and turn our main attention to the Roman or Visigothic period, that is to say to the superstructure. When attempts are made to explain why Valencia became Castilianized more rapidly than Catalonia, the reason given is that a Celtic element, akin to that of Castile, stretched from Celtiberia to Segorbe, a region where to-day Aragonese and not Valencian is spoken. But this identification of Segorbe with the *Segobriga caput Celtiberiae* of Pliny cannot be accepted, among other reasons because it is based only upon a resemblance of names, and this resemblance disappears when we learn that in the Middle Ages the form was Soborbe, not Segorbe. Segobriga, the capital of Celtiberia, must be placed in Cuenca, on the hill known as Cabeza del Griego. The proximate cause of the rapid Castilianization of Valencia was that it was reconquered, half by the Aragonese, half by the Catalans, and the remote cause must be sought not in ethnography, of which we know hardly anything, but in the administrative systems current in Roman, Visigothic and Moslem times when Valencia was a suffragan diocese of Toledo. It was for this reason that the Archbishop of Toledo claimed jurisdiction over the Valencian churches reconquered by James I. The Castilian spirit of Valencia thus goes back to the superstructure, not to the contact the Celts had with the primitive Edetani. The same is true for the mediaeval kingdoms. We cannot explain them as the result of the rising of indigenous nuclei which are either unknown to us, or have no connection with these kingdoms. On the other hand we find that they do coincide in some points with certain details of the Roman-Gothic superstructure which is known to us, as for instance, the extension of Navarre under Sancho el Mayor as far as the Oca mountains which were the boundary of the ancient Tarraconensis province. It is easy to explain why historians are always interested in the superstructure seeing that it is this that gives to the people its most complete and elaborate system of life. It is the work of representative men produced by the people itself or the assimilation by them of influences from outside. We do not deny that the action of what we call the *infrastructure* may also be the object of history, but this *infrastructure* must not be taken as the essential form of the Spanish people hampered in its growth by the superstructure. If the superstructure were only a deformation, and if it had been supported

o

under protest not only as far back as the time of Raymond Berenguer IV but as far back as Rome itself, that is to say 2,000 years ago, we should have to conclude that the Spanish people had shown an inconceivable passivity which amounted to non-existence. But let us be clear on this point: the form of life of the Spaniards throughout these 2,000 years has not been a perpetual mistake, nor was the superstructure artificial; it was in fact the normal structure, the most natural one that the Spanish people could select in the particular historical circumstances in which it was involved.

LOCALISM AS AN ACCIDENTAL DISEASE

The mediaeval kingdoms served their purpose and endured because they grew up gradually in opposition to adverse forces from without which were attempting to disrupt violently the ancient, well-consolidated unity. They came into being and maintained themselves as a defence against threatening catastrophe. On the contrary the federalism, cantonalism, and nationalism of modern days have come to destroy the unity of many centuries and have not succeeded in establishing themselves. Far from representing authentic Spain they belong only to an abnormal and transitory moment, a period of weakness that cannot be prolonged without grave danger to the country. They appear as a disease which attacks a nation, when its strength is low, for all disease consists in the struggle for autonomy of some organ which refuses to co-operate with the unified functioning of the body. Localism has always existed side by side with unitarism, but in moments of pathological weakness both one and the other become exacerbated. Differences of temperament, language, interests between the component parts exist in every nation, but in Spain these are felt with peculiar acuteness owing to the difficulty of understanding the long-term advantages of association. On the other hand, in the unified state there often is a failure to appreciate the problems of the region; there is, in fact, a lack of that strong and just spirit of co-ordination whereby each part of the nation feels itself assisted in a way which it is forced to recognize as equitable. Sometimes what happens is that extravagant concessions are made to the autonomous regions, and they are given protection which injures the other regions.

On other occasions there is a severe repression of legitimate aspirations and attempts are made to suppress violently the symptoms of the disease without trying to cure it at its roots by wise and steadfast government.

Chapter V

The Two Spains

It is not only the struggle of the localist spirit against the spirit of unity that weakens national cohesion. We must also bear in mind the unusual vehemence in which differences of political ideology separate Spaniards from one another, thus breaking down the moral unity of the mass of the people. This needs two preliminary explanations.

ISOLATION AND COMMUNICATIONS

The element of austerity in the Spaniard's character, with its lack of interest in novelties, leads him to pay little heed to the spiritual currents that flourish in the more advanced countries. This is the reason why Spaniards so fiercely oppose one another, some advocating isolation from the outside world, others, on the contrary, considering it necessary to establish active intellectual communications with those foreign peoples who lead in culture. The personification of this struggle is Padre Feijóo, who was unwearying in his fight against isolation.

In these alternations between activity and passivity, the tendency to retire into seclusion predominates. The clearest proof of how far the spirit of seclusion prevails may be found in the peculiar lack of interest of the Spaniard in travel. Saavedra Fajardo laments bitterly that there is no taste for 'wandering, the mistress of Prudence'. He adds that northern nations are to be praised for their curiosity, 'which leads them to reconnoitre the world and learn languages, arts and sciences. Spaniards, who with greater ease than the rest could become acquainted with the world, seeing that their rule extends on all sides, are those who remain in closest seclusion in their countries, unless when the call of arms drives them abroad.'

This lack of the spirit of travel becomes a serious limitation. The Venetian ambassador Paolo Tiepolo,[1] when describing the Court of Philip II in 1562, makes a distinction between the Spaniards who have never left their country and those who have travelled in foreign lands. The first, he says, 'do not try to understand anything beyond what they see, and what they have learnt from their nurses, and thus they utter the strangest and most unreasonable statements imaginable: the others, on the contrary, are prudent, wise, tolerant, and always attend to what is honourable no less than what is useful'. This substantial difference, noted by Tiepolo, is one which has always existed. Even though one need not be as bitter as the Venetian in describing the stay-at-homes, yet we always note a radical difference between the Spaniard, whether he be scientist, priest or industrialist or whatever else, who has travelled, and the man who is satisfied to live in isolation. Unfortunately to-day there is the same exaggerated unwillingness to move about noted by Saavedra Fajardo; even more so, for to-day that extensive monarchy no longer exists nor those foreign wars. Amongst the many who are aware of this disease let us take the case of the Countess Pardo Bazán. Realizing that she was an out-and-out Spaniard she imposed upon herself the following precept: just as the Church orders us to confess our sins once a year, so culture ought to order every Spaniard to go outside his country once a year, and more than once, if he notes in himself any symptoms of mental stagnation. But if a wise law were to lay down that those who did not carry out more or less the cultural precept of the Countess Pardo Bazán should not be allowed to hold administrative posts, Spain would remain without rulers. For all that, it is clear that the habit of travel is not always a sure test; the only essential point is to feel the necessity of getting into intimate spiritual intimacy with the foreigner. There are some who feel this keenly and yet have never left their country, as was the case of Padre Feijóo, and there are others who travel as their trunk does. But in the end, with or without travel, the fact is that isolation prevails in Spain and seeks to justify itself on the principle that the Spaniard has

[1] The illustrious Venetian family of Tiepolo rendered great services in diplomacy. One of the family, Paolo Tiepolo, who was killed in 1585, was Ambassador in Spain, 1560, and also in France and Rome. The Account of his Embassy in Spain is dated 1562.

very little to learn from foreign peoples and that it is most
essential to preserve unimpaired all the traditional forms of life
and thought and keep them free from any contact with foreign
influences which would only weaken them and imperil their
existence. All Feijóo's diatribes against those two prejudices
have as much meaning to-day as they had in his time.

EXCLUSIVENESS AND TOLERANCE

That same austerity which dominates the Spanish character
may be the cause of the poverty of its impressions and reactions.
There is an absorbing interest in what is considered the principal
thing in life, and indifference towards what is considered of
secondary importance, that is to say, complete absorption in one
object, and disregard of anything else. This is a great quality in
the case of enthusiastic action, but a great failing, even perilously
near negligence, when dealing with the many connecting causes
that make up the complexities of life. In this way the restriction
of interest goes to the opposite extreme of exaggeration. Pliny,
who had been an imperial procurator in the Peninsula, and was
well acquainted with the Spaniards, attributes to them two
principal qualities: physical endurance and vehemence of spirit,
vehementia cordis. Donoso Cortés[1] said, most aptly, that 'the
historical characteristic of the Spaniard is to exaggerate in
everything.'

Spaniards are always prone to exaggerate. Either they are in
the depths of depression and consider themselves inferior to the
rest of the world, or else they reach the extremes of national pride
and believe that they are the new Chosen People. Their climax
of power in history was magnificent and exhausting, an exclusive
consecration to a high ideal upheld in opposition to the most
powerful adversaries with a complete disregard of their own
wants and necessities.

The same exclusive trait and the same disregard for their most
urgent needs occur in their internal disputes. Every Spaniard is
prone to consider his own opinion as the only one possible. Those

---

[1] Juan Donoso Cortés, 1809–1853, Marquis of Valdegamas, was at first a liberal,
but later evolved towards rigid Catholicism which he explained in his book
Ensayo sobre el catolicismo, el liberalismo y el socialismo, 1851.

who differ from him he merely despises, if the matter is of secondary importance, and he betrays not the slightest curiosity to know about them; if the differences are capital he immediately condemns them as intolerable, without taking into account the good points which must always exist in any diversity of opinion, no matter how wide of the mark it may be. He is unable to conceive the fruitful co-existence of discrepant principles, worthy of respect as containing some possibility of being right. As a result, in Spain difference of opinion degenerates into a contest of irreconcilable animosity.

Larra, during a critical period of the nineteenth century, imagined the mortal struggle as taking place between the two halves of Spain, an idea which Fidelino de Figueiredo expanded in a fine book of ample historical vision, 'As duas Espanhas'. In that book he described the struggle which began in the eighteenth century between the two tendencies, namely whether the direction given to national life by Philip II should be re-established or abolished. This tragic dualism in Spain is so true that we must consider it extending back beyond these two centuries, in fact, all through Spanish history, for it is a necessary result of the inborn tendency to extremes that we have described. The struggle between opposite tendencies, especially between tradition and innovation, is the normal state in all peoples; but in Spain this struggle occurs regularly in a most bitter form whereas it only takes place at critical moments in other countries. Here, in Spain, frequently no agreement can be arrived at by both tendencies, especially with regard to the most urgent and vital problems which arise, because the Iberian Peninsula is either exposed to the influences that pour in from the two continents which she links together, or else she retires into the isolation that is due to her remote geographical position.

This struggle between different tendencies should be carefully noted as it appears in the different historical epochs, for it has consumed a great part of the historical energy of the Spanish people, but to the truce in the struggle, when the two opposite forces managed to unite in harmony, we owe the most fruitful moments of national life.

BETWEEN AFRICA AND EUROPE

One of the taunts that has been repeated most often by foreign countries is that which compares Spain to Africa. It was already referred to by Feijóo and formulated later by Alexander Dumas: 'Africa begins at the Pyrenees.' Unamuno, influenced by Martin Hume's unfortunate 'History of the Spanish People', converted this taunt into a formulation of a programme, by proposing the preferential cultivation of those qualities which distinguish the Spanish people from its neighbours in Europe. This he did because he considered that the affirmation of the Africanism of Spain was the first step in a process of evaluation which would one day lead to the influence of Spain on the other modern peoples. We, on our side, answer that although we are unable to recognize the African elements that Hume and Unamuno discover in this or that Spanish quality, nevertheless the Africanization of Spain at different periods was a historical process which repeated itself more often than is believed, only that it does not imply a difference or an inferiority to western culture, but rather the reverse.

On the occasion of the Punic wars we learn for the first time how the two Spains faced each other, one of them the ally of Hannibal and the other of the Scipios. Early in the struggle Spain decides its European destiny from the moment when the Saguntines sacrifice themselves to preserve their Roman alliance—so extremely heroic an act that it was not even fully understood by the Romans themselves (*'fidem socialem usque ad perniciem suam coluerunt'*, says Livy in a tone of wondering admiration). And this Punic Africa, Africa Minor, after being the seat of Carthaginian culture and the dread rival of Latin culture, became one of the most prosperous provinces of the Roman Empire. When political and intellectual power had passed from the Italians to the inhabitants of the provinces, after the Hispanic century which stretches from Mela and Seneca to Trajan and Hadrian, there came the period from the second to the fourth century when Africa took the lead with Apuleius, Septimius Severus, Tertullian, Saint Cyprian, Arnobius, Saint Augustine, and Martianus Capella. This period was followed by the hegemony of Gaul, between the fourth and the sixth centuries.

This Africa, so noble a portion of Western Latin civilization, lived on a par with Spain, not in opposition to, but in deep community with all the culture of Christian Europe. Africanism then meant the same in Spain as Europeanism did later, that is to say the tendency to shake off cultural isolation. To this Africa the Galician Paulus Orosius travelled in order to receive inspiration from the great father of the Church, Saint Augustine, and in the following centuries, even when intellectual supremacy passed back to Spain, during the period of Saint Isidore, the African Church continued in close relations with the Visigothic. This inclination towards Christian Africa is clearly visible in the historical treatise of Saint Isidore, '*De Viris Illustribus*', where, among the religious men of recent memory there commemorated, he sets next the fourteen from Spain, eleven from Africa, another eleven from Italy, while he mentions only four names from Gaul. The Spain of Saint Isidore, which was in such close relationship with Africa, casts a brilliant beam, the last before the beacon of antiquity was extinguished over the dark ages. It was the Iberian Peninsula, the link between the two continents, that under the influence of the Hispano-Roman Saint Isidore produced the last flowering of Latin-Mediterranean culture which was to be followed by the long period of collapse until Latin-German culture began to bloom in the centre of Europe.

In the political history of that Visigothic age one can also perceive an opposition between the Spain that unites itself to Byzantine Africa and the other which leans upon the Frankish Kingdom, and doubtless to this dualism was due the ferocious partisan spirit which destroyed the Gothic monarchy in its last seventy years. In vain the clergy in its Toledan councils tried to exercise a moderating influence over the extremes that were at war with one another, by urging the kings to use pity and indulgence rather than vengeance and cruelty with their opponents, so that they might be able to rely on the hearts of their subjects against external enemies. In vain were those warnings included in full in the '*Lex Visigothorum*' as an urgent necessity in the government of the kingdom; the antagonism between the two halves raged implacably, and the confiscations and murders reached such a pitch of violence that the Frankish historian Fredegarius gave it the name of 'Gothic disease', thus signifying the grafting of German roughness on to Hispanic exaggeration. The irreconcilable duel reaches its tragic end with the handing over of the kingdom to external enemies, when the family of Vitiza asked for help from Africa.

By that time the conquest of Africa by the Arabs had gravely disturbed the balance of life in all the Western Mediterranean, especially in Spain. Africa with its magnificent Latin civilization and its profound Christian spirit, so admired by Saint Isidore, had become Islamic Africa, torn away from the western world to be united henceforth to the Asiatic East. The party of Vitiza, helped by the Africans, were the victors, and drove the partisans of King Roderick to seek narrow refuge in the mountains of Asturias. The counts and bishops of Vitiza who are personified in the famous Julian and Opas reached such a pitch of arrogant intolerance that, setting their party before everything, they did not hesitate to enslave their religion and their country by handing them over to the Moslem auxiliaries. Half of Spain annihilated the other half, but Spain in its entirety fell into Mozarabic serfdom beneath the African yoke.

When little by little the defeated party rose again in Asturias, the only survivor of free Spain, we must not think of a partisan movement of opposition, but of a struggle between two states that occupy separate territories and have separate and distinct governments. Southern Spain, *El Andalús*, although it developed an Islamism that was, to a great degree, Hispanized in customs, art and ideology, remained in isolation from Europe and united to the Afro-Asiatic cultural world. Northern Spain, though steadfast in its Christian spirit, nevertheless was subjected to a great degree to the influences from the south, at a time when Arabic culture was far superior to Latin, and it then accomplished its high historical mission of being the link between the two worlds of the east and the west.

EUROPEANISM AND MEDIAEVAL 'CASTICISMO'

Later, when the cultural superiority of the Arab world over the Latin world ceased, once the inrush from the south had spent itself, there was no question of a struggle between the influences from Africa and those from Europe. Nevertheless, in the north the struggle between two tendencies and two Spains began under different conditions. Only one of the two continents to which the Iberian peninsula serves as a link is now important, but the influences from European life reach her late because of her remote position, a distant shore to which only the strongest waves could reach, leaving behind many others to break on nearer shores. And frequently adverse historical circumstances produced long periods of life apart from, and in disagreement with, the rest of the West. And every time that the isolation ceases or diminishes the results of this separation are felt; the struggle breaks out between those wishing to correct the effects of isolation, by adapting the life of the Peninsula to that of the rest of Europe, and those of the opposite tendency who wish to maintain intact the ancestral heritage of culture.

The longest period of isolation which Spain suffered with regard to Europe was that caused by the hegemony of Moslem Córdoba, from the eighth to the tenth century inclusive. Already at the beginning of that hegemony, Northern Spain, the offspring of Mediterranean culture, that is to say, of Graeco-Latin antiquity, felt itself cut off from the new nordic culture of Latin-German origin which had begun in the Europe of the Carolingian dynasty. The relations between Alfonso the Chaste and Charlemagne imply the existence of a primitive party of *afrancesados*, as they used to say in the eighteenth century, or *europeizantes*, as they said in the nineteenth, and from their opposition to the rest of their countrymen sprang the legend of Bernardo del Carpio. Precise information on those primitive parties can only be found in the eleventh century, referring to the ecclesiastical reforms and the substitution of the Roman rite for that of Saint Isidore.

This is the most typical example of the cultural isolation produced by Spain's remote geographical position. She had given great splendour to a national Church which was a glorious example owing to its ancient councils, its discipline, its liturgy, its hymns and its sacred music, but as a result of its traditional isolation it was unable in its succeeding evolution to influence the liturgical development of the universal Church, as might have been expected, owing to its own high qualities, nor did it manage to take its share in the general evolution. For this reason, after

four centuries had passed, it found itself at loggerheads with
Rome when Gregory VII, with the help of the monks from Cluny,
proposed to unify the rite. The remedy for such prolonged isolation was bound to be difficult and hard, a noble and much-
loved portion of tradition had to be uprooted, and it was necessary to receive a host of foreign clerics, who would implant the
new patterns of ecclesiastical life intended to replace the
national ones. At this time Sancho el Mayor of Navarre and his
two grandsons, Sancho Ramírez in Aragon and Alfonso VI in
Castile, as well as the Cid in Valencia, became 'Europeanizers'
in the sense that they led the party which favoured the introduction of the reforms imposed by Rome and the occupation of
the principal ecclesiastical posts by the monks of Cluny. We know
that there was a traditionalist party, very hostile to these reforms,
and its stubborn opposition in defence of the Toledan rite showed
itself in 'judgements of God', trials by combat and court in-
trigues. The bitter struggle between traditionalist and innovating
Spain in this liturgical question is known to us because it was of
great interest to the clerical historians of those days. But with the
exception of this episode which concerns the religious sphere, we
know nothing of similar episodes which must have occurred then
in other spheres of life.

Because of its connection with the liturgy, we have one piece of
evidence which enables us to say that, broadly speaking, the
Europeanizing party in its triumph behaved in no violent or
authoritarian way towards the opposite party, but with considerable moderation. I refer to the substitution of French for
Visigothic script. By virtue of this change all the books of the
Hispanic past became illegible, and thus the cultural continuity
of the country was cut off and a new era began in which all
Spanish books would have to be rewritten in the new script and
the majority of them would be substituted by others copied from
those in other countries. But this change was, generally speaking,
carried out very gradually and spontaneously. Alfonso VI and
the Cid continued to use in their chancelleries the Visigothic
lettering; only in prayer books was there an ordinance imposing
French lettering, but in all other documents the change was
made in special instances and took thirty years to accomplish, a
fact which indicates a gradual acceptance on the part of the

traditionalist party. This signifies that there was a spirit of accommodation, which, when applied to all orders of life, was the cause of the great prosperity of this period. The sorrowful determination to sacrifice the past, a feeling which would seem inconceivable in modern days to the traditionalists in Spain, but was welcomed in those days by the noblest figures of the early Spanish Middle Ages, was taken in order that Spain might make up for its former long period of isolation and incorporate itself into the life of Europe, but it was carried out after securing a happy agreement between two antagonistic parties. Spain renounced a great part, indeed a glorious part, of its past, and yet kept its own spirit which enabled it to create its greatest poetical hero in the person of one of those innovators. The 'Poema del Cid' welcomed the all-powerful French influence and gave it a typically Spanish poetic form, and at the same time, with a noble spirit that was ethical as well as artistic, renewed the ideal of epic poetry both Spanish and French. Spain lived in this period of renunciation in its last heroic age, the most original of them all and the most magnificent.

In the following two centuries we can readily note the continued influence of Spain as an innovator, when numerous Frankish colonies were established in the principal cities of the Peninsula; when Alfonso VII appeared as a modernizing king imposing feudal principles on the ancient empire of León, and generously welcoming to his court the Provençal troubadours; when at the same time Archbishop Raymond of Toledo encouraged the founding of schools where Arab, Jewish and Christian scholars collaborated in a series of works, which, when communicated to the learned centres in Europe, opened a new era in mediaeval science. Soon afterwards the poets of León, Rioja and Aragon imported from France a perfect syllabic form of verse,[1] boasting that it was superior to the primitive Spanish metre. This reform was similar to the one so much resisted by Cristóbal de Castillejo, when it was a question of Italian influence.

Immediately afterwards came Alfonso X who gathered into

[1] The metrical reform introduced from France by Gonzalo de Berceo about 1230 was the stanza of alexandrines or lines of twelve syllables. The reform attacked by Castillejo (1490–1550) was the hendecasyllabic Italian line of verse introduced by Garcilaso (1503–1536) about 1525.

his court the learned of the three religions, for he was as eager to sift the wisdom of the East as of the West and paid as much attention to the new Roman Law as he did to the old laws and customs of Spain. He was the first European king interested in secularizing culture, which he did by expressing his vast encyclopaedic knowledge in a vulgar Romance tongue. An echo of the violent opposition that was aroused by his audacious novelties still reaches us to-day when we read of how he was reputed to be an impious blasphemer. But all the opposition against reform was unable to prevent his success, and his historical and legal works were translated by scholars all over Spain into Catalan and into Portuguese. His oriental works were translated into French and had an influence on Dante. The Astronomical Tables were studied in Europe for various centuries and were read and annotated by Copernicus himself. During all this great movement of the twelfth and thirteenth centuries, now that the forces working for innovation and those working for tradition were happily reconciled, Spain underwent a deep transformation and reached one of her historical peak points. She assimilated the abundant influences of the East as well as those from Europe, and she accomplished in the most brilliant way her true destiny, which was to serve as a link between the two heterogeneous worlds of Christianity and Islam. At the same time that an impulse was given to traditional institutions whether social or political, she carried on the century-old war to recover the soil of the fatherland. In that war the greatest conqueror of all was one who was both king and saint, Ferdinand III, and whose epitaph, written in different languages, proclaims him to be a king who was tolerant to infidel cults in mosque and synagogue.

UNIFICATION: THE DUAL CHARACTER
OF THIS EPOCH

As a contrast to the magnificent development during the epoch of Alfonso VII and Alfonso X we must recall another powerful influx of new ideas and customs, strangely contemptuous of the traditional foundations of public life. The general decadence caused by the break up of the Middle Ages reduced Spain to a very low level of depression, and this was increased by the degenerate character of Henry IV. The throne itself set the foolish example of belittling and insulting all national feelings. Moorish customs were openly adopted; the war of reconquest was wilfully impeded; scorn of the laws was actively encouraged and corruption became the order of the day among all the officers of government and justice. Religion was openly jeered at, and people boasted of their bestial materialism, while at court the immoral practices became a public scandal.

The traditionalist party at first showed their opposition by proclaiming the anti-king Alfonso; afterwards they chose Isabel, Princess of Asturias. And the great success of the movement personified by Isabel consisted in not limiting the reaction to a mere party movement, but in a prudent uniting of all the forces at their disposal. The characteristic quality of the Catholic monarchs was their earnest determination to select the right man for the right place, which prompted them both to attract to their side even their enemies, converting them into collaborators, and to co-ordinate and harmonize the two antagonistic tendencies. Once this double task had been carried out, traditional Spain succeeded in restoring all her values, which before this had been perversely and wantonly tramped underfoot. With exemplary zeal law and morality were made the rule for the people, and social order was reimposed after an implacable internal war had been waged against the powerful elements of disorder and anarchy. It was then decided to complete once and for all the conquest of Granada, and undertake the reforms which would raise the dignity of the religious institutions. But through all this restoration of tradition the spirit of reforming Spain was present, introducing elements of perfection which had been unknown before. A notable example was the new plan adopted for organizing and directing the war against Granada. Another was the admission of the middle class into the high administrative posts. Above all we should mention the firm anti-isolationist policy which attracted to Spain all the modern currents of the European Renaissance. The former uncouth barbarism was now combated by Spanish humanists educated abroad, and by learned Italians, French, Greeks and Jews invited to court, to the noble houses and to the Universities of Alcalá and Salamanca. The young nobles, who formerly led a life of slothful ease, were now obliged by the Queen to attend the classes given by these foreign scholars. And so, all through these acts of the monarchs we notice a desire for culture and education, and this culminates in the decree of 1480 which enacted that works of the intellect should be imported into the country free of customs dues, tithes and all other taxes, for it was seen that the merchants 'every day brought in good books in great quantities and this redounds to the profit of all and ennobles our kingdoms'. This enthusiastic and continuous attempt to harmonize and make full use of both tendencies is the true cause of the immediate prosperity that ensued.

In addition to all this work of co-ordinating the elements which had operated in the past, we should lay special stress upon a new and prevailing thought of the Catholic monarchs, which, although it, too, was rooted in the Middle Ages, yet was more decidedly directed towards modern times. The tendencies towards absolute kingly power and the national personality of the State, both of them aspirations which the Renaissance inculcated into princes, became more prominent in the Catholic monarchs, and with truly Spanish originality they fused these ideas with the mediaeval universalist idea which the national states with their local ideas of autonomy were trying their best to combat. The Spanish state would henceforth be based upon the unity of the Catholic faith and its ever-increasing propagation. And this design, owing to the grandeur of its scope, prevails over all others if it meets opposition. Thus the broad, tolerant spirit of the Middle Ages, practised by the great kings, who were both warriors and saints, ends now with the expulsion of the Jews and the violent baptism of the Moors of Granada *en masse*, to which must be added the new system of the Inquisition which had been set up. This implantation of religious intolerance at the end of the fifteenth century is the great change which divides the history of the characteristically Spanish cult of extremes into two completely distinct epochs. At the beginning, under the Catholic monarchs, intolerance was necessary to a certain extent in order to unify the nation in its European spirit by the suppression of foreign religions. Nevertheless, it is also worth noting that the cautious attitude towards Europe, with regard to printed books, makes its first appearance in 1502, in contrast with the confident optimism of twenty years before. It was now necessary to get a previous government licence to sell or print books, under penalty of a heavy fine and disqualification. This restriction by censorship was at the start a mild one, but as time went on it was to grow more severe and became the favourite method to be followed by those who aimed at intellectual isolationism.

THE INCREASE UNDER CHARLES V

In spite of these restrictions, during the period of Charles V isolationism was suppressed as never before. The price paid for this suppression was indeed heavier than in the period of Alfonso VI to which we referred before. The two aspects of abnormal intensity which we mentioned then as characteristic of such great changes, namely the influx of foreign counsellors and the violent attacks made on important traditional principles, were now to be witnessed in full force. First of all we have the inrush of Flemish followers in the suite of the grandson of the Catholic monarchs when he entered Spain, then we have the overthrow of vital political institutions after the defeat of the Comuneros at Villalar[1] and the substitution of new forms of government. But in the midst of the fierce struggle, young Charles heard from his own followers the crudest and most humiliating truths, which induced him to substitute for the violence shown at the beginning a respect and love for Spain. Thus it was the War of the Communes which caused the Hispanization of the Emperor, and the consequent enthusiastic association of Spain with the vast imperial plans. As a result there came about an active and fruitful interchange between Spaniards and foreigners in the government, in the army, in the court, and in all orders of life.

Charles V, a staunch Catholic as well as tolerant by nature, was the best fitted to be the leader of this the greatest and most spontaneous opening of the Spanish mind to all the problems that were agitating the world, and the result was that the spirit of Spain extended its influence over all fields of action in Europe and in America, in its aspiration towards *One Monarch, one Empire, and one Sword*. At that time the history of Spain became

[1] Villalar was the place where, on 23 April 1521, the Comuneros were defeated. They had tried to impose upon Charles V the authority of the Castilian Cortes. The war of the *Communidades* lasted one and a half years.

P

the history of the universe in the old world as well as in that which had been recently discovered.

When he perceived that all his plans for saving the spiritual unity of Europe had failed, Charles retired to Yuste, but although isolationism then began, Spain still continued to be the centre of universal history during the greater part of the reign of Philip II.

EXCLUSIVENESS PREDOMINATES

Philip II on assuming with determination the decision to maintain the Catholic unity of Europe counted upon the loyal adhesion of a traditionalist majority who saw their ancient convictions linked with the extraordinary political development of the nation which now had reached the summit of its power. This great triumph caused the spiritual unity of the Spaniards to increase its strength daily, and to maintain it they needed, at all costs, to preserve it from dangerous ideas that were current in other countries, those, in fact, against which they were fighting. But the precautions they took ended by being altogether out of all proportion. In the early years of his reign, in 1558, Philip II prohibited, under penalty of death and confiscation, the importation and publication of books without a licence from the State Council, lest those books might contain heresies, new-fangled notions against the faith, or 'vain matters' that might give evil example. Let us note how the penalty had increased, for in 1502 it only consisted in a fine and disqualification. In the following year, 1559, Philip II also prohibited Spaniards from studying abroad except at Rome, Naples or Coimbra, or in the Spanish college at Bologna. He gave two reasons for these restrictions: first because Spanish universities 'are daily diminishing and in bankruptcy'; that is to say, he took the absence of the students as a cause, whereas it was only an effect, of the bad state in which the Spanish universities found themselves. The second reason was that the intercourse with foreigners involved the students in extravagance, dangers and distractions. And so, as he did not find in the world any universities free from dangers except those at home or practically at home, he closed the doors and windows of the decayed Spanish schools so that the inmates might breathe nothing but their own confined air.

Nevertheless, though this was the period during which Spain reached one of its moments of greatest unanimity, yet the conformity was to a large extent only apparent, and was possible owing to the severe repression carried out by the enemies of progressive thought who were ready to persecute the slightest trace of non-conformity, even the new ideas, not in any way heretical, of a Fray Luis de León or a Brocense,[1] at whose trials the crowd of domineering reactionaries had actually to be restrained by the tribunal of the Inquisition itself. And in spite of the unanimity which had been achieved we can observe some deep divergencies of opinion, even with regard to the central idea of Counter-Reformation policy, namely the religious repression in Flanders, though the dissenting element was only able to operate within very reduced limits.

The theologians, who were first consulted in 1565, gave it as their opinion that, taking into account the dangers that would ensue for the Church from the rebellion and imminent war, the King might, without any danger to his royal conscience, allow the cities of Flanders to have the freedom of worship they asked for. But Philip II, declaring himself opposed to this opinion, swore that he would never allow the religious unity to be broken, for he did not wish to be lord over heretics who did such offence against God. In this the King, more zealous than the theologians, was interpreting faithfully the opinion of the great majority of his subjects. The man charged with the carrying out of his inflexible zeal was the Duke of Alba, who, swayed by his self-denying loyalty to the crown, insisted upon bearing the responsibility for all the odium which his severity would arouse. By displaying his accustomed harshness he carried out to the entire satisfaction of his master the repressive policy which the King was determined to carry to the bitter end. The Duke summed up the reasons for this policy in a biting phrase: 'It is far better to preserve by war for God and the King a kingdom that is impoverished and even ruined than, without the war, preserve it entire for the benefit of the devil and the heretics, his disciples.'

Pirenne believes that if the Duke of Alba had been twenty

[1] Francisco Sánchez (*El Brocense*), reviver of Spanish humanism, was professor of Greek and Latin at the University of Salamanca during the last quarter of the sixteenth century. He and Fray Luis de León were accused to the Inquisition by the rigid elements dominating the University of Salamanca at that time.

years younger he would not have thought thus; for his thoughts were those of the ancient Spaniards who had been trained in the holy war against the Moors. This is not the case. This was no mere archaic conception, but the usual Hispanic exaggeration backed up in this case by the unbounded passions which were stirred up in Europe by the religious question among both Catholics and Protestants. Philip II was twenty years younger in accordance with Pirenne's dictum, but he was as rigid in his views as Alba or more so. Gregory IX considered the Massacre of Saint Bartholomew as a fortunate day for Catholicism. We, therefore, must not blame in any way the severity of the first decision that was taken. The error of Philip II was in not seeing that, when it came to repressing ideas, if he did not succeed with the employment of violence once and for all at the outset, he would never do so, but would make the situation worse by keeping up so constant a policy of executions that it became endemic, for blood that has been spilt serves but the one purpose of making proselytes for its cause. And to the error of the King we must add the error of the majority of the Spanish people.

This majority paid no attention to a considerable minority which foresaw the future, namely that the Low Countries, driven into poverty and ruin, would be shared out between God and the heretics, under worse conditions with war than would have been the case without war. Many Spaniards, some of them very distinguished men, saw this coming. Arias Montano, from 1568 on, and above all in 1573, disapproved of the harsh repression carried out by Alba, especially in the case of the punishments inflicted at Naarden and Zutphen. That cruel war, he said, was just a squandering of many millions and 'the loss of countless souls and lives of Spaniards as well as of the enemy'. It was an urgent necessity that the Council of Troubles[1] should not serve merely for the purpose of chastising the rebellious, but should also raise the moral tone of the corrupt Spanish administration and enable His Majesty to recapture the affection of his vassals. Likewise the Secretary Esteban Prats asserted in 1572 that the sackings carried out by the soldiery, added to their extortions, violence, raping and vile deeds, 'had been the chief cause (not heresy as some tried

---

[1] *El Consejo de los Tumultos* was the French *Conseil des Troubles*. It was distinguished by its rigour in putting down disturbances.

to prove) for driving the Flemish people into despair'. Similarly, Don Francisco de Alava, the Prince of Eboli, the royal chronicler Furío Ceriol, and many others, condemned the war which the Duke of Alba was waging as a tragic error, and they maintained that more thought should be given to Spanish maladministration than to heresy.

The opposition against the war extended all over Castile, because this was the kingdom that paid the heaviest amount of tribute, and even though it was dangerous to oppose it because of the King's decision to carry on, there were protests on all sides. At the end of the reign, when the money had still to be found for war and the finances of the country were exhausted, it was decided, about January 1595, to impose a new tribute on flour. Then there was published an anonymous pamphlet, attributed with certainty to the jurist Gonzalo de Valcárcel, which courageously stated the point of view of the minority: if God has abandoned England and Flanders for their sins, we shall gain nothing by killing heretics, while without any war at all God preserved Bavaria from heresy. The many religious wars that Spain has fought since the days of Charles V against Germany, France, England, and Flanders show that the patient is not to be cured with that medicine; in fact it is a proof that the cure is a failure: 'What has our paying the flour tax here to do with making them give up their heresies over there? Can it be that France, Flanders, and England will be more virtuous in proportion as Spain is poorer? A remedy for the sins of Nineveh[1] was not found by increasing the tribute in Palestine so as to pay for the expedition to conquer them, but rather in sending there some one who would convert them.' And the anonymous protest adds: 'It is said that Castile is long-suffering and will bear all the burden, but it has no longer the strength: the towns are becoming depopulated, the estates are lying fallow, the farmers flee to the mountains as they cannot pay the tributes.' This dark picture and these arguments show how damaged materially and how reasonable intellectually was this dissenting portion of Spain's population. They obtained the trifling satisfaction of foiling the flour tax, not by their arguments, for these met with no response, but owing to the widespread exhaustion of the country.

[1] An allusion to the Old Testament, Book of Jonah.

We have regarded it as quite natural that in the beginning a
severe repressive system should have been used against the dissenters, for this was the prevailing one everywhere in the baroque
period; but, later on, even the extreme limit of poverty which
Spain reached was not enough to impose the opinion of the
minority in the face of the war party which remained impregnable and immutable in its high resolve. The thought of making
Spain the champion of the unity of the faith was certainly one of
noble abnegation, and it enabled Spain to preserve for modern
Europe a precious reserve of Catholic spirit, of moral values, all
in fact that could be saved from the high universalist conception
of the Middle Ages. But this result would have been now acceptable to the world generally if heed had been given to the minority,
which, during the thirty years from Arias Montano to the
licenciate Valcárcel, clamoured for a strongly Catholic Spain, but
a tolerant one. The minority considered that the religious war
was a mistake, for it placed Spain in a critical situation with
regard to her enemies and kept her deprived of strong allies, who
would have prevented the animosity against the power of Spain
from becoming, as it did, general throughout the world.

But the isolationism of Spain was not based upon this question
of high politico-religious ideals alone. It was also believed that
dealing with foreign countries was prejudicial from an economic
point of view. The 'Eulogies' of Spain which were written from
time to time ever since ancient days had convinced the Spaniards
that Spain was an exceptionally rich country, and as it was so, its
inhabitants did not need to busy themselves in industry as
foreigners did in their more sterile lands. This note of exaggerated optimism, which was already rife in the Middle Ages, still
prevailed in the psychology of the Counter-Reformation. The
topic of Spain's fertile soil was brilliantly developed by Mendez
Silva, by Mariana, by Fray Benito Peñalosa, by Juan Manuel de
la Parra, by all in fact, in terms that make Saint Isidore's
famous Hymn of Praise seem tame by comparison. Spain is self-
sufficient, Spain can satisfy her own needs, and far from needing
foreigners, she actually finds them a disturbance. Quevedo considered that Spain was the prey of foreigners, who, on account of
the poverty and bleakness of their lands, came to Spain to enrich
themselves with the rewards they earned by their industry.

Gracián in his '*Criticón*' resolutely asserts the advantages to be
obtained by isolation. In this sense Critilo answers the observation of Andrenio: 'Spain is far apart from the trade of the other
provinces and at the end of the world,' with the retort: 'It should
be still farther away, for all come in search for it and swallow all
the best things it produces: England its generous wines, Holland
its soft wool, Venice its glass, Germany its saffron, Naples its
silks, Genoa its sugar, France its horses and the whole world its
doubloons.'

When we admit this spirit of isolation, this reluctance to having
dealings abroad, how can we explain the cultural greatness of
Spain in the golden centuries? We must realize that this with-
drawal from the rest of Europe, no matter how active it was, only
existed in matters that touched high politics and religion, while
in the general sphere of culture the isolating tendency did not prevail until a late period. Spain was the chosen people among all
others for the defence of religion, and she might live apart in
splendid isolation. Her pride and satisfaction was well expressed
by the ambassador Mendoza: 'God is powerful in heaven, and
the King of Spain on earth'. But beneath this splendid arrogance
there was another contrary feeling, excessive too, of over-valuing
other peoples who led a kind of life which was less austere than
that of the Spaniard. This feeling is noted frequently in the
literature of the period and confirmed by Ambrosio de Morales
at the time of greatest political power, about 1570. He says: 'We
Spaniards of this age have a strange loathing against our own
products: we scorn them as if they were the poorest and meanest
in the universe and we set the highest value on foreign languages,
clothes, victuals, usages and customs.' This discontent Gracián
shows again in the same dialogue of Critilo and Andrenio when
he says that when they begin to speak ill of Spain they do so feeling sure that Spaniards will not consider it a crime. 'They are
not,' he says, 'as suspicious as the French; they are more kind-
hearted; they embrace all foreigners but they do not value their
own people; they are not great admirers of their own country.'
This means that the free and open criticism of their own country
and the feeling of dissatisfaction, which seemed a novelty
peculiar to the eighteenth and nineteenth centuries, already
existed in the sixteenth and seventeenth centuries, and it is to be

hoped that this frame of mind will never disappear altogether, for
it is the most potent force against isolationism. Although Philip II
closed the doors and windows of the universities, and although
Spain believed itself to be a people set aside by God for His service, this was counteracted by the Spaniards themselves who
spread over all Europe, exercising their own fruitful powers of
self-criticism. The Spain which, according to Morales, appreci-
ates foreign languages and customs, or embraces all foreigners,
according to Gracián, prevails and expresses its own soul tem-
pered by communion with other peoples. The culture of Spain
continues its greatness, because when Valdés and Garcilaso led
the way by their admiration of Italy they did so with a profound Hispanic consciousness; Ignatius de Loyola, after studying
at Alcalá, went to Paris to make himself universal-minded; Lope
de Vega, although he felt 'genuinely Spanish' in body and soul,
yet sought eagerly the approbation of the Italian and French
humanists; Mariana refused to shut himself up in a blind,
enthusiastic Hispanism, but demonstrating the truth of the
Spanish characteristic noted by Gracián, earned the reproof of
having too little enthusiasm for his own country. Finally, the
authentic Spain did not shut herself in, but rather broke out of
her isolationism, and in every true Spaniard we find the traditional spirit and the spirit of innovation working together in
perfect harmony, producing both the mediaeval and those late-
maturing fruits in which the mediaeval mingles with the modern.

QUOMODO SEDET SOLA!

The deterioration increased and the policy of isolation produced grave consequences, for it was now regarded as Spain's
destiny, accepted proudly but sadly as a legacy inherited from the
glories of the past.

In 1609 Quevedo, with the words from Jeremiah, '*Quomodo
sedet sola!*' ringing in his heart, opened his tract '*España Defendida*'
with a motto in the style of the prophet: 'All our foes opened their
mouths against us.' He sees Spain a victim of 'a stubborn
persecution', and the Spaniards 'hated by all nations, for all the
world is for them a prison and a punishment'; but in spite of all,
solitude is steadfastly to be desired, for Spain receives all evil

through her communication with foreign peoples; she would not know what excesses in eating and drinking were if the Germans had not introduced them, nor unnatural vice had not Italy taught it to her, nor would the Inquisition have anything to do had Melanchthon, Calvin or Luther never existed. Nevertheless, in spite of these assertions, the sense of solitude becomes embittered, for the disillusion of the extremist Spain of Philip II still lies over the country like a pall of lead. Quevedo thinks that the God of armies helped Spain in the battles of the Cid, at Navas de Tolosa, in the enterprises of Vasco da Gama and Cortés, in the achievements of Cisneros who halted the course of the sun at the taking of Oran, but that golden age is now a thing of the past. Spaniards no longer wear iron armour unless it be to deck the statue on their tomb; they dress in effeminate luxury, 'repenting that they had been begotten men'. On all sides are to be seen insolent married women who boast of their adulteries and men who find the bond of marriage to be a lucrative one. And so when Quevedo in this doctrinal pamphlet remembers from time to time his satirical vein he gives us a very valuable historical commentary on his own burlesque works. The vices against which he there fulminates are not mere defects of normal society deformed and exaggerated in order to produce literary effect, but they are, as it were, a fetid swamp in which the clear stream of a glorious past has lost itself, a past that is still close enough to create all the greater sense of affliction at its loss. Those vices are a sorrowful proof of the corruption which has taken the place of the virtues which have recently vanished together with the spiritual qualities which inspired the creation of the Spanish Empire.

Quevedo, who was the echo of isolationist Spain which was beginning to sink into disillusion, believed that the cause of so great a decline was the peace which the nation enjoyed. 'Although in my opinion,' he says, 'Spain never enjoys peace, she only rests as now from the fatigues of arms, in order to return to the fight with strength unimpaired and fresh courage' against Turks, against heretics and against idolaters of the Indies. In this sense and with this hope Quevedo moderates his pessimism, although peace, namely the peace with Holland, had only been running for very few months, too short a time in which to produce such deep decadence. But in the end wars will start again and the ancient vigorous qualities will return, enabling Spain to carry on her Catholic destiny which is perpetual and immovable. Quevedo in 'Spain Defended', argues about isolation and war, like the majority of his fellow citizens. He reasons from abstract political ideas without paying heed to the inexorable realities.

Twenty years later, the hard reality became only too evident. An obscure Benedictine, Fray Benito de Peñalosa, wrote the truest description of the extreme exaltation which led Spain to wear herself out in her task, accepting with resignation all the poverty which accompanied her greatness. This is clear from the title of the book, which is: 'Book of the five excellences of the Spaniards which depopulate Spain for its greater power and expansion' (*Libro de las cinco excelencias del español que despueblan a España para su mayor potencia y dilatación*, 1629). These 'excellences' are: religion propagated and defended all over the world, the great abundance of theologians and jurists, the arms that have won the greatest empire ever known by man, the nobility with its unevenly distributed privileges, and American gold which has been spent prodigally. Effectively Spain suffers from her own excellences: she is great in purpose and in deeds, but insensitive to her own injuries; and being without the necessary flexibility to adapt herself to changing times and peoples she remains immovable in her isolation from all countries.

But the dangers of such a situation became evident. Quevedo denounced the risks of isolation when he introduced the concept of 'solitude' into the adaptation he made of a saying of Seneca:

> *Y es más fácil, oh España, en muchos modos*
> *que lo que a todos les quitaste sola*
> *te puedan a ti sola quitar todos*
> ('Tis easier, O Spain, in many ways
> for all to take from thee alone
> what thou alone didst take from all).

Years afterwards Quevedo sees that already the enemies are beginning to take away from Spain her prizes. He sees that the Spanish empire not only weakens in her basic ideals, as he had been aware before, but also her material strength was mouldering away. The wars have returned, certainly, in great numbers, but they were unsuccessful wars leading up to the national misfortunes of Catalonia,[1] Roussillon, Portugal[2] and Recroy.[3] Quevedo in 1645, eighteen days before his death, relieved his feelings in a letter to Francisco de Oviedo, saying: 'From all sides come very bad news of utter ruin, and the worst of it all is that every one expected this would happen. Señor Don Francisco, I do not know whether the end is coming or whether 'tis already come. God only knows; for there are many things which seem to exist and have their being, and yet they are nought but a word or a figure.' Quevedo had lost altogether that steadfastness and that belief in the future which had sustained him in the days when he wrote 'Spain Defended', and when he believed that the 'modesty, virtue and Christianity' of Philip III, once the war activity of Spain should begin again, were sufficient to save the country from the decadence that was descending upon it.

So great, however, was the old belief that Spain was the chosen people, set apart by God for the purpose of battling for the Catholic unity of Europe, so vast still was the power of the nation in both hemispheres, so brilliant also was the cultural activity that flourished during the centuries of expansion and growth; so much, too, had been achieved, in spite of the final adversity, that there was no possibility for the dissenting party in Spain to make full use of its dissent and secure an entry into the new vital currents of Europe. Would it have still been possible to turn the national activity of the country in a new direction? Would this have saved the country? Even though Spain had already lost all hopes in the possibility of success for her ancient policy yet she preferred to slumber on in that policy, without the strength to create new national projects in accordance with the new times which the progress of the different peoples had brought to Europe.

INNOVATING SPAIN COMES INTO ACTION

The isolationist spirit met with strong resistance from the moment of the War of Succession. The two aspects of abnormal

[1] The rebellion of Catalonia in 1640–1652 to hand the province to Louis XIII of France; Roussillon, which was acquired by Ferdinand the Catholic in 1493, rebelled with Catalonia in 1640 and remained in the power of Louis XIII.

[2] Portugal was incorporated in the dominions of Philip II in 1580 and became independent in 1640.

[3] Rocroy, town in the Ardennes where the Conde de Fuentes was defeated on 19 May 1643. This marked the end of the military supremacy of the Spanish Infantry.

violence which we noted in other outstanding periods (Alfonso VI and Charles V) were bound to reappear again at this time. On the one hand the invasion of foreigners occurred owing to the fact that the armies of France, England and Austria fought on Spanish soil during the first fourteen years of the eighteenth century, followed by the arrival of a host of ministers, courtiers, technicians, either Italian or French, who under the new dynasty of the Bourbons took part in the Government and the life of Spain. Then on the other hand the uprooting of traditional ideas and usages frequently was carried out in an authoritarian manner, by means of government decrees which aroused discontent, protests and even riots. All the forces of innovation, if they did not level the traditional walls of isolationism, yet breached it in many places and allowed in many influences from outside. Spain now found that the great events of history had definitely decided against her, for a new concept of public life had grown up in the two countries that had been her bitterest enemies, namely England and Holland, and had spread throughout Europe. The religious question, which had caused the shedding of so much blood in the two preceding centuries, could not be solved on the field of battle or by state compulsion, and so was to be left to the inviolable sanctuary of the individual conscience. The State aimed exclusively at dealing with the problems concerning material and intellectual culture. In this field of action the backwardness of Spain in comparison to other countries, owing to its isolated life, was enormous. This was noticed by many Spaniards who were discontented with the past, and this section of public opinion, which in former days had been unable to give voice to its views, now found support in the actions of the State which had been inspired by the new dynasty to introduce a progressive policy.

But now, from the beginning of the eighteenth century, the spiritual unity of the Spaniards, which during the two previous centuries had appeared to the external world to be strong and unbroken, with the exception of small and accidental schisms, shows the deep antagonism caused by two ideologies which frequently reached a climax of exaltation. The points of divergence might vary according to the times, but in the end the struggle was always for religious motives. When the mediaeval toleration began to be restricted by the Catholic monarchs, intolerance was necessary for a meritorious purpose, namely that of achieving the necessary national unity, so that the Spanish people might launch out into great external enterprises. Now, in modern days, when national unification was not possible under that militant spirit of Catholicism, which at the time of the European struggle had been so highly successful as a unifying force, an intolerant zeal lasted on throughout half the country, wrecking by its ceaseless antagonism all the benefits of unity which had been achieved in the past. It is not that the anti-Catholics were numerous; they were in fact very few. But the intolerant anti-Progressives looked upon any one who proposed new-fangled notions as a downright enemy, even though those ideas were in no way a danger to religion. And vice versa, out-and-out modernizers pushed on their schemes without any regard for religious interests.

From the beginning an attempt was made to put Spain into intellectual communication with the European countries from which for two centuries she had tried to isolate herself. Feijóo[1] laments the exclusiveness of both sides; on the one side are those whom he calls *nacionistas*, which is the same as 'antinationals' for they admire in unmeasured fashion foreign nations and everything in their own country seems to them uncouth and barbarous. On the opposite side are those who believe that their land contains all the treasures and virtues that are to be found in the world, and they look down with scorn upon the other nations, making fun of their advances in arts and sciences, for they believe that foreign books bring nothing new save futile frivolities. Feijóo takes up his position between one party and the other, but owing to the exigencies of the times he found it much more necessary to incline to the side of the innovators in order to combat ceaselessly the prejudices, superstitions and the backwardness of the isolationists. These declared themselves the sworn enemies of all that was done or thought by the 'foreigners, who are either heretics or well on the way to be so', and so they wished to close all entrance to what they called 'the infected air of the north'—a

[1] Fray Benito Jerónimo Feijóo (1676–1764), Benedictine, represents in Spain the new ideas of the eighteenth century which he set forth in his *Teatro crítico universal*, eight volumes, 1726–1737, and his *Cartas eruditas y curiosas*, five volumes, and various other works. Consult *Las ideas biológicas del Padre Feijóo*, by Gregorio Marañón, second edition 1941.

phrase, added Feijóo, 'which became the stock one in such matters, and a most efficacious method for hallucinating many good Catholics, but as ignorant as they are Catholic.' These ignorant people, in great alarm, insistently opposed the valiant Benedictine, but Ferdinand VI gave him his protection and prevented them from attacking him (1750). Feijóo achieved lasting fame and his success was due to his moderation and his comprehensive judgement. 'No other Spaniard,' says Marañón justly, 'did as much as Feijóo to incorporate our soul in the soul of the world without tarnishing its traditional innocence. He felt the longing for renovation that was characteristic of his century without destroying a single one of the roots of his national tradition.'

Nevertheless the secularizing policy of the Bourbons did not bring so complete a change as is generally believed, for it did not by any means favour modernism at any price. The new kings, although they did not put religion before anything else and allow it to guide their actions as the Austrian monarchy did, yet always allied themselves strictly with the Catholic feeling in the country. The ministers of the government used to pay attention to the fears and misgivings of the traditional extremists and often supported them by linking them with their own political suspicions. As a result they often looked askance at authentic innovations, no matter how much these may have respected the rooted beliefs and customs of the nation. The government supported the ideas of 'Enlightenment' and 'Progress', which were inspired by the French, and also the sciences, arts, and industries; in order to make up for two centuries of isolation they brought in foreign technicians, and they sent young Spaniards to study abroad. But they always acted with the utmost caution for fear lest some danger from an intellectual source, no matter how remote or fictitious it might be, would imperil the monarchical or religious system. For this reason the Inquisition and the strict civil censorship still continued functioning. All this policy of limitation was necessary at the beginning, in the interests of prudence, but afterwards it was carried on too long.

Two representative names will enable us to understand the difference between the 'Enlightenment' of the authorities and that of the truly independent spirits, no matter how moderate and prudent they were. Forner, who had been educated at the

University of Salamanca, was, in accordance with the spirit of that centre of learning, a 'scholastic' or a 'peripatetic' as the phrase went there, or a 'Gothic' as such students were nicknamed. He spoke with scorn of Descartes, Leibnitz and Newton and praised only the sciences reputed to be 'useful to mankind', namely theology, moral philosophy, jurisprudence and medicine. He defended passionately government censorship and isolationism, for he believed that Spanish libraries were none the poorer because in them were not to be found Rousseau, Helvetius, Bayle, Voltaire, and a host of other authors of disquisitions on useless and frivolous subjects (the futilities of foreign books, according to the isolationists censured by Feijóo). Against Forner, Cadalso took up the cudgels on behalf of the 'modernists' or *ilustrados*, for he believed that scholasticism and Aristotelianism, which his opponents considered to be as sacred and eternal as religion itself, were upheld only from sheer mental laziness. For this reason he encouraged those students who studied secretly the positive sciences 'in order that they might not be called barbarians by the foreign students'; and it was to be hoped that in a few years the whole scientific system of Spain would change as a result of the study of forbidden books in which the students would discover 'a thousand truths not in any way opposed to religion or fatherland but only to idleness and prejudice'. As this reading and writing had to be done in secret, Cadalso could not utter such opinions in public. He wrote sorrowfully to Iriarte that in opposition to the ignorant people who believe Spain to be the best country in the world, there are those who see the evils and know the remedy for them, but they have to retire into some corner, for those who speak out are made to keep silence. And the two statesmen, Aranda and Floridablanca, who were considered advanced Voltairians, were the very persons who ordered Cadalso to keep silence and not to publish the 'Moroccan Letters' and to limit himself to being 'exclusively military'. On the other hand they encouraged Forner to publish his *'Apologia'* (1786) wherein he shows himself to be Aristotelian and 'Gothic'. This shows plainly the cautious limitation of government reforms. Even the idea of the utilitarian value of intellectual culture remains unaltered. The only activities of the intellect which bring immediate profit to man as enumerated by Forner are those described by Quevedo as 'solid sciences', opposed to other lucubrations of the intellect which are superfluous, vain and harmful. Thus on this occasion as well as formerly there is the same misgiving about pure science, which must be studied secretly, as Cadalso said.

The Cadalso thus condemned to work in silence was in reality a moderate man well-balanced in everything and always maintaining his position between the two opposing tendencies. On the one hand he censured those who would live only according to the customs and thoughts of former days, that is to say in the ancient Spanish manner, and he proves to such people that they are unable to understand the 'genuine national qualities'. Something they appreciate as being most Spanish, the costume of the day, was a novelty that dated only from the Austrian dynasty. On the other hand he is more severe in his criticisms of the opposite exaggerations, and he especially attacks those who believe that they are distilling the quintessence of modernism when they speak badly of their country and listen joyfully to foreigners who satirize her, from the hairdresser and the dancing-master upwards; he ridicules the young lady who is inconsolable in Madrid, who is 'ashamed of being Spanish', and all this because she cannot find in the shops of the capital a ribbon of the colour she wanted.

In spite of the fact that the authorities with their extremely limited sense of modern life promoted the work of Forner and prohibited that of Cadalso, though there was no very deep change in the scope of cultural life, yet there did take place a change on the practical side. When the practical concerns of the State, so long neglected, received full recognition, innovating Spain made some advance after its long period of inactivity. The first mutual concessions which were made between the two opposing tendencies opened a period of considerable advance, the most outstanding cf modern times, which culminates in the reigns of Ferdinand VI and Charles III.

This movement, though basically moderate, as it was an unfamiliar ncvelty after the long preceding period of weakness, seemed to its opponents to be excessive, and even the ultraconservatives of to-day consider it exaggerated. Doubtless there were excesses, some of them of regrettable violence, such as the expulsion of the Jesuits, but the general idea of the reform was

moderate. Nevertheless, as the collision between the two antagonistic forces, which formerly had been hardly perceptible, now
became apparent and even acquired unusually high relief, it
seems as if the schism between the two Spains took place for the
first time in the eighteenth century. There is no doubt that it was
one of the strongest and most definite cleavages, for to find
another as deep and tumultuous we should probably have to go
back to the eleventh century.

So strange does the innovation introduced in the eighteenth
century appear that it affects our whole assessment of the national
life. Most marked is the concept of 'decadence' envisaged from
two opposite viewpoints. Modernists like Cadalso believed that
the prosperous period ended with the Catholic monarchs. After
them began a long period of decline. The policy of Philip II exhausted the strength of the country to no purpose and left Spain
completely ruined materially and two centuries behind the rest
of Europe. These arrears have to be made up urgently, by shaking
the country out of its apathetic stagnation. On the other side the
traditionalists denied this idea of decline; they considered that
the reign of Philip II and the action of the Counter-Reformation
were the zenith of Spain's glory, and they held that this action
must be maintained and continued in spite of its defeat in the
international political field, at least as an internal rule of conduct. In this way the nation would save, at any rate, the pure
essence of Spain, with the contamination of which by the corruption of modern European civilization there had set in a fatal
disorder which it was necessary to check.

The opposition of Spain to Europe during the time of the
Counter-Reformation had now been transferred to within the
country itself, and we find a purist Spain facing a Europeanizing
Spain, two halves that cannot easily reach any mutual agreement
which will ensure harmonious and continued action. The men
who were most capable of creating this harmonious action, such
as Cadalso, were unable to exercise any decisive influence. Later
on Jovellanos,[1] a man whose new ideas of the 'Enlightenment'

[1] Gaspar Melchor de Jovellanos (1744–1811), in the transition between the
eighteenth and nineteenth centuries, is the principal writer on social, economic
and political questions. He was also a lyric, didactic, and dramatic poet. He was
exiled from 1790 to 1797 and was again exiled in 1798 and a prisoner between
1801 and 1808.

were balanced by a deep love for his country, and a genuine respect for the history of Spain, one therefore who stood for harmony between the two antagonistic Spains, and could have inspired a truly progressive movement of deep significance, had no
political power at his disposal and was in fact repeatedly persecuted by the state authorities.

THE TWO SPAINS IN CIVIL WAR

The Napoleonic war enabled progressive Spain, hitherto
rather timid, to realize that she had come of age; and now that
she was released from the trammels of absolute monarchy, she
could, for the first time, hold advanced political opinions, thus
intensifying the opposition between contrary ideologies. The
struggle which had declared itself all over Europe between
revolution and tradition now broke out in Spain with the
greatest violence. On the one hand the Constitution of Cadiz, as
radical as that of any other nation, suddenly introduced very
advanced reforms and contemptuously overwhelmed the deeply-
rooted conservative spirit of the country; on the other hand the
reaction when it came cancelled with a stroke of the pen all that
had been done, as though nothing had happened since Charles
IV, as if the people had not lived in a few years a period of
deliverance from worn-out notions.

More than ever half of Spain denied the other half. The
Constitutionalists of Cadiz did not try for a single moment to
limit their aspirations by considering what was the force
represented by their opponents; they considered the force as non-
existent. Likewise the reactionaries thought that nothing in the
Constitution was worthy of respect, and they, too, imagined that
the Constitutionalists were of no account in the country; they
were only a set of reprobates worthy to be chastised by the Angel
of Extermination, both themselves and 'their families even to the
fourth generation'. And when the Extermination by Ferdinand
VII came, it was carried out in such an implacable way that it
frightened the very foreigners who were intervening in favour of
Ferdinand VII, such as the Duke of Angoulême, the enthusiastic
Catholic and lover of Spain Chateaubriand, Louis XVIII, all
those, in fact, who were in vain trying to make the absolutists
come to some kind of harmonious agreement with the liberals.

Shortly after came the final consequence of extremist opinions, namely civil war, which is always apparently either a war of succession or secession, but one which never ends, even though blood ceases to be shed after the peace has been made. All the forces of the nation were engaged in an exhausting struggle on behalf of insoluble problems concerning the practice of state activity, and forgot the urgent collective enterprises which must be accomplished if life in common is to have any meaning. The two Spains while fighting for the highest principles neglected all the immediate aims, namely those essential to their life in common.

Larra in '*El día de difuntos de* 1836' ('All Souls' Day 1836') seeing the Carlist war extend all over Spain, and remembering the rising of the sergeants of 1812 against the monarchy and many other bitter struggles, finds nothing but death and tombs on one side as well as on the other: '*Here lies the Inquisition; it died of old age*'; '*Here rests freedom of thought; died in infancy*'; '*Here lies military discipline*'; '*Here rests Spanish credit*'; and finally the most depressing epitaph of all: '*Here lies half Spain, it died at the hands of the other half.*'

And so the mortal duel between the two halves continued like a horrible nightmare. Already traditional Spain appeared to be dead, and a French traveller (Théophile Gautier), when noting the irreverent behaviour of the Madrid populace during the procession of Corpus Christi in 1840, and the emptiness of Seville Cathedral, now only visited by occasional tourists, concludes: 'Spain is no longer Catholic.' But then (1842) when Balmes asked himself anxiously: 'Is it true that Spain is still Catholic?' he could answer hopefully: Catholicism is the strongest regenerative force that the Spanish nation possesses. This took place under the banner of Espartero. Soon afterwards under the opposite banner of Narváez, liberal Spain was, in theory, condemned to sterility and death, when Donoso Cortés, who had recently been converted from liberalism (1848), urged on by the exaggeration which he himself confessed was the 'historical characteristic of Spaniards', denied to his former liberal colleagues even the smallest capacity for good. His infallible political axiom, following the traditionalism of Bonald, was that nothing which did not follow the dictates of Catholicism could be

Q*

acceptable, seeing that human reason always produces evil unmixed with good and follows error as a mother follows her child.

And this exclusive idea, whether expressed as here in the form of a definite system, and as such disapproved by the Church, or whether believed unconsciously and practised diligently, was the guiding-force of the Spanish right-wing thinkers.[1] In vain were voices raised in favour of a more moderate policy. Balmes once, in 1845, under the same banner of Narváez uttered the warning that it was necessary to pay some attention to the 'new Spain that imitates the foreigner'; it was a wise policy to offer ways and means whereby it might reform and evolve, 'for we must not count too much upon repressive measures.' But Balmes decided to keep silent, for he found himself derided by the ultra right-wing extremists as a liberal cleric, a Spanish Lamennais. Even Pope Pius IX, whom Balmes so much admired, was called 'the liberal pope' by these extremists of the right-wing.

This extremist policy continued inexorably. Menéndez Pelayo, even in the early years when he was rigidly right-wing (1877), was accused of being lukewarm by the ultra-Catholics, disciples of Donoso Cortés. On the opposite side those who kept repeating that 'Spain is no longer Catholic' were legion. And so the struggle continued without any attempt being made by either side to understand the other. Governments formed from both sides followed one another, lasting two, four or six years, but rarely longer. Generally the periods of right-wing rule lasted longer as such governments were more determined and unified in their views, but all the time there was the same mutual intolerance which sent the ship of state tossing from side to side, never allowing it to follow a fixed course.

OPPOSING CONCEPTS OF HISTORY

The concept of history that belongs to each of the two ideologies spreads deeper and wider in the nineteenth than in the eighteenth century. It continues to pivot on the period of greatest prosperity reached by the nation and the subsequent

[1] For lack of any better terms, I use these old parliamentary expressions of right and left, which by their vagueness have varied greatly in meaning at different periods. (Author's note).

decline. This theme of decline became an obsession entailing two questions; first of all: When did this decline begin? or to put it another way, What is the historical character of the events which determined the decline? Secondly: What consequences ensue for the present as a result of the events which ended the preceding state of prosperity?

The traditionalist thinkers approved totally the part played by Spain in the sixteenth and seventeenth centuries, for it was then that the nation reached its zenith of power and glory, and produced the most brilliant examples of her activity in all walks of life. The thought and action developed in that golden age were essentially true to the Spanish genius and should be taken as a programme that Spain should follow always, unless she wishes to renounce her essential spirit. The decline developed as a result of having abandoned the guiding force that operated in those golden centuries. Menéndez Pelayo believes that this unfortunate abandonment began with the expulsion of the Jesuits or perhaps in the last decade of the eighteenth century, that is to say at the time when Charles IV held his Voltairian court, and the 'Encyclopédie' was the order of the day. Maeztu,[1] who was more particularly concerned with isolationism, considers that the change in ideas took place a little earlier, about 1750, when the Marquis de la Ensenada was already in power; he it was who invented scholarships for study abroad which were responsible for the introduction into the Peninsula of the spirit of foreign peoples. This was for Maeztu indeed an evil day, for if in former centuries Spain had too much neglected material interests and science, on the other hand, it must be recognized that while the Europe of Galileo and Descartes was creating modern science with its more positive results, Spain kept its *Philosophia perennis*, which was the most valuable of all knowledge. The result, therefore, of the sinister change which took place in intellectual and religious matters was that Spain interrupted its true history in order to imitate France, and for the past 200 years she has been losing her soul in the effort to be what she is not.

To these views the anti-isolationist thinkers reply that the material and scientific backwardness of the country recognized

[1] Ramiro de Maeztu (1875–1936), journalist, essayist and principal exponent of the *Hispanidad* movement in his *Defensa de la Hispanidad*, 1934.

by both sides is a proof that Spain cannot be in the right against all the other countries. They believed, as did Cadalso, that Spain abandoned its true course, not in the eighteenth but in the sixteenth century, when she took up a position of isolation in Europe, and was left behind culturally. Costa indeed holds that real Spain ends with the death of Cisneros. Every good liberal of the last century thought that Charles V, when he crushed the Communes, acted as a bloodthirsty despot. Following this line Macías Picavea considered the Austrian dynasty to be a foreign body which, when grafted on to the Spanish people, paralysed its natural evolution. Everything that happened afterwards was a disaster, says Castelar in his rhetorical manner, and nothing is more lamentable than that great Spanish Empire stretched out over the planet like a vast shroud. Thus was denied the essential and permanent identity between the ideals of the two golden centuries and the spirit of the Spanish people, and this negation was upheld by well-known writers in different fields of knowledge who cover the last quarter of the nineteenth and the beginning of the twentieth century. The oldest of those writers, Juan Valera, directs his arguments in 1876 against those who considered that for Spain to recover her lost prosperity it would be necessary to return to a social, political and religious state similar to that of the sixteenth century. Such people, he thought, did not take into account the inevitable evolution of human affairs. What produced that greatness in former ages cannot produce it now, and it would be necessary to demonstrate whether those ideas and customs of the past were the cause of the greatness or whether they were the cause of the corruption and rapid decline, for there is no doubt that the infirmity leading to decline under the Austrian kings was overweening pride, a belief that, like the Jews, they were the chosen people, and it was this obsession which estranged Spain from the rest of Europe. Later came other thinkers, who, while considering the link with the past necessary, sought for the true Spanish tradition not in its particular manifestations in the golden centuries but in the innermost recesses of the people's soul, the rock foundations on which alone can any true structure be built up. To this belief were due works such as those of Costa concerning primitive customs and the politico-legal significance of mediaeval popular poetry, and also the tendency to encourage youth to travel and acquire an intimate knowledge of their fatherland not only in its present, but in its past by studying its archaeology, history, landscapes, geology, crafts, folk songs and regional customs. It was the same desire to conciliate both the old and the new spirit that made Ganivet say that without doubt it would be necessary to continue the spirit of traditional Spain, but not with the same aims in view, for the motives of the past led Spain to interfere in European affairs, which was 'a monstrous absurdity', whereas if on completing the Reconquest Spain had only concentrated on her internal activity, she might have become a Christian Greece. 'Generally speaking,' says Ganivet, 'tradition, contrary to what is believed, cannot produce an energetic impulse, because in intellectual life the past, although it is powerful as a centre of resistance, is weak as a spur to action.' Unamuno is more categorical, for he considers that Spain by mixing herself up with European affairs contradicted her true nature. He thinks that in order to continue our tradition we do not need to copy the ideas of the past, but to delve into the *intrahistorical* depths of the Spanish people and extract from there the forces which once vitalized those ideas and which may vitalize others, for what is 'eternal' in the spirit of the people will survive only on condition that what is 'historical' is forgotten.

This manner of considering tradition not as an immediate and invariable mentor but as an inspiration, correct though it be, is not easily understood by everybody, and all that the majority generally extract from the doctrine is a scornful rejection of the sixteenth and seventeenth centuries, without discovering any positive values to take their place, so that this rejection is equivalent to a denationalization. In spite of Costa, Ganivet or Unamuno, the left-wing parties were very little inclined to study and point out in historical traditions any aspects that coincided with their own ideology; they were never interested in selecting a traditional idea which tallied with any of the basic principles of liberalism; they only remembered the 'monstrous absurdity', the 'shroud extended over the planet'; they generally saw in the sixteenth century only what they considered to be inapplicable to the present, and they failed to see that essential and enduring historical element, which can always be reassimilated and is fertile for ever. The quest for what is eternally pure and genuine does not mean, as Unamuno insists, that one should forget historical tradition, for there is no opposition, since this 'eternal' spirit underlies all history. It betrays lack of understanding not to appreciate in Spanish history the noble and fruitful part played by the country in the sixteenth century, wherein the only fault was that Spain did not evolve in accordance with the unescapable necessities of modern life. In the antagonism between the two Spains this historical pessimism was a definite sign of the inferiority of the left-wing parties. Urged on by their intolerant party feeling they abandoned all the strength of tradition to their enemies, and allowed their right-wing opponents to win entire profit from the solid support of Menéndez Pelayo who with unmatched art and learning exalted all our bygone history, calling it a glory of the past and a guide to the future.

But Menéndez Pelayo, though in mature years he rectified the extremist views of his youthful polemical writings, and though no one better than he could have achieved the conciliation of the two antagonistic groups, did not succeed in doing so. He saw that the adverse historical judgement of the left-wing party was gaining ground owing to the state of mind created by the disaster of 1898. He saw a continual increase among the intellectuals of this tendency to reject the past, and at the end of his life he became bitterly pessimistic as he watched 'the long, slow suicide of a people, who, deceived by garrulous sophists, grimly liquidates its own past, makes mock of its ancestors, and rejects all that in History made them great'.

Certainly the mood of general pessimism made those who wished for a renewal of values take a still more gloomy view of Spanish history. Formerly it was admitted that there had been a brilliant period of prosperity followed by a long decline which began, according to some, with Philip II, and according to others, with Charles III or Charles IV; but now a negative pathological note is used to characterize all past history. As early as 1912 and 1913 Azorín severely questioned the prosperity created by the Catholic monarchs, as described by Ganivet, saying: 'Spain has never, even in her most brilliant century, the sixteenth, had a moment of genuine vitality.' In 1920 the Duke of Maura wrote a striking, fully documented work to show that the capital defects now considered to have been the causes of the decline could be observed in every period of Spanish history from Ataulf to to-day. Spain has not been suffering a decline from the sixteenth century, but ever since the Middle Ages she has been suffering from 'congenital atrophy of the noblest organ of national life, namely civic spirit', though this illness is not an irreparable hindrance to great indiv'dual actions. About the same time Ortega Gasset, in a memorable essay of 1921, maintained with his great authority that Spain has not suffered a decline in modern days, but has been in bad health ever since the time of the invasion of the Goths. She suffers from a constitutional deficiency—the absence, or, at least, the scarcity of directive minorities capable of leading the masses of the people, and she also suffers from the fact that the masses in Spain are so refractory to any discipline. This it is that has produced 'invertebrate Spain'.

In thus rejecting the idea of decline we are really affirming the characteristics of the Spanish people which have lasted throughout the centuries. We are inclined to go further back in the study of basic characteristics, noting them not merely in the days of Ataulf[1] but even as far back as Indibil[2]; and we should consider those examples not only from the pathological aspect so dear to the pessimists of the post-1898 period, but as signs of a vitality which does not cease to be normal because its defects and qualities do not tally with those of neighbouring countries. With this idea in view historical works have been written, and we find that the generation of '98 has co-operated in revaluing the past. Azorín, always among the leaders, goes as far as denying the reality of the well-worn theme of historical decline (1924). Baroja, who had given such impulse to this belief, with his mournful references to Spain, the Country of Gloom, in 1935, even if in spite of Menéndez Pelayo's defence he does not think highly of the achievements of Spanish science, yet considers that Spanish culture, as a whole, is one of the three or four most

---

[1] As the allusion to Ataulf, the first Gothic king of Spain in the fifth century, implies that the characteristics date from the beginning of the Middle Ages, so the name of Indibil, an Iberian chieftain of the third century B.C., links these characteristics with the Ancient World.

[2] Indibil was a prince of the tribe of the Ilergetes at the time when the Scipios began the Roman domination of Spain in the years 212 and 205 B.C.

important in the world. But this new current of understanding, barely initiated, has had no time to produce results.

SPANISH EXCLUSIVENESS RECEIVES INTERNATIONAL SUPPORT

During the first third of the present century the Spanish exclusiveness of the left- and right-wing parties found formidable support in the complex reaction which had taken place in Europe as a result of the crisis of liberalism. This reaction brought in the rule of *the collectivity*, the supremacy of the State, whether communist or nationalist, and the new dictatorial state in Europe would admit no dissenters in its ranks, and only allowed the existence of the so-called 'one party'. The expression itself is a contradiction in terms; a party which wishes to be all and do without the other parties. This exclusive policy fitted in admirably with the usual Spanish intolerance, in fact it strengthened it. It was not enough to refuse to compromise with the antagonistic half of Spain, it was necessary to suppress it totally so as to become all-powerful. The monarchy in its last phase found itself driven to deny with due solemnity the other Spain. This took place on the occasion of the visit of Alfonso XIII to Rome in November 1923. The King in his speech at the Vatican announced to the Pope that Spain to-day continued the Spain of Philip II which battled in the name of the Church: 'If like another Urban II in defence of the persecuted faith you start a new crusade against the enemies of our holy religion, Spain and her king will never desert the place of honour.' The King affirmed the unanimity of the country, saying: 'These are wishes of my whole people,' and he went on to remind His Holiness especially of 'the consecration which at El Cerro de los Angeles, amidst the applause of all my subjects and in presence of my government, I made of Spain to the Most Sacred Heart of Jesus'. But in his reply Pius XI, precisely the Pope who consecrated the world to the Sacred Heart, did not consider it opportune to deny in this way the existence of the problem of the two Spains, and he gave a fatherly warning, reminding the King that among the great and noble Spanish people 'there are also unhappy children of ours, though still most beloved of us, who refuse to draw near to the

Divine Heart; tell them that we do not exclude them on that account from our prayers and blessings, but, on the contrary, our thoughts go out to them, and our love.' Thus the Pope, even on this occasion of diplomatic courtesy, did not refrain from denouncing and correcting as a political error the affirmation of a single Spain, ready to crusade as a 'chosen people of Providence', as the king's speech put it. He did not offer one word of thanks for the suggested crusade, but on the contrary, he gave warning that the Spain which did not conform to those views should be borne in mind. What a catastrophe, and what a deluge of blood would have been avoided if both sides, instead of denying the existence of the opposing Spain, had recognized it mutually and tried to win it over by genuine affection, as Pius XI did, recognizing it as an inevitable fact which needed charity and comprehension.

The right-wing partisans continued to look upon those who were in dissent not as an integral sector of the nation, but as its enemies. They called the opposite side 'anti-Spain' and 'anti-fatherland', in imitation of the 'anti-France' used by Charles Maurras, and the 'anti-Italy' used by Marinetti. But in Spain this word 'anti' was applied to everybody, no matter how patriotic he was, if he did not unconditionally belong to the ultra-right-wing party. The left-wing parties, likewise, felt the same determination to suppress their adversaries. They, through the voice of Azaña, proclaimed that Catholic Spain had ceased to exist on the exact day, the twelfth of April 1931, when the republicans triumphed in the elections. They alone were the fatherland; their opponents were a set of despicable cave-dwellers, and if the latter on their side thought it necessary to suppress the eighteenth and nineteenth centuries, the triumphant republicans declared that the history of Spain had been a mistake from the days of the conversion.

ONE SPAIN

Larra lamented over half Spain as dead, yet the deceased rose from the tomb to continue the mortal struggle. A hundred years later, when Azaña proclaimed the death of Catholic Spain, the latter rose and it was republican Spain which fell. This was the fated destiny of the two sons of Oedipus, who would not consent to reign together and mortally wounded each other. Will this sinister craving to destroy the adversary ever cease? Evil days indeed have come upon the world when extremism of a kind that leaves that of Spain far behind appears on all sides, and when a ferocious cleavage such as had never before existed makes national life in common impossible in many countries, owing to the mad exclusive tendencies which have gripped the dominant parties in the state. Mussolini called the twentieth century the era of collectivity, the century of the State; but for Italy and Germany this century lasted only a couple of decades, and we do not yet know how the democracies will fare after the victory which they share with communism. Nevertheless, in spite of the all-powerful collectivism which has achieved its unanimity only at the cost of a ruthless and exclusive policy, the individual will again win back his rights, which allow him to disagree, to rectify and invent afresh, for it is to the individual that we owe all the great deeds of history.

To suppress those who think differently and crush projects for what our brothers believe to be a better life, is to sin against prudence. And even in questions where one side sees itself in possession of the absolute truth as against the error of the other side, it is not right to smother all manifestations of error (as it is impossible to suppress the side itself), for then we should reach the demoralizing situation of living without an opposition, and there is no worse enemy than not to have one. There is a great deal of wisdom contained in the humorous wish expressed by Ganivet that Spanish Catholics should remedy their lack of opponents, and bring here some Protestants or heretics on hire, so as to act as a tonic to the Catholicism of the peninsula.

The hard reality of events is bound to strengthen toleration, that priceless fruit of the experience of the noblest peoples, not to be destroyed by the collectivist extremism now spread over the world. It is not one of the half-Spains that will prevail as a single party and write the epitaph of the other half. It will not be a Spain of the right or of the left, but that integral Spain for which so many have longed, the Spain that has not amputated one of her arms, but makes full use of all her capabilities in the laborious task of winning for herself a place among the peoples that give an impulse to modern life. Two organs necessary for existence must enter into function. First, a traditional Spain unshakable in her

Catholicism which, hating violence, not only avoids coercion of the dissident, but shares with them in brotherly fashion the interest taken by the State in the common welfare; thus offering to the innovators, as Balmes suggested, possibilities of evolution and reform. Secondly, a new Spain, full of the spirit of modernity, non-isolationist, interested in foreign standards but not idly subject to them: her originality rooted, as Unamuno said, in the 'eternal', not in the 'historic'. She will look on the past achievement of her people not, as did Castelar, under the similitude of a funeral shroud, nor with merely cold respect, but with affectionate interest in that Spain of old which shed such brilliance on important periods of universal history.

The sorrows of Spain, one and eternal, deeply felt by all who in their thoughts on history rise above the dissensions of the past, will bring about the needed reintegration, in spite of the fierce storm of antagonisms that rages in the world. The normalization of our existence demands that every Spaniard, in fruitful sympathy with his brother, should give play within himself to the two tendencies of tradition and renovation, the two forces that produce by their intimate struggle the greatest benefits for humanity; those two souls which Unamuno said he bore within himself, that of a traditionalist and that of a liberal, in unending but fruitful discussion. It was this double impulse which made Menéndez Pelayo at one time exalt the intolerance of sword and bonfire, and later on point out that the truly Christian thing was 'not to kill any one'. This too made him at first despise the literary fame of Galdós and afterwards choose the most solemn occasion to pay him a warm tribute, grieving that he had once attacked him 'with violent anger'. This calm and understanding spirit will make it possible for Spaniards to live in concord on their native soil; not in unanimity, for that is neither possible in a world handed over by God to the disputes of men, nor is it desirable, but at least united for a common Hispanic purpose which inevitably cannot be the same as that which united Spaniards in the Golden Age. If Spaniards can join together for the great collective tasks before them, if they can agree in establishing an era based on justice and selectivity free from party prejudice, they will at last bring to an end these tossings of the ship of State and set her on a steady course towards the high destinies of the nation.

Barcelona

T A R R A C O N E N S I S

C A R T A G I N E N S I S

C A N T A B R I A

G A L E C I A

L U S I T A N I A

B E T I C A

Santander
Oviedo
Santiago
Braga
León
Salamanca
Coimbra
Lisboa
Pamplona
Zaragoza
Burgos
Segovia
Madrid
Toledo
Valencia
Córdoba
Sevilla
Granada

S. FRANCISCO XAVER
EL CANO S. IGNACIO
A. DE GUEVARA
A. CABEZÓN
J. PONCE DE LEÓN
F. DE VITORIA
M. F. QUINTILIANO
B. GRACIÁN
F. SALINAS
M. J. M. V. MARCIAL
PRUDENCIO
TEODOSIO
S. JUAN DE LA CRUZ
S. JUAN DE LA CRUZ
P. DE VITORIA
STA. TERESA DE JESÚS
DUQUE DE ALBA
F. CISNEROS
M. DE CERVANTES
LOPE DE VEGA
TIRSO DE MOLINA
F. DE QUEVEDO
P. CALDERÓN DE LA BARCA
D. DE SOTO
F. DE ROJAS
J. DE MARIANA
F. PIZARRO
P. ALVARADO
H. CORTES
V. Nº DE BALBOA
B. ARIAS MONTANO
V. Y. PINZON
TRAJANO
HADRIANO
P. DE VALDIVIA
H. DE SOTO
OSIO
M. A. LUCANO
M. A. SENECA
L. A. SENECA
L. DE GONGORA
G. Fª DE CÓRDOBA
D. VELÁZQUEZ
B. E. MURILLO
F. DE HERRERA
MATEO ALEMÁN
A. DE NEBRIJA
A. CANO
A. DE BAZÁN
LUIS DE GRANADA
L. C. BALBO
L. J. M. COLUMELA
PAMELA
J. DE MONTEMAYOR
JORGE DE MONTEMAYOR
GIL VICENTE
P. OROSIO
L. DE CAMOENS
M. CANO
GARCILASO DE LA VEGA
LUIS DE LEÓN
P. RIVADENEIRA
T. DE MOLINA
GUILLEN DE CASTRO
L. VIVES
J. RIBERA

36
0
4
8
40
36
246

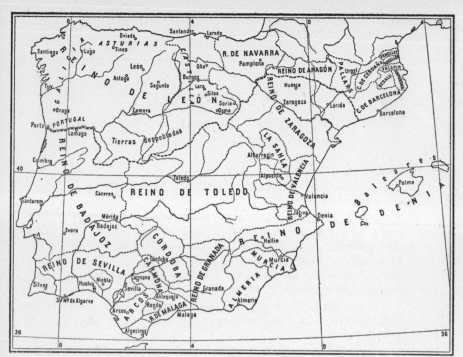

CHRISTIAN AND MOORISH KINGDOMS AT THE MIDDLE OF THE 11th CENTURY

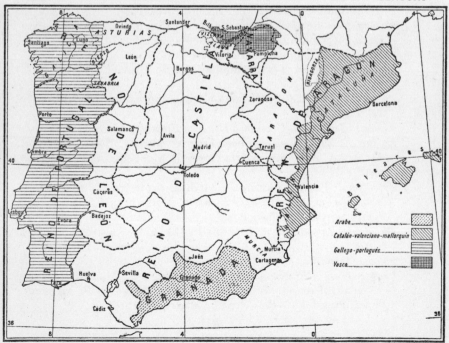

THE MEDIAEVAL KINGDOMS AND DIFFERENT LANGUAGES IN THE 13th CENTURY

BIBLIOGRAPHY

OF THE PRINCIPAL WORKS BY
D. RAMÓN MENÉNDEZ PIDAL

La Leyenda de los Infantes de Lara, Madrid, 1896; 2nd ed. 1934.

Crónicas Generales de España. Catálogo de la Real Biblioteca. Manuscritos, Madrid, 1898.

Notas para el Romancero del Conde Fernán González, Madrid, 1899.

Poema del Cid, Annotated edition, Madrid, 1900.

'El Condenado por Desconfiado', por Tirso de Molina, Madrid, 1902.

La Leyenda del Abad Don Juan de Montemayor, Dresden, 1903.

Manual Elemental de Gramática Histórica Española, Madrid, 1904.

Primera Crónica General de España que mandó componer Alfonso el Sabio y se continuaba bajo Sancho IV en 1289, Madrid, 1906; 2nd ed. 1916.

Cantar de Mío Cid. Text, grammar and vocabulary, Madrid, 1908. Vol. I.

L'Epopée castillane a travers la littérature espagnole, translated by Henry Mérimée, with a preface by Ernest Mérimée, Paris, 1910; 2nd ed. in Spanish, Madrid and Buenos Aires, 1945.

El Romancero Español. Lectures given in Columbia University, New York, on the 5th and 7th of April 1909, under the auspices of the Hispanic Society of America, New York, 1910.

Cantar de Mío Cid. Text, grammar and vocabulary, Madrid, 1911. Vols. II and III.

Poema del Mío Cid. Introduction, text and notes, Madrid, 1913. Ed. La Lectura.

Manual Elemental de Gramática Histórica Española, Madrid, 1914.

La Serrana de la Vera, de Luis Vélez de Guevara, published by R. Menéndez Pidal and María Goyri de Menéndez Pidal, Madrid, 1916.

Antología de Prosistas Castellanos. Madrid, 1917. 3rd ed. 1920.

Manual de Gramática Histórica Española, Madrid, 1918; 4th ed., with corrections and additions.

Documentos Lingüísticos de España—I: "Reino de Castilla", Madrid, 1919.

Estudios Literarios, Madrid, 1920.

Un aspecto en la Elaboración del Quijote, Ateneo de Madrid. (Lecture given at the inauguration of the course, 1920–21, by R. Menéndez Pidal, President of the Ateneo), Madrid, 1920.

Introducción al Estudio de la Lingüística Vasca, in *Cursos de metodología y alta cultura. Curso de lingüística*, Barcelona, 1921.

Poesía Popular y Poesía Tradicional en la Literatura Española, Oxford University Press, 1922.

El Rey Rodrigo en la Literatura, Bulletin of the Royal Spanish Academy, 1924.

Poesía Juglaresca y Juglares, Aspects of the history of the literature and culture of Spain, Madrid, 1924.

Floresta de Leyendas Heroicas Españolas, compiled by R. Menéndez Pidal.

Rodrigo, el último godo Vol. I: "La Edad Media", Madrid, 1925.

Orígenes del Español. Estado Lingüístico de la Península Ibérica hasta el siglo XI, Madrid, 1926.

Flor Nueva de Romances Viejos, Madrid, 1928; 2nd ed. 1943.

La España del Cid, Madrid, 1929, 2 vols.

The Cid and his Spain, translated by H. Sunderland, Foreword by the Duke of Alba, London, 1934.

The following works of Menéndez Pidal have been reprinted in the Colección Austral, Madrid and Buenos Aires

De Cervantes y Lope de Vega—No. 120.

Antología de Prosistas Españolas—No. 110.

Poesía Arabe y Poesía Europea—No. 190.

Flor Nueva de Romanceros Viejos—No. 100.

Castilla, la Tradición y el Idioma—No. 501.

Idea Imperial de Carlos V—No. 172.

Estudios Literarios—No. 28.

El Idioma Español en sus Primeros Tiempos—No. 250.

Poesía Juglaresca y Juglares—No. 300.

Homenaje Ofrecido a Menéndez Pidal, 3 vols., Madrid, 1925.

INDEX OF NAMES